REVIEWS
LIVING BRAVE IN LOVE

Oh the glorious mysteries, trials and tribulations of love. It's certainly what makes the world go round and you'll find insight into its many dimensions in the vivid stories of love found, lost and re-found in the pages of this book. Reading the inspiring stories is a sweet journey that has me pondering what love really is and how it is indeed the essence of life and our reason for being. Savor this one and take its messages to heart. It will enhance your life and comprehension of what makes human beings tick.

-**Kristi Hall**, author, speaker, and the creator of Conscious Connections, a global community for business women on a mission to make a serious impact.

Love is the core need for all of us, yet poses some of the most difficult challenges we encounter in life. The love stories from numerous contributors which are told in *Living Brave In Love* inspire and nurture us in opening more fully to this greatest of all spiritual expression. With vulnerable and authentic hearts, the authors also reveal their own personal struggles and successes in living and loving. This compassionate book gently invites us to trust life, to care lovingly for ourselves and for others, and to live courageously and expansively. With its inclusion of a wide range of wisdom, insight, and experience, *Living Brave In Love* generously supports us in creating our own story of beautiful and joyous intimacy.

-**Kathy Juline** is the author of *It Is About You,* editor of *365 Science of Mind,* and a frequent contributor to *Science of Mind* magazine.

Curiosity is the hallmark of the human heart. We wonder if we are in love, if we are loved and how those around us love and are loved by one another. It is this curiosity that drives multi-billion-dollar film and publishing industries and is responsible for the empires of Cadbury and Kleenex. *Living Brave In Love* pulls back the polite curtain which hides our neighbors' secrets and gives us a glorious glimpse into the true story treasure trove that is the lost and found of love. Those brave enough to share their unvarnished stories are the heroes and Hilda and Mary Beth have managed to satisfy our curiosity while leaving us hungry for more. A glorious glimpse into the true story treasure trove that is the lost and found of love...Heidi Lamar

-**Heidi Lamar** is the owner of Spa Lamar, Scottsdale Arizona's oldest resort-style day spa, since 2004.

LIVING BRAVE IN LOVE

Stories of Intimacy Lost and Found

LIVING BRAVE IN LOVE

STORIES OF INTIMACY LOST AND FOUND

Hilda Villaverde and Mary Beth Stern

JONES MEDIA
PUBLISHING

Jones Media Publishing

10645 N. Tatum Blvd. Ste. 200-166

Phoenix, AZ 85028

www.JonesMediaPublishing.com

Cover design by J. Tabor Design

jt@jtabordesign.com

Interior Line Art by Ron Fusselman

rjfuss@gmail.com

Cover photography by Lynne Ericksson

lynneericksson@me.com

Printed in the United States of America

ISBN: 978-1-945849-09-1 paperback

DEDICATION

Hilda Villaverde: Dedication
I dedicate these words to my father
Dionicio Villaverde
February 8, 1925 – September 13, 2004
whose search for love never ceased.

The fear I held for him as a child has released me and I can now see the
innocence of his love that stopped me from loving.
May he rest in peace.

Mary Beth Stern: Dedication

To the men in my life. . .
I dedicate my words to my father, Frank, who enthusiastically embraced
life and loved and supported his five daughters unconditionally.
July 1, 1930 - April 13, 2016

To my patient and kind son, Thomas, who is the supportive and loving
husband and father I envisioned he would someday be and to my son,
Mark, who with zeal, passion, and commitment will also be a loving
husband and father.

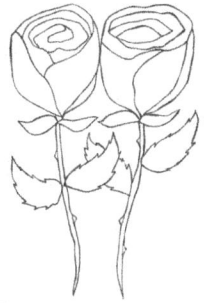

CONTENTS

PREFACE

Hilda

There is so much to love—I don't know where to begin the process of writing about it! I will begin with what I don't know. I don't know how others love. I don't know how I have managed to love and feel loved.
—Hilda

In our first book *Living Brave—Women, Stories, and Pathways to Thriving*, I wrote that I had never considered myself to be brave and that every decision I had ever made, personal or professional, had been motivated by my overwhelming feelings of fear. With an even greater intensity of my fears, my motivation for love was driven by the necessity to feel accepted and protected. Although I don't believe these motivations are unusual for most women desiring love, I do know that falling in love, for me, was not only frightening, but also confusing. I give credit to my father's Latino-Mexican heritage for the passion that coursed through my veins. Although not as strong as it surges through my younger sister's veins, nevertheless, the portrayal of the sensual Latino, hot-blooded lover most certainly formed in our genetic pool. They seek romance no matter what! My father was indeed a romantic looking for the thrill of love and emotional connection in every area of his life. By day my father worked as a laborer in a copper mine, but in the evenings and weekends he had his music. As a musician and singer, my father listened to music, sang dreamy songs, and played the drums and the accordion much of his time at home. The sounds of big band tunes and rhythmic dance music literally vibrated our small, wooden home while he practiced to play with Bobby Pool and his Anglo hometown band. On other days, as he practiced to play with the Mexican band, we listened to the heart-throbbing lyrics of mischievous men and sensual women

1

coming in and out of heart-wrenching relationships. The words of painful and unrequited love filled our home through the melodies and lyrics and also through the ongoing, complicated relationship of my parents.

My mother's Spanish-European heritage was not romantic but much more serious and organized. She worked hard to keep our home safe and stable and cared for us by making sure we were clean and well fed, displayed good manners, and attended school. I find it interesting that as I write these words, I can more clearly see the vast differences between my parent's personalities. And I am able to accept that both characteristics live equally within me. My father, his heart filled with fervor to experience romantic love, and my mother, craving safety and stability, were most of the time in conflict in their relationship. Their marriage was a dangerous dance of, "Come here because I love you" and, "Go away. You disappointed me. I don't love you anymore." Without a moment's notice, their tempo could change from affection to disdain with this tango of emotional turmoil lasting for thirty-two years until their divorce. Hence, my childhood introduction to love with the deep-seeded doubts about true and lasting, intimate love left me frightened and confused. Despite this, I have managed to fall in love, be deeply hurt by love, succumb to love again, and eventually been able to feel loved and cared for over the years. Notwithstanding, my marital partnerships have transformed from divorce into lasting friendships, a pattern that my mother also followed with my father after their divorce.

Thank goodness for years of good therapy to explore, decode, dissect, and, finally, assemble the "real me" as a whole person whose aspiration to love and be loved has at last made sense.

When the opportunity to collect and publish stories of how others love came to Mary Beth and me, we decided to take a chance on love once again and discover for ourselves how others love.

This book is a collection of stories of how others love...bravely.

Your own life story of love begins the instant you are born and is still unfolding at this precise moment while reading these words. I am sure that your story includes falling in love, being hurt by love, and finding love again. This natural progression of love seems to be present in every life story that I have had the opportunity to hear, read, or personally experience. But love we must, for according to Dr. Erich Fromm in *The Art of Loving*: *"Love is what we are starved for. Love defines us; it is the answer to the problem of human existence."* Fromm goes on to boldly state: *"The world is one great object for our appetite, a big apple, a big bottle, a big breast; we are the sucklers, the eternally expectant ones, the hopeful ones—and the eternally disappointed ones."*

Continuing to read *The Art of Loving*, I was also reminded that what I do know about love is that we all undeniably have the great desire, the *appetite*, for experiencing it again and again no matter the disappointments that may occur. As social creatures, there is a deep longing to be connected and to be cared for by another. Love keeps us eager within our own thoughts and emotions about the one we love and we crave to be kept alive in the thoughts and emotions of them. Or, at least, that is what I have come to know through the stories of those who have honestly shared their feelings of wanting to be thought of...by their lover. How many times, when completely immersed in the throes of an intensely affectionate relationship, have you wanted to ask, "Have you thought of me today?" We want to know that someone has a soft spot in their heart for us and a place for us within their thoughts.

Our own stories are not unlike the ones that you are about to read. They are the collective experiences of others just like you and me making choices for love. At times thriving in a partnership, at other times disappointed, and once again, confused by the inability to find the *right* partner. After all, we are the *"internally expectant ones, the hopeful ones—and the eternally disappointed ones"* that Eric Fromm writes about. We cannot stop this process because to be human is to need others and that certainly includes loving others.

No less is our desire to hear the stories of others caught up in their excitement for experiencing love. In another book that I published several years ago, *Blow Dry This*, I stated that, *"We are all voyeurs at heart, endlessly curious about how others are living their lives—comparing, contrasting, judging, damning, or admiring. We pretend that we don't want to know, that we are not interested, but the truth is—WE ARE! Sometimes with a morbid curiosity, other times with just a passing fancy, we want to know about the lives of others, so that we can better understand and accept our own reality. I have also come to believe that above and beyond the curiosity to understand and accept ourselves, there is a prevailing, instinctive motivation that exists in each and every one of us...and that is the quest for happiness, not fleeting happiness, but the kind of happiness that deeply satisfies the soul."*

It's not that complicated: we desire love because it makes us happy. And aside from the quest for happiness, there is also our profound need for survival. In his 1998 ground-breaking, national best-selling book, *Love and Survival, 8 Pathways to Intimacy and Health,* Dr. Dean Ornish writes: *"Our survival depends on the healing power of love, intimacy, and relationships. Physically. Emotionally. Spiritually. As a country. As a culture. Perhaps even as a species."* Although his research on human health and survival began with his scientific study of diet and exercise, he quickly discovered that, *"Love and intimacy are at the root of what makes us sick and what makes us well, what causes sadness and what brings happiness, what makes us suffer and what leads to healing."*

We have all heard the saying, *"When the student is ready, the teacher will appear."* Although this quote is attributed to Buddha Siddhartha Gautama Shakyamuni, the true origin is unknown. However, I am certain of its validity. The teacher, Dr. Dean Ornish, has once again come into my life. I am now re-reading his book on love and survival and those ambiguous 8 pathways to intimacy and health that I did not connect with years ago, but that have now come into my life in an expression of "if only I had known." Perhaps I did not think I needed the knowledge of health and survival. After all, I was young and still tightly wrapped in my fears from my childhood, and, in spite of those fears, I possessed youthful invincibility. But certainly this one statement would have helped me on my journey of living happier and more fully. Here is Dr. Ornish again with one of my *now* favorite remarks: *"I think there is great value in living fully and making mistakes, if you survive and learn from them, because then your knowledge is authentic: it comes from your own experience. Great mistakes can lead to great wisdom, if we pay attention, learn, and stop repeating them. As William Blake wrote many years ago, 'If the fool would persist in his folly, he would become wise.' Robert Frost wrote, 'The only way out is through.'"* It would have served me well to have unraveled myself earlier in life and loved more, allowing myself to come up from the darkness of my frustration and confusion and perhaps discovering the authentic me sooner. And, of course, forgiven myself and moved on to love again without the baggage of guilt and apprehension. Certainly, I would have worried less and taken life lighter like Scarlet O'Hara in *Gone with the Wind* when she announced, *"I'll worry about that tomorrow!"* I'm sure I'm not alone in these thoughts.

Adding to the health of the physical and emotional body, Dr. Ornish delves deeply into the benefits of a spiritual belief, advising that a more loving perspective towards all that is placed in front of us would be a spiritual practice worth considering. Writing of techniques to use to either keep our hearts open or closed, to live in love or fear, he uses a harsh example of this realism to get his point across: *"The same hand that caresses can also kill. The same voice that soothes also can attack. Sexual intercourse can be an expression of deep love and a return to the source of transcendent union and oneness or, in the case of rape, it can be one of life's most isolating and destructive experiences...When the intentionality and motivation are an open heart, then our actions tend to move us closer to intimacy and healing rather than isolation and suffering."* To be able to transcend from violence and fear and victimization to an open heart demands a spiritual practice that is not an occasional doing but a daily practice of forgiveness, non-judgment, and transcendence of pain into service to each other. After all, what happens for one happens for us all. In lifting oneself from a darkened time in our lives, we can help lift others into their light.

In a more current book written by Dr. Sue Johnson, *Love Sense: The Revolutionary New Science of Romantic Relationships*, she writes: *"We hunger for love, yearn for it, are impelled to it but we haven't understood it. We have given it a name, acknowledged its force, and cataloged its splendors and sorrows. But still we are confronted with so many puzzles. What does it mean to love, to have a loving relationship? Why do we pursue love? What makes love stop? What makes it persist? Does love make any sense at all?"*

Dr. Johnson, a clinical psychologist and distinguished research professor who developed Emotionally Focused Couple Therapy, is immersed in the newest leading-edge psychology exploring the significance of human connections and their relation to our physical, mental, and spiritual well-being. She has won numerous awards for her work and continues to train thousands of therapists throughout the world in her method of counseling. She gives much of the credit for her conclusions on romantic relationships as being crucial to our survival to Dr. John Bowlby, *"a conservative and British rebel who changed the landscape of love and loving forever. His insights are the foundation on which the new science of love rests."* Dr. Bowlby is credited with the development of Attachment Theory which Dr. Johnson explores and gives relational significance to in her book. This impactful statement from her book, *Love Sense*, only begins to summarize her enormous and remarkable work in the field of romantic relationships and Dr. Bowlby's Attachment Theory: *"We've long assumed that as we mature, we outgrow the need for intense closeness, nurturing, and comfort we had with our care-givers as children and that as adults, the romantic attachments we form are essentially sexual in nature. This is a complete distortion of adult love.*

Our need to depend on one precious other—to know that when we 'call,' he or she will be there for us—never dissolves. In fact, it endures, as Bowlby put it, 'from cradle to grave.' As adults, we simply transfer that need from our primary caregiver to our lover. Romantic love is not the least bit illogical or random. It is the continuation of an ordered and wise recipe for our survival."

Yes! Romantic love makes complete sense. For as Dr. Johnson writes in her last chapter of *Love Sense*, *"In my opinion, the only game worth playing is that of building a more humane society, a society that fits with our core nature as social and bonding animals and offers us a real chance to find secure, lasting love relationships—those that allow us not only to survive but also to become fully and optimally alive."*

Just in case you are not yet convinced that love is fundamental to our health and that it's the natural order of human existence, I have another influential book to share with you. Dr. Amy Banks, author of *Four Ways to Click: Rewire Your Brain for Stronger, More Rewarding Relationships*, was an instructor of psychiatry at Harvard Medical School and is currently Director of Advanced Training at the Jean Baker Miller Training Institute at the Wellesley Centers for women. From my perspective, the title, *Four Ways to Click*, did not offer a strong, descriptive, mental representation of the extensive research on the neuroscience of relationships that has obviously gone into the writing of her manuscript, but the book offers the reader an enlightened awareness of the true nature of love. Dr. Banks writes this about the four pathways for creating more rewarding relationships: *"I find it helpful to think about our human brain's need for connection in terms of the four major neural C.A.R.E. pathways...When you are in healthy relationships with others, your brain sends messages that help you feel: Calm, Accepted, Resonant, and Energetic."* She goes on to explain that the health and strength of the pathways are influenced early on by our childhood relationships and that the pathways are reshaped continually throughout our adult lives in the context of our relationships. *"That's right: our relationships sculpt our brains,"* she exclaims as she delivers a formidable argument for being in healthy relationships.

I find it fascinating that in Dr. Banks' private practice one of her specialties is therapy for people who suffer from chronic disconnection, especially during a time when people are seemingly more connected than ever. But we all know that if you have 500 friends on Facebook or Instagram or whatever is popular in the Internet world of connections...it can still be very lonely sitting in front of your device...home alone. Her book offers practical steps, using the neural C.A.R.E. pathways to retrain the brain toward authentic and more loving relationships.

Dr. Banks proves the point that the brain is naturally wired with the need for a genuine connection with others! Here is a quote from *Four Ways to Click*: "*We are just not as healthy when we try to stand on our own, and that's because the human brain is built to operate within a network of caring human relationships. How do we reach our personal and professional potential? By being warmly, safely connected to partners, friends, coworkers, and family. Only then do our neural pathways get the stimulation they need to make our brains calmer, more tolerant, more resonant, and more productive.*"

She adds, *"Isolation will kill you. Relationships are crucial to feeling happier and healthy relationships equal healthy body."*

I must confess that the analyses of the complexities of human interactions and the psychological concepts of neurological communications that each author has spent a lifetime researching are beyond my mental capacity to completely understand, but I am grateful to have found their voices and their publications and to be able to share a very small amount of their findings with you. I highly recommend them to you on your personal journey to a healthy and loving relationship.

My point in discussing their conclusions was simply to position us all in the same direction as we prepare to read the stories of how others love and to learn a bit more about why they love.

Off to the movies we go...searching for love.

Besides reading, searching the Internet and interviewing an array of people, Mary Beth and I began to watch a variety of movies to expand our research on love and intimacy. Starting with the romantic classics, we included *Casablanca, Gone with the Wind, Breakfast at Tiffany's, The English Patient, Doctor Zhivago*, and *Out of Africa* for the pursuit of happiness and the heartache that they still deliver. Although these movies are so old that half of the generations in our world today have never even heard of these award-winning movie marvels, they still reflect the rhythm of falling in love, losing at love, and some, but not all, recapturing the ability to love again.

A bit more contemporary but still considered old movies, we included *When Harry met Sally, Pretty Woman, Ghost, Love Actually*, and *The Notebook*, and the most recent movies to date concerning love lost and found, *Me before You* and the *Legend of Tarzan*! How many times has the Legend of Tarzan been revised anyway? Nevertheless, Jane falling in love with a muscle-bulging, rugged, gorgeous man with no manners who can only say "You Jane, Me Tarzan" while jabbing his finger into her chest confirms my belief that women still think there is always hope for change or, at the very least, the possibility for *improvement* with any man. Although this newest version of Tarzan has him settled and gentrified as John Clayton III, Lord Greystoke, wearing clothes and without the traditional loin cloth, it's still an all-time favorite love story that viewers enjoy watching. Myself, I missed the loin cloth.

The list of opportunities for being entertained by the movie industry is ever increasing with made-for-television movies and the ability to watch movies on many devices. Who would have ever considered watching a full-length motion picture on a hand-held tablet or a 5 1/2 by 2 1/2 inch telephone? And yet, as long as there is a link to a device, there is a movie available. Our curiosity as to how others live their lives is alive and thriving. And as the authors above, Doctors Ornish, Fromm, Johnson, and Banks agree, our brains were designed to feel connected and, along with an inquisitive nature, to understand how others live and love. So...we're off to the movies searching for love.

Comparing the movies of the past to the most current films, we could not help but notice the advancement, not only in technology with over-the-top special effects, but also with the fast-paced, demanding lives of the characters on the screen that have become much more complex, dramatic, and challenging. Falling in love is not as easy as just meeting someone and developing a relationship. Most likely, the relationship will be fraught with circumstances beyond what our parents could have ever imagined. We have arrived at a point in our human evolution that we have become desensitized, not only to the language, the explicit sexual scenes, and the extreme violence portrayed in the movies, but our brain's demand for dopamine release to elicit even more excitement for our imaginations keeps us asking for more and demanding it from our personal relationships.

What we have also rediscovered while watching the movies is that fear and bravery will always be in the story line and in the characters of every movie. As we stated in our first *Living Brave* book: *"There is always the beginning of the story, the development of the situation at hand and the introduction of the characters, followed by the problem, infused by fear and more fear and then the solution and the bravery in becoming, followed by the climax, and then the conclusion."* Fear is most certainly an emotional draw for eliciting the bond between viewer and movie that makes it worth watching. And when the story line is infused with a complex pursuit for happiness, challenges, miscommunications, loss of love...well, the more the better—more viewers, more recommendations for the movie. Although some movies will entertain, inform, educate or inspire us, most do attempt to illustrate...how others love.

Love and the Internet

Aside from books, movies, and personal interviews, Mary Beth and I poured over the Internet reading articles on relationships and marriage, what works and what doesn't, how and why to do it this way or that way, and endless opinions and discoveries on how to love. In our Google search, we found there are 435,000,000 (million) stories of love in addition to a plethora of Internet sites for finding true love. This may come as a surprise to some of our younger readers, but in the days before the Internet, the search for the pleasure of falling in love was a mystery and possibly included sheer luck. Some people attended college specifically to find the perfect mate. Others depended on family and friends to make the introductions and still others met at work or at bars. At our hair salon, we have been privy to every scenario imaginable of meeting the love of their lives, many involving pure luck.

Today, the Internet is the cosmic luck pathway for finding that special and perfect person to love. We cannot even begin to mention all of the methods for searching because by tomorrow, they might be obsolete. We can only say this: on the Internet, you have options to choose from—partners who want a customary relationship, as in a man and woman, with or without sex, younger or older, same race or mixed race also. Then there are other options—gay, lesbian, bisexual, transgender, and other options whose preferences I still don't understand. And to think that not too long ago, I thought that a friend with benefits was too much for me to comprehend. No matter the application of the Internet used for finding the perfect connection, the outcome is still the same—falling in love.

By now we have established that people are driven by the desire to love and be loved. Or as Sigmund Freud revealed, *We are all driven by the desire of pleasure.* Love is one of the pleasures of life that we have the ability to benefit from. Along with other pleasures we include children and families, success and experiences, delicious food and beverage, travel and friendships, homes and hobbies, books and toys, and let us not forget the delight of a fabulous new wardrobe. But all of these pleasures include love; we love our children, families, successes, etc., and we will indeed grow and expand ourselves into the desire for greater pleasures. The more we love, the more there is to love.

The love we cannot see

There is a spiritual aspect to some of the research on human nature, the brain, and its pathways to intimacy for health and survival that I believe screams loudly to have us take notice and recognize that there is something much larger than our physical bodies that compels us to be in love. At times, with no direction of where it will take us, we jump in and do it all over again...even if the circumstances are not "just right" or the caller is not "the perfect one". We long for it, we hunger for it, and we will undeniably love again. It's helpful to know that as humans, living both physical and spiritual lives, the physical, mental, and emotional capabilities that we know exist, but also the spiritual essence we ignore and deny until we have no other answer but to say, "Something made me do it".

We will not find this part of us within Google or anywhere else on the Internet, because for now it still remains within us available in the quiet spaces that are not connected outwardly. The spiritual component of who we are—the inner certainty and reliance that we will survive and grow and transcend our ill-prepared childhoods and adult tragedies to love once more—is waiting and ready with confidence to connect yet again. Because that which created us, desires to recreate Itself again through us and through everything that exists, it is, after all, only One. We are created from the One, having an experience of love not only because our body craves it, but because there is something beyond our understanding that begs to experience the life force within our being to be connected to one another and to help each other succeed in surviving. What happens for one happens for us all.

Mark Nepo, poet and philosopher who has taught in the fields of poetry and spirituality for over thirty-five years and is a *New York Times* # 1 bestselling author, writes on the pursuit of universal knowledge and love. In his book, *The Book of Awakening: Having the Life You Want by Being Present to the Life You Have*, he emphasizes a view of love and Oneness. Allow me to share a small part of one of his daily writings from December 24, *"In a Burst of Oneness... Oneness is what the faithful of all paths have called Love. And in the illumination of Oneness called Love, all that's left is willingness toward birth, an urge to be touched by something timeless and fresh. All that's left is the want of deep parts in strangers. To relish the waking over being awake, the burning over being burned, the loving over being loved.*

When we can be—no matter how briefly—at one with what we have in common with all life, we are rewarded beyond attachment and ownership. This is the difference between becoming a singer and becoming the song. This is the best of ambition: that the dancer melts into the dance, and the lover melts into the act of love, and the builder melts into the thing being built, until in a burst of Oneness, dancer and lover and builder are one."

There is much that I appreciate about Mark Nepo's writing, but mostly that his writings are a collection of his stories. A quote from one of his teachers, Muriel Rukeyser, is worth sharing: The world is not made up of atoms, it's made of stories."

One must be brave to love.

Louise Erdrich, one of my favorite novelists, wrote this declaration in her novel, *The Painted Drum*: *"Life will break you. Nobody can protect you from that, and living alone won't either, for solitude will also break you with its yearning. You have to love. You have to feel. It is the reason you are here on earth. You are here to risk your heart. You are here to be swallowed up. And when it happens that you are broken, or betrayed, or left, or hurt, or death brushes near, let yourself sit by an apple tree and listen to the apples falling all around you in heaps, wasting their sweetness. Tell yourself you tasted as many as you could."*

Although her quote gently frightens me, I appreciate her insight and delivery. I'm also glad that Louise Erdrich gives us a good ending; *"Life is tough, but love yourself enough to be glad for the taste of life that you took in".*

While interviewing the women who contributed their stories to our first *Living Brave* book, Mary Beth and I discovered an immediate intimate connection to them as they shared their stories with us. We had asked the women to answer a series of fifteen questions in three areas of their lives: Physical Strength, Mental Clarity, and Spiritual Courage. The questions varied from identifying physical health issues to the mental abilities they used to navigate through difficult times and the methods they used to create a spiritual vision of hope for themselves. Their answers uncovered an undeniable theme of a strong desire to survive, a perseverance to get through the next challenge, and a passion for getting to the next stage of their lives without recognizing that they were indeed living bravely. After collecting the answers and seeing them come to life in the book as their life stories, we discovered that people live brave lives, want to belong and feel connected, and want to love and feel loved. For many of them and for those of us who have been deeply hurt by life's circumstances and relationships, it has taken courage to begin the process and to allow ourselves to love again.

Although only one woman wrote in her answers that she loved herself, we have come to believe that love for one's self is at the core of thriving. Although self-love is not usually looked upon favorably in most relationships, we now know that this is actually a good place to start!

Let me explain the above statement: in order to love another, we must first create an intimate relationship with ourselves. Who are you? What do you value? What do you stand for and in which areas of your life will you not compromise your beliefs, desires, and, especially, your well-being? Once you have defined your answers to the questions above and established an intimate relationship with yourself, not in a pompous or narcissistic manner but an honest view of your strengths and weaknesses, your chances of connecting with another honest and healthy person could be so much easier. However, we don't always take this path to falling in love. Most of us want to believe that we know how others will love us. We think they love the same way we do. Nor do we ask the questions: Who are you? What do you value? What do you stand for and in which areas of your life will you not compromise your beliefs, desires, and, especially, your well-being? I know what you're thinking...only a mature person recognizes this train of thinking. Hence my new view of marriage—no one should marry until the age of thirty, forty, fifty, or whenever maturity has found its way to you! Those fortunate couples who met, married young, and have grown up together have been able to establish the answers to those questions within their partnership and they have indeed been very blessed. We have included several of these stories in our book. We hope that you will enjoy their insights and advice to young lovers.

Our goal in writing *Living Brave In Love, Stories of Intimacy Lost and Found* is to share the stories of men and women who have come forward to give a biographical sketch of their personal journeys of falling in love. None of our contributors found this process effortless and some decided not to participate. We completely understood their choice and are grateful to them for their honesty. And we are grateful for those who have endured the writing and rewriting, the editing and writing after editing. We appreciate the time and effort that went into rehashing and, for some, reliving the feelings of the excruciating circumstances that inevitably expanded their love muscle. And, through them, we will increase our own knowledge of how others love.

In the beginning of this introduction, I wrote that I did not know where to start the process of writing about love and that I wasn't sure how I had managed to love and feel loved, but now I know.

One must be brave to love.

INTRODUCTION

Mary Beth

Perhaps you find it a bit peculiar that two women in their 60's both unmarried and neither one currently in a relationship, have collaborated on a book about love and long-term relationships! However, it's the very fact that we're both single at this stage in our lives that drew us to the topic of love and what it is that creates enduring marriages and relationships. I am fascinated by the long-term marriages of my sisters and friends as I observe the joys and sorrows of their relationships. I am encouraged by the joy and hope I see in my oldest son's marriage and in my daughter's and son's relationships. I certainly have had my share of joy and heartache and at this age I have become quite reflective on my past relationships and two marriages. While I enjoy the autonomy and freedom of single life, I do recognize the beauty of loving, intimate relationships.

Love and relationship is certainly a mystery to many. Thomas Moore aptly subtitled the title of his book, *Soul Mates; Honoring the Mysteries of Love and Relationship* and introduces *Soul Mates* by writing, *"The Heart has its own reasons. When we try to understand why relationships come into being and fall apart, why some families are nurturing and others devastating, why some friendships endure long absences and bitter arguments while others fade, we come face to face with the unknown core of the human heart."*

While each relationship is unique, is there a common thread? We're all familiar with the buzzwords for successful relationships: communication, honesty, integrity, intimacy, unconditional love. And in reading Hilda's preface, you know we read books and digital articles and watched romantic movies to gain insight. It was in interviewing the contributors to our book that I personally gained insight, found some of the answers to my questions regarding relationships, and have reconfirmed my feeling that loving relationships are indeed the greatest gift of all. We hope in reading this book, that you too will be encouraged to enter into a relationship if you have been hurt in the past, commit more fully to the relationship in which you are engaged, or share what you have learned with someone who may need a bit of encouragement.

In our first book, *Living Brave—Women, Stories and Pathways to Thriving*, Hilda and I share stories from the lives of 29 women we interviewed. The women do not necessarily see their lives as ones of bravery and yet to those who read their stories, it is quite evident that the ability to overcome life's challenges clearly required bravery. We received an enormous amount of positive feedback on *Living Brave* and its interview format which lead us to our second book, *Living Brave in Love* in which we follow the same format.

In *Living Brave in Love*, you will hear the voices of the women and men we interview, their stories of bravery: venturing into a new relationship after leaving a difficult one; staying committed when hurt so deeply by a partner; ending an abusive relationship. Simply sharing one's deepest feelings with a lover or spouse requires bravery. The book opens with "Falling in Love, Lost at Love, Recapturing Love". The contributing voices have compelling stories of heartbreak, abuse, and disappointment but each individual moves on to find a loving relationship or at the very least to be open to a new relationship. Additionally you will find a section of the book titled, "Committed Couples . . . The Rewards of Long-Lasting Partnership", in which we share stories from couples whom we interviewed in long-term marriages. They each share their upbringing; religious backgrounds and beliefs; raising children while experiencing both joy and heartache; and combating major health issues. Most of our couples do not see their behavior throughout their marriages as brave--- they persevered because it was the right thing to do and because they love and support their spouses. We carefully chose the word "rewards" in the title, "the rewards of long-lasting partnership" because it became evident in interviewing the couples and writing the book that a solid, loving, long-term relationship is indeed a reward bestowed on those who persevere with love.

With love and hope in your heart, enjoy the voices of the women and men we present who share their stories in an effort to encourage you to be brave in loving again, in loving more deeply, and in sharing your love unconditionally.

PART ONE

PHYSICAL CONNECTION

"I believe in the compelling power of love. I do not understand it. I believe it to be the most fragrant blossom of all this thorny existence."

Theodore Dreiser

CHAPTER ONE

FALLING IN LOVE

"You learn to speak by speaking, to study by studying, to run by running, to work by working; in just the same way, you learn to love by loving."

Saint Francis de Sales

Hilda

In all of my years of writing, I had yet to interview a man and ask for his personal life story. Mary Beth and I were pleasantly surprised and a bit taken aback by the honesty and deep reflection that we experienced when we met with Lonnie; especially when it came to expressing his feelings about his health.

I have known Lonnie socially through his wife for many years and had heard that he had recently struggled with some health challenges. It surprised me, because upon meeting him, one would consider him the picture of perfect physical condition. Aside from being a very handsome man, his posture and physique radiate well being.

When we met for our interview, he was his usual, confident and relaxed self that I have always known him to be. We discussed the *Living Brave In Love* questions that he had already answered and reviewed his commentary. At the time that we asked him to contribute to our book, we did not know that a few years back he had authored his own book: *From the Heart, Experiences, lessons and stories to help make your life easier*, a book that gives practical advice on life skills, such as relationships, money, self-esteem, and finding one's purpose.

While reading his book, I was inspired, entertained and enlightened and decided to take his practical advice that only he could give. Abandoned by his mother as an infant, raised by a distant and stoic father, Lonnie managed to become a man who embraces others into a circle of acceptance and unconditional love. He is proactive with his health challenges and leaves no stone unturned in both main-stream medicine and alternative modalities for recovering his wellbeing. In both his professional life as a marketing specialist and in his spiritual life as a minister, Lonnie has evolved into a man whose integrity is his word and his world. Allow me to introduce a man who learned to love by loving.

LONNIE, 67

> *"Telling the truth is the foundation of a long-lasting relationship. You must be truthful and be ready to expose your hidden faults as well as your attributes."*

Lonnie attended Ohio State University where he earned a bachelor's degree in industrial design. His first job was with an internationally recognized design studio north of Columbus, Ohio. He worked there as a designer and photographer for more than three years.

In the spring of 1975, Lonnie moved to Phoenix and worked as an account representative for an advertising agency for more than two years and then founded his own design firm. He also taught graphic design part time at Arizona State University from 1976 through 1984 as a visiting lecturer and later as an associate professor.

Currently, Lonnie is a marketing consultant to a small number of high-tech, business-to-business clients that he manages from his home office in Phoenix. His clients range from companies that provide information technology support for colleges and universities to design and manufacturing for medical and aerospace. Lonnie develops websites, logos, trade show exhibits, and other marketing materials. He also writes technical white papers highlighting processing techniques and produces videos for his clients.

In addition, he is a Religious Science minister and supports his wife, Michele, who is the senior minister at Creative Living Fellowship in Phoenix, Arizona. He is the author of *From the Heart, a guide to life*, a book that gives practical advice on life skills, such as relationships, money, self-esteem, and finding one's purpose. It's a collection of stories and events in which Lonnie tells of the mistakes he made in his life's journey so that the reader can learn from them and not have to make the same mistakes that he made. Also, it's pretty funny. It's available from Amazon in print and digital versions.

Title: From the Frying Pan into the Fire

Physical Connection

WHERE WERE YOU BORN AND RAISED, AND WHAT CAN YOU TELL US ABOUT YOUR CHILDHOOD SURROUNDINGS AND CIRCUMSTANCES?

I was born in Cleveland, Ohio, and grew up in North Olmsted, a suburb west of Cleveland. My parents were divorced when I was three years old, and my father got custody of me, which was unusual at the time since the mother typically got custody. My father was sixty years old when I was born so there was a significant "generation gap" that was always very uncomfortable for both of us. My father was an editor for the *Cleveland Plain Dealer*, the morning paper, which meant that he left for work about the time I was coming home from school and arrived back home around two o'clock in the morning. We rarely saw each other. From the time that I was six years old until fifteen, we rented a room in a private home in order for someone to be around monitoring me.

I didn't have much contact with my mother in my early years, and the last time I remember seeing her was during the winter of 1956 when I was seven years old. I tried to contact her in the late 1980's to no avail. By hiring a private detective, I found out in the late 1990's that she had died in 1991. I also learned that she had received letters that I had sent her to reconnect, but she never responded.

Since my father was gone so much of the time, we rented a room from a family on a small farm. There were chickens, a couple of horses, rabbits, and fields of corn, tomatoes, and other vegetables, along with several fruit trees. It was a "gentleman's farm" that provided me with a rural experience in an urban setting. The family we were living with ostensibly left me alone and I longed for some type of "normal" family relationship. I didn't much care for them since the father usually came home drunk at night from his job as a construction foreman, and his wife was the long-suffering type who was never happy. None of my friends were from broken homes and I felt isolated most of the time. I remember going to my friend Johnny's house one afternoon and coming upon a spanking he was receiving from his father. Johnny was in the back yard near his swing set while his father was whipping him with his belt. Johnny was screaming in pain and I was thinking at the time, not, "Ow, that must hurt," but instead, "I wish my dad would pay that much attention to me".

Since my father was not able to attend many of the school functions because of his job, I felt embarrassed by his absence. In addition, he was the same age as the grandfathers of my peers so I was also embarrassed when he was able to attend events with me. Being from a broken home was unusual. I didn't know anyone in my school who didn't have both parents at home. Due to these factors, I chose not to participate in most of the social events of the school. I retreated from family events and dreaded graduation since I knew none of my real family would be there to support me.

My father died when I was a senior in high school. He had retired in 1965 and we moved to a house next door to a veterinarian. I worked construction in building the veterinarian hospital during the summer of 1966. The doctor and my father agreed to have the doctor be my guardian in case my father died before I was 18. After my father died in December of 1966, I spent the next few months with the doctor and his family until I graduated from high school in 1967. I attended college that fall and came back to North Olmsted and stayed with the veterinarian and his family in the summers to work construction. I was a union laborer in Cleveland, which financed my college education during the several summers that I worked.

TELL US OF A TIME WHEN YOU FELL DEEPLY IN LOVE—THE ATTRACTION/CONNECTION, THE CIRCUMSTANCES, YOUR AGE AT THE TIME, AND HOW LONG IT LASTED. WERE THERE ANY "RED FLAGS" AT THE BEGINNING OF THE RELATIONSHIP THAT YOU WERE AWARE OF BUT DID NOT ACKNOWLEDGE?

I had one major girlfriend in high school with whom I was smitten. We dated during my last two years of high school. However, ours wasn't a smooth relationship, and we "broke up" practically every week.

When I was twenty-two, I met a girl who was living in North Olmsted while I was living in Columbus. She was a horse owner and we went on several rides together in the fall of 1972. Ours was a long-distance relationship in which I would drive the hundred-plus miles to Cleveland each weekend for a whirlwind romance. Within a couple of weeks, we decided to get married that next spring. I was in love with the idea of being in love since we didn't really know each other and the only time we had with each other was a perpetual date.

Red flags popped up all over the place, but I paid no attention to them because this was someone who wanted to be with me and that was all that mattered. We didn't share the same taste in food, and our friends weren't compatible. She was involved with horses and the horse show circuit as a trainer. I wasn't happy hanging around the horse show crowd and the requisite event settings across the country. But it was fun for a few months since there were quite a few celebrities from the movies and television involved in the scene and my wife was a riding instructor to some well-known personalities.

After the wedding, I took her on a dream honeymoon to Paris and St. Tropez, which is on the southern coast of France. I had been there the year before and wanted to recreate the excitement that I had felt visiting France. We had a good time in Paris, but she wasn't happy about the train ride across the country and certainly didn't enjoy much of St. Tropez, a sleepy little fishing town inhabited by locals as well as the jet set. She didn't enjoy the adventure and missed her surroundings. By the time we came home, I was ready to give her back to her father.

We endured seven years of marriage and divorced in 1980 after becoming aware that we were wasting our lives. I desperately wanted the marriage to work and I considered it a huge failure on my part to have to follow in the steps of my divorced parents.

Emotional Responsiveness

WHAT DID YOUR PARENTS MODEL IN A RELATIONSHIP FOR YOU AS A CHILD?

I had no overt modeling from either of my parents, either positive or negative. My mother was absent most of my life. She was only involved in my life up to the time I was five. We had very little of a relationship. I don't ever remember her saying that she loved me or even receiving a hug from her. My father and I had no deep relationship either. He characterized it once as "Two ships passing in the night," and he was correct. My father died when I was a senior in high school. I distanced myself from feeling abandoned by either of them through the rationalization that it was better not to feel anything than be hurt by dashed expectations. I always had the sense that I was hovering above my body watching my life from a distance.

WHAT WERE YOU LOOKING FOR IN THIS RELATIONSHIP?

I was yearning to be recognized, be loved, and be respected for who I was. I was yearning for a real and solid relationship. But that always seemed to be elusive.

LOOKING BACK, DID YOU AND YOUR SPOUSE SHARE THE VALUES THAT YOUR PARENTS MODELED?

My wife wanted me to be the father figure to which she had grown accustomed. Her father was a very Germanic authoritarian and ruled the family with a firm hand. She was looking to me to be the dictator in the family and would do things to test me. She constantly challenged me to put her in her place. That was not how I viewed a loving relationship. I wanted an equal partnership in which we both had responsibility to support each other.

WHAT CHANGED? WHAT OCCURRED FOR YOU TO FEEL THE LOSS OF THE RELATIONSHIP?

We continued the long-distance relationship right up until the wedding and didn't experience living with each other until the honeymoon. That was a huge mistake. We didn't take the time to get to know each other and to experience everyday life before the marriage. We didn't have to think about matters such as money, who did the dishes or anything involving plans for the future. There was no discussion about the mundane events of washing clothes or how much it cost to live. We were young and everything was focused on living in the moment.

Once we started living together, it was evident that we had very little in common. We had very few compatible interests and two entirely different sets of friends. We would agree to go to a party, but at the last moment, she would refuse to go—not giving a reason—just refusing to go. On several occasions, she acted strangely; she said inappropriate things and sometimes screamed for no apparent reason. I found out, well after our divorce, that those spells were flashbacks attributed to LSD that she had taken in college a long time before we met. Our marriage was a constant strain and I remember very little of the years we spent together; seven years almost entirely wiped from my memory. Once we decided to get a divorce, I felt completely defeated and that I had failed myself as well as failing the relationship. I repeated the tragic ending that my parents went through and through which I suffered. The only saving grace was that we had brought no children into the world.

The end of our marriage was the beginning of my literal jump into a disregard for my personal safety. At the time, I had no idea why I was doing the things I was doing, but I was compelled to live on the edge. I bought a motorcycle and raced it as fast as I could on the highway. I took up skydiving and opened my chute closer and closer to the ground with each jump. I became a SCUBA diver and dove in some of the most dangerous waters. I became a pilot and flew faster and more powerful airplanes, twisting them through the skies— which led me to competitive aerobatics. I had friends who were into the drug scene and I made it clear to them that I would steal a plane to fly guns to South America and drugs back across the border for no less than one hundred thousand dollars. I didn't really care if I lived or died because I didn't think anyone really cared for me. I was emotionally numb.

The only normal part of me was my business. I operated my businesses and kept my employees happy. I was very good at the design and creativity of advertising, and my clients were all very happy, too. My employees thought I was a dare devil and encouraged me to keep pushing the envelope. Some of them said that they lived vicariously through my exploits. They didn't see how empty I was inside.

Spiritual Surrender

DID YOU AND YOUR SPOUSE SHARE THE SAME SPIRITUAL BELIEF?

Spirituality was never an issue between me and my first wife. We never discussed it or made it a factor in our lives. The only time that it mattered was when we were getting married and had to meet with the minister before the wedding. I'm sure he asked us some questions, but I have no idea what I said at the time. We never went to church together or even talked about the existence of God.

WHAT ATTRIBUTES DID YOUR SPOUSE BRING TO THE RELATIONSHIP, POSITIVE OR NEGATIVE?

Neither of us was the "bad guy" in the relationship. Both of us were responsible for jumping into marriage without seriously considering what marriage really means. We were both young and naïve about what constitutes a healthy relationship and didn't listen to our internal warning systems. However, we also both realized that our lives are too important to waste on a failed marriage and that there was no future in staying together.

WHAT OCCURRED TO BRING YOU OUT OF THE DENIAL OF YOUR SITUATION? HOW DID YOU FIND YOUR WAY BACK TO TRUSTING YOUR DECISIONS AND RECAPTURE YOUR ABILITY TO LOVE AGAIN?

After the divorce, I started dating other women; lots of women. I didn't know it at the time, but I was constantly looking for the next conquest and treated women in a cavalier manner. There was one girl who I dated for more than eight years but, all the while, jumped into bed with scores of others.

During the 1980's, I was into many death-defying adventures. I did sky diving, SCUBA diving, learned to fly airplanes, and raced motorcycles at excessive speeds. I didn't value my life and also didn't think I would live to be 40. I approached dating with the same attitude, little realizing that I didn't want to be abandoned again. I was the one to have one foot out the door at all times. I wanted that control so I wouldn't be hurt again.

Jean was the exception. She truly loved me, and our relationship lasted the longest, more than eight years. However, she had no idea that I was dating other women at the same time. Then Lisa came into my life. She and Jean were polar opposites. Lisa was an early riser and nurturer. Jean practically awoke after dark and loved dancing and the social life. Together they were an almost ideal woman for me, more thrills to add to my life. I started dating Lisa exclusively, too. For more than two years neither knew of the other. My life was a constant whirlwind and I needed to keep track of all the lies I was telling them.

It was fortunate that Lisa and Jean travelled in different circles and at different times of the day although they lived fewer than three miles from each other. There were several times when the two worlds would have collided, but fate intervened and kept them apart. The holidays were particularly difficult, but fortunately, Lisa's family liked to celebrate early and Jean's preferred celebrating late. Then, there was my 40th birthday, a seemingly monumental event. Lisa threw a surprise party for me a week before my actual birthday since she needed to go back to Michigan to see her father. Jean threw a surprise party for me on my birthday with two couples in attendance at both parties. It appeared that I lived a charmed life. I thought I really cared for both of them but couldn't make a commitment to either. I took two weeks of vacation in the spring of 1989 to make a decision on which one to choose. This life was wearing me down, and I knew that it could not go on forever. I booked two weeks at a Club Med in Mexico to be alone and think, but my ways didn't change. I met a television newscaster from Texas. She and I started a brief affair and I had accomplished nothing but complicate my life further. Little did I know that soon after I returned to Arizona, my life was about to collapse upon me.

Lisa became suspicious and followed me a couple of times to Jean's apartment. She contacted Jean, shared stories, and together the two of them confronted me one evening with the lies that I had been telling them. I was surprised, devastated, and truly sorry for the way I had treated them. Neither of them deserved the way I had treated them and I was remorseful.

My ego was crushed and I knew I deserved the emotional beating the two of them pummeled me with that night. However, it was also the release of a huge weight from my soul. That resolution had been waiting to happen for years, and my bruised and battered ego welcomed it. I silently vowed to never treat a woman that way again. How could I since I was never going to date again!

Two more events occurred that took me deeper into despair. A couple of days after the confrontation, the police notified me that my office had been broken into. Early one Saturday morning, I met the police and gave a report before starting to clean up. Not much had been stolen, but several items were smashed, a large window needed to be replaced, and there was a general mess everywhere. It took me several hours to deal with the police, the insurance, and the mess. I arrived home that afternoon to find that my apartment had been broken into while I was at my office. I suffered another mess and several items this time had been stolen. I'm sure that neither of the girls had anything to do with either of the break-ins. I knew that this was an opportunity for a complete house cleaning, a purge. I wasn't mad. I felt that I deserved it.

Then Michele entered my life less than two weeks later. I met Michele through business. She had enjoyed meeting me so much that she wrote a letter asking if I would be free to meet and "take it from the professional to the personal." Michele appeared to be smart, pretty and sure of herself; someone whom I could admire. Although I didn't think I could date again this soon, or ever, I almost immediately said yes to her invitation, and our first date was less than a week later on Halloween, 1989.

We had a very nice time on our first date dining and dancing and we mutually agreed to a second date. Our second date consisted of seeing a movie. Afterward I needed to be completely honest with Michele. I risked telling her of my past indiscretions and the way I had treated women badly in the past. Regardless of how it would turn out, I had to tell her the truth and live with the consequences. She deserved to know the truth about me early in the relationship and I had vowed to be honest. After I said my piece, she was honest with me and talked about her two failed marriages and a string of relationships that had typically ended poorly. It was a huge burden lifted from me to tell the truth to her and to be seen as the person I really was rather than who I pretended to be. Actually, it was a relief for both of us to be honest and build a potential relationship on the truth.

NOW I UNDERSTAND AND BELIEVE THAT... My actions toward women were the result of my feeling abandoned by my parents. I didn't acknowledge the hurt their actions had caused me. I feared being abandoned by women so I had to have control over the relationship. I equated sex with love and suppressed any sign of emotion within me. I attempted to use thrill seeking as a replacement for emotional feeling. Going higher, faster, farther, and deeper was never enough. It was a substitute for accepting who I am and allowing that to be seen by someone who might truly care for the real me. It was a substitute for being vulnerable.

WHAT ADVICE WOULD YOU GIVE TO YOUNG LOVERS ENTERING A NEW RELATIONSHIP?

Telling the truth is the foundation of a long-lasting relationship. You must be truthful and be ready to expose your hidden faults as well as your attributes. Of course, this doesn't have to happen all in one night as Michele and I did. That was a pretty extreme way to do it, but it worked for us and we have been happily married since 1991. Truth, mutual respect, and a genuine concern for the happiness of our partner are the factors we attribute to our blissful marriage.

In addition, we value the individual personalities that brought us together in the first place. We support each other in our uniqueness and never try to change the other person. Contrary to some points of view, we have found that a successful relationship does not have to be work. It comes down to recognizing what you value—some transitory event such as dirty socks on the floor versus the relationship? A scratch on the car or the relationship? A difference of opinion on the décor or the relationship? Being right or the relationship? For us, maintaining a long-lasting and deep relationship wins over petty issues every time.

MY MYSTICAL JOURNEY TO JOHN OF GOD

At the age of 63, I had open heart surgery in December 2012. I had two valves replaced, a triple bypass, and an aortic reconstruction. A few days later, I had a pacemaker implanted to stabilize my heartbeat. In just a few weeks at the beginning of February, I was starting physical rehab and I was feeling better. Eight weeks later I was losing energy and didn't feel as well. My health started to deteriorate. The pacemaker was pressing against the muscles of my chest which affected the ligaments and tendons in my left arm. The tendons would constrict, and I needed a massage about once every two weeks to relieve their constriction. I couldn't lift my left arm above my shoulder without pain. I continually felt strange, disconnected, and wasn't sure I would wake up in the morning. It was a struggle to walk a few yards.

I was back in the hospital the first week of January 2014. The doctors said that my heart was performing at less than ten percent of capacity. There was nothing else they could do for me but perform a heart transplant. That was not the way I saw it. I did not want to be opened up again and suffer through the agony of an additional surgery. I had heard of a healing mystic in Brazil by the name of John of God. I had done research about his healing and knew that visiting him was the answer for me. I needed to go alone. Michele wasn't so sure about the whole thing, but she recognized that this was what I wanted so she relented.

For someone who didn't have the strength to go from the car to the grocery store, travelling several thousand miles to Brazil was ludicrous. I arranged to have guides in Brazil, but it was a rush to get the reservations and visa for the last week of February through the first week of March, the soonest I could go.

Somehow, I made it through the flight from Phoenix to Atlanta with a six-hour layover in Atlanta before a nine-hour flight to Brasília, the capitol of Brazil. A short two-hour van ride West, and I was in Abadiania, the little village in which John of God has a campus that's called the Casa.

My guides were the best I could have chosen. They had arranged Oprah's visit the year before and were personal friends of John of God. I stayed at their hotel for the two weeks. The first night was an orientation regarding what to expect and protocol. We sat outside listening to the guides tell us that this experience would be different for each of us and we had the potential to be transformed in profound ways. They said that it was all about the love of God and that the encounter with John of God could potentially reveal the reasons for our physical illness.

I had known that I was loved. I was loved by my wife Michele. I was loved by the congregation at the church. I was loved by my friends. But I never felt such an overwhelming embrace by God as I did that night. Almost everyone left after the orientation and I was left with my roommate, Jim, whom I just met that evening. Waves of emotion overtook me and I started to sob uncontrollably. I felt the love of God embrace me, and it was the sweetest and most profound feeling I had ever encountered. I embraced Jim, who was certainly startled by my behavior, but he let me cry.

From that moment to now, the tendons in my left arm no longer restricted movement or caused me pain.

John of God sees thousands of people each week. He is in the Casa on Wednesday, Thursday, and Friday of each week. He performs physical surgery on people who, without anesthetic, are presented to him on stage. I witnessed several surgeries in which he makes incisions with a scalpel and probes into various parts of bodies with his fingers. I was no more than fifteen feet away, witnessing people standing in front of him during the short surgeries. He also performs "spiritual surgeries" in which people are prescribed to sit within the Casa in a state of meditation while hundreds of others hold a meditative state for their benefit in the same building.

I sat through two spiritual surgeries not knowing what to expect. In the first, my mind was flooded with the most intense violet color. I was again bathed in serenity and a feeling of being loved. The second spiritual surgery was about the same but less intense. I also had the most vivid and intense dreams that I have ever experienced. Each of them reinforced the idea that Spirit was sup-porting me in recovery.

My health has slowly improved since then. In fact, I went back to the gym a few months after returning from Brazil and more than a year later, my wife and I signed up with personal trainers. I have been performing aerobic and weight exercises that I never thought I would be capable of doing again.

I have not told my cardiologist that I went to see John of God. I'm not sure how he would take it. He is a naturopathic doctor and I may let him know in the future. In reviewing an annual blood test a few months ago, he asked if I had any questions. Normally, Michele would attend those sessions, and she always had good questions that I would not think to ask. I told the doctor that Michele would be eager to know the results, and he said, "Given the state that you were in during the winter of 2014, I never expected to see you standing here again. Tell her this is a miracle."

* * *

From Chapter 12 of Lonnie's book, *From the Heart*, is this writing that I think captures the sensitive yet strong essence of a man who has come full circle of living in love:

Chapter 12—Now What?

"I firmly believe that we are put on this planet for a purpose. The discipline of philosophy was created to ask, answer and argue about life's most basic questions such as, 'What is the purpose of life?' I don't want to put any philosophers or college professors out of business but I believe our purpose, simply put, is to learn, to love and to teach. Of course, each of those concepts is a never-ending pursuit in itself, if we do it right. We never want to stop learning because there is always something to learn. We never want to stop loving because it is a constant process with ourselves, our partners and with everyone we meet. We never want to stop teaching because there is always someone who can benefit from our knowledge and our experiences."

Live brave.

Falling in Love

"If we are a metaphor of the universe, the human couple is the metaphor par excellence, the point of intersection of all forces and the seed of all forms. The couple is time recaptured, the return to the time before time."

Octavio Paz

Hilda

There are many aspects of owning a hair salon that I genuinely appreciate, but the most significant to me is the opportunity of getting to know people. Nancy is a comparatively new client to our salon, just under two years in which she has quickly become a salon treasured friend. Many of our clients have been with me for over forty years and although that is a long measuring stick to differentiate between the new clients and the long-term clients, my point being... although relatively new, Nancy is already a favorite.

At a time when happiness and the meaning of life are being highly explored, it has become evident that at the center of genuine happiness and living meaningful lives are relationships; loving, caring and sincere relationships. Our client Nancy is that woman who brings together women who form those relationships. Through her sense of humor, generosity and caring nature she draws to her a love that most would undoubtedly welcome. We feel fortunate to have attracted her into our lives. While preparing to introduce her, this favorite poem came to mind:

Reason, Season, or Lifetime

People come into your life for a reason, a season or a lifetime. When you figure out which one it is, you will know what to do for each person.

When someone is in your life for a REASON, it is usually to meet a need you have expressed. They have come to assist you through a difficulty; to provide you with guidance and support; to aid you physically, emotionally or spiritually. They may seem like a godsend, and they are. They are there for the reason you need them to be. Then, without any wrongdoing on your part or at an inconvenient time, this person will say or do something to bring the relationship to an end. Sometimes they die. Sometimes they walk away. Sometimes they act up and force you to take a stand. What we must realize is that our need has been met, our desire fulfilled; their work is done. The prayer you sent up has been answered and now it is time to move on.

Some people come into your life for a SEASON, because your turn has come to share, grow or learn. They bring you an experience of peace or make you laugh. They may teach you something you have never done. They usually give you an unbelievable amount of joy. Believe it. It is real. But only for a season.

LIFETIME relationships teach you lifetime lessons; things you must build upon in order to have a solid emotional foundation. Your job is to accept the lesson, love the person, and put what you have learned to use in all other relationships and areas of your life. It is said that love is blind but friendship is clairvoyant".
—Unknown

Allow me to introduce Nancy to you.

NANCY, 72

"One of the greatest protective devices we have, if we can learn to use it, is our memory."

Nancy is a resident of Phoenix, Arizona, with two adult daughters and four wonderful grandchildren. Initially, she was a practicing nurse but then went to work for a law firm as a legal nurse consultant working on medical malpractice and personal injury cases. She is retired and enjoys gardening, bridge, travel, reading, her family, and her many friends.

Title: Loving John, Our Story

Physical Connection

WHERE WERE YOU BORN AND RAISED, AND WHAT CAN YOU TELL US ABOUT YOUR CHILDHOOD SURROUNDINGS AND CIRCUMSTANCES?

I was born in the early 40s close to the end of WWII to a 22-year-old legal secretary and an officer in the Army stationed in Europe. My mother and biological father were married right before the beginning of the war when my mother was 18. I never met my biological father. I also never knew much about him except what I was told by my aunt. He was a pilot during the war and when he returned home, he had what we now know as post-traumatic stress disorder.

My earliest memories are of living with my grandparents and my mother in southern California. I know these were happy days because of my memories of my dog Sutsy and my grandfather who would feed me sweets behind the backs of my mother and grandmother. He had a wonderful sense of humor, and I remember him teaching me how to eat dog biscuits on the back porch with Sutsy. And I remember lots of laughter.

When I was two years old, my mother divorced my father and remarried when I was four. The divorce was never discussed, and I don't remember ever actually being told about it; I just grew up knowing. My stepfather adopted me. I never considered him my stepfather; he was always my dad. My grandfather had died before my mother remarried and most of the time after that is a blank.

My next memories are of living in a suburb of Los Angeles with my parents until we moved to Phoenix when I was fifteen.

My senior year in college I was dating a sophomore, and we were married at the end of my senior year. We had pizza and fraternity parties in common. In those days everyone seemed to marry whomever they were dating their senior year. I had just finished college and passed my state nursing exams. My husband was in his second year of pre-law. We were divorced in 1985 when our daughters were eleven and thirteen. He was a good man, great father, and good husband. We had simply married too young and had little common ground for a life together. Eventually, the negative aspects of that marriage would help me form the guidelines I would need to live a successful life and make the decisions I made.

TELL US OF A TIME WHEN YOU FELL DEEPLY IN LOVE—THE ATTRACTION/CONNECTION, THE CIRCUMSTANCES, YOUR AGE AT THE TIME, AND HOW LONG IT LASTED. WERE THERE ANY "RED FLAGS" AT THE BEGINNING OF THE RELATIONSHIP THAT YOU WERE AWARE OF BUT DID NOT ACKNOWLEDGE?

In May of 2000, I was working as a nurse consultant in a downtown Phoenix law firm with Carol, a nurse-attorney who was part of our "Nine." "The Nine" was a group of very close women friends who worked at the firm. Some of us had known each other thirty years. We became as close as sisters. Our story was told in the book *Living Brave: Women, Stories and Pathways to Thriving.*

Carol and I were working late and decided to have a glass of wine and relax. Midway through the evening, we started talking about our dating lives and comparing stories. She had been through a series of get-togethers for coffee with single men during which she felt that she had been interviewed. Up to that time, the highlight of my blind dates was with a nice gentleman who was the father of a ten year old who was a friend of my 10-year-old daughter. The two of them had cooked up this plot to get us together, and there is nothing more relentless than two ten year olds with an agenda. I think they had long plans for ditching their siblings and starting a new family life together as sisters. In any event, taking advice about dating life from two ten year olds cost me fifty IQ points. On the good side, I swore I'd never date again. Of course, that didn't last, and I continued to date throughout my 40s and 50s. Most were long-term relationships that I ended for a variety of reasons.

However, that evening with Carol would change my life. Carol was ten years younger than I was and had been fixed up by Chris, one of the secretaries at our law firm, with John, a gentleman who played golf with Chris' husband. John's wife had died the previous year in a bicycle accident. He was one of those people everyone loved, and his friends couldn't wait to find him a girl-friend. Carol spent the next forty-five minutes telling me how much fun she had with him, what a nice man he was, and how he loved to travel. Carol's description of John and the date she had with him conjured up the picture of a knight in shining armor in my head. She had decided not to date him, how-ever, because she was concerned about their age difference; he was 12 years older than she was. In any event, two glasses of wine later I asked her to call our mutual friend Chris to see if she would give John my phone number, tell him about me, and if interested, have him call me.

In the twenty years I'd been divorced I had never done anything like that. I had to look up the word *brave* when I started to write this, and I think that moment for me was the bravest I've ever been. It was so completely out of character for me, but this finally led me to my dear, wonderful John. It's so hard to explain us, our love, what we had, or why we were given this tremendous gift.

This is our story:

A few days after Carol called Chris, John called me and asked me out to dinner, not coffee but dinner. That was interesting. I was used to people and their coffee dates which doubled as a quickie interview. I don't remember much about that telephone conversation, but I do remember that he wanted me to pick a restaurant I really liked not far from my house, so I wouldn't have far to drive home. I was impressed because it seemed such an uncommonly nice gesture to think of that. I arrived a little early at the Fish Market, and John was already there. I later discovered this was just like John, to make it a point to arrive early so I would not have to wait alone.

Years later, my ex-husband would describe John as a real gentleman. He belonged to a generation that would not have considered going to dinner with a single woman, even in a group setting, and not paying for her dinner. He opened car doors, walked on the curbside of the sidewalk, and had wonderful manners.

It's surprising how many times you can leave after an evening with someone new and they know nothing about you. I was greeted by John's smile and lots of questions. He was interested in everything about my family and me. We had a real conversation. I can't tell you what we talked about, but I do remember the laughter, always the laughter. We spent the next two-and-a-half hours talking about everything. When we said goodnight, he asked me to go to dinner the next weekend. I felt like I was saying goodnight to an old friend.

John and I met in May and continued to date throughout the summer. His wife had died the previous year in a bicycle accident, and he hadn't done much dating. They had been married for thirty years. I was surprised that he was really, really good at dating. I think it was his charm. He was such an open, warm person. He loved meeting new people, and many became his friends after meeting him for the first time. It was a pleasure to be able to introduce him to my friends. As I stood beside him and watched him interact with all types of people, it made me so proud of him, and I felt so lucky to be with him.

Golf was his passion, and after a game, he could describe every hole and repeat all the disgusting jokes he and his friends had shared. There was such a joy in him when he related these stories. Before we were married, he told me that he didn't need to play as much golf as he did, and that after we were married, of course, he'd be happy to stay home more on the weekends and spend time with me. I could not imagine depriving this man of his golf. I told him as long as he could manage to show up for Christmas, my birthday, and our anniversary, his golf was not a problem, and I really enjoyed hearing him talk about it. I could not imagine keeping him home on Father's Day. It seemed to me the best gift he could be given would be a golf game.

He asked me if I was interested in learning how to play. At the age of fifty-eight, I really, really wasn't. I had never been very athletic, and my coordination was pathetic. But, by this time, I loved this man beyond reason, and I was going to learn to play golf and love it. I took several lessons before we were married, but it's too depressing to describe what kind of golfer I was. Fortunately, John was the most patient man I ever met. He would play golf with me at any time even though my drives usually managed to go about four feet. I could make it to the green in thirty-two shots. My vocabulary was a little off too. For some reason, I could not seem to remember that the driving range was not called the "striking zone." John thought it was the funniest thing he had ever heard. So life went on throughout the summer and early fall. We were becoming a real couple and I, the 16 year old in the relationship, was completely gaga. This man was an anomaly and at least I was smart enough to know it.

In November one of my best friends had a sixtieth birthday party. It was an extravaganza and we all had a great time. On the way home in the car, unexpectedly and very casually, John said, "What would you think about living together?" I went into the kind of shock where the blood drains straight out of your head. The first thought in my oxygen-depleted mind was that my parents would have a frigging fit. They were not raised in this kind of world and simply would not understand it. That thought rolled out of my head onto my tongue and out my mouth before I could edit myself. His calm response to this was "Well, then, what would you think about getting married?" My first thought was "Yippee!" Before this, I hadn't even given marriage a thought. What I did know was I wanted this man desperately, and I wanted him forever. However, I managed to refrain from actually saying "Yippee!" and with a huge grin on my face, told him that I thought that would be wonderful. This whole conversation took place in his usual calm manner while he was driving home and while I was flipping out in the passenger seat.

I was 58 years old and someone had just handed me the biggest gift of my life. After calling my parents, who were thrilled, I told my daughters. Fortunately, they also adored John. However, unknown to me, I apparently had a reputation within my family of breaking up with men after a year or two of dating. My youngest daughter, who was twenty-seven at the time, looked straight at me and said, "If you hurt this man, I just want you to know we're going with him." This was the first time I had an inclination that my friends and family felt I was some kind of serial dater.

I was surprised to learn that John wanted a big wedding. He suggested our local country club and said he would arrange for a band to play. He said I should do anything else I wanted to do. We had the time of our lives planning this wedding. We were now both 16 year olds looking toward the future like young people.

On Christmas Eve in front of our Christmas tree and the fireplace, John dropped to one knee unexpectedly and surprised me by formally proposing marriage and bringing out an engagement ring. He had also called my 80-year-old father and asked for his permission to marry me. In this day and age, I had to ask myself "Who is this guy?"

The next several months were taken over with planning the wedding, attending wedding showers, and dinner parties. Our friends were almost as delighted as we were. At one of the showers, we received a very special gift from Julie, one of our friends who has a very irreverent sense of humor: The book *365 Days of Sex*. It was, of course, John's favorite wedding gift, and Julie became one of his favorites of all our friends.

I had always been a horrible dancer, limited to the box step, so John spent days teaching me to dance in our family room. It was such great fun. I truly felt like a young bride-to-be. The wedding was a celebration for everyone.

Before we were married, John had said casually "You know if you don't want to work you don't have to. I can take care of us." I loved my job, but the thought of being at home, taking care of our house and my husband, was just too tempting. Plus, I knew John wanted to travel and plan for his retirement in five years, so I happily quit work and got started on the best seven years of my life.

Emotional Responsiveness

WHAT DID YOUR PARENTS MODEL IN A RELATIONSHIP FOR YOU AS A CHILD?

One of the greatest protective devices we have, if we can learn to use it, is our memory. Forget the things that harm us and get on with our lives—a statement I am sure many mental health professionals would violently disagree with, but it served me well. I haven't thought about the years growing up on Ocean View Drive since I was in my 30s or 40s and for good reason. I don't mean to imply that I was unloved or abused. I was not, but the words that come to mind to describe growing up as an only child in a house with two parents who had no emotional or physical connection to each other at all that I could see, would be *depression* and *anxiety*. Maybe it was simply a different era. My parents were quiet, well-educated, fairly formal people. We didn't kid around and I don't remember a lot of laughter.

WHAT WERE YOU LOOKING FOR IN THIS RELATIONSHIP?

It was certainly not marriage. I had been single for twenty years, and I loved it. I think it stemmed from being an only child. Although I had hated being alone growing up, I had learned to entertain myself and books became my best friends. I loved being alone, so for the twenty years before I met John, I was perfectly content with relationships which are now called having a "friend with benefits." I don't think I would have resisted falling in love, but I would have resisted marriage. I didn't consciously think about it, but on some level I knew that being with someone twenty-four hours a day would probably not work out very well for me or for him. What a shock it was to find out how really wrong I had been for twenty years.

LOOKING BACK, DID YOU AND YOUR SPOUSE SHARE THE VALUES THAT YOUR PARENTS MODELED?

No, because I never felt my parents had any real intimate connection on any level. John and I, on the other hand, were just the opposite.

What changed? What occurred for you to feel the loss of the relationship? To what extent was it hurtful, physically, financially, mentally, and emotionally?

Early in 2006 I noticed that when John would walk down the hall on the tile floor it sounded like he had something called foot drop; one of his feet slapped the floor as he walked. I asked him to see a neurologist. The day of the appointment I could not go with him so he went alone, neither of us suspecting this was going to turn out to be a devastating and major life-altering event. John was home sitting on the couch when I got home. He had a very serious expression on his face. He told me the doctor had done a very thorough neurological exam and told him that he had ALS (amyotrophic lateral sclerosis also known as Lou Gehrig's disease). He had just been handed a death sentence. Although I was a nurse, the shock of what he told me left me with an inability to even remember anything specific about ALS other than it was fatal. I remember that I was in complete and absolute denial that this could possibly happen to us. I told him that I was going to make an appointment with another neurologist. I took him to see a close friend who wasn't convinced this was ALS. He had given us some hope, and I clung to that hope for two-and-a-half years, despite knowing the diagnosis was true. But I also didn't want John to give up hope. There are new discoveries all the time in medicine, and I wished and begged and prayed that he would be one of the miracles. I also talked to John frequently about this, and as only John would, he never did anything to take my hope away even though he also knew better.

I don't think in my entire life I was ever so glad I was a nurse as I was the day he was diagnosed because the one thing I did know with absolute certainty was that I would take care of this man and no one else would touch him. The next two-and-a-half years were a very gradual decline; mostly, John's movement was affected. He went from wearing leg braces to a walker and then a wheelchair. Although his general health did not diminish as is usual with ALS patients, he was bothered by the disabling effects and what he knew was coming. He began to have some bowel problems which required my attention and which I think was humiliating for him. He was always able to feed and dress himself and could transfer in and out of the wheelchair with a little help. But I knew he was thinking about what the coming months were going to be like, and, knowing John, I knew he was concerned about me.

Eventually, he stopped eating. As much as we tried to encourage him by making him special foods he liked, he had made his decision, and it was a conscious one. He gradually became weaker and spent most of his time in bed. I was turning him every two hours, day and night, and trying to make him comfortable. But I wasn't sleeping. I would wake up at night trying to think of things I could do to help him, to make his life better, to make him comfortable. I would stay awake making lists in my head. Finally, one of the nurse practitioners in our group of "The Nine" put me on medication for depression and anxiety so I could continue to function.

Although I didn't know it was the last week of his life, my exhaustion prompted me to call Hospice of the Valley, and I hired a nursing assistant who would help me turn John during the night. It was a peculiar arrangement. She would sit at the end of the bed coloring in a child's coloring book while we slept, and she would wake me every two hours when we needed to turn him. For the last couple of weeks of John's life either one or two of "The Nine" had been present in our home most of the time to keep me company and take care of me. The last night Janie and Kathy and my two daughters stayed with us. John was not responsive for several days before he died. The night John died I was sound asleep in bed next to him so emotionally exhausted I didn't realize when he was gone. When the girls called the mortuary and they came to pick him up, I did not even wake up. Janie and Kathy removed all of the heavy equipment and supplies from our room, and I never woke up or even turned over during that process. The next morning when I woke up John was gone.

I can't describe that morning. When I go back and remember that day, the pain feels the same as it did that morning. Most of the next few weeks were a blur. Just about the only thing I remember was spending a lot of time in bed just looking over at John's side of the bed or standing in the shower screaming and sobbing, "Give me my husband back. I want him back. This is wrong. Give him back to me." This would go on until the shower water was cold, and I could no longer stand up. Over the next few months one or another of "The Nine" called me or brought food by to check on me almost every day. They wanted to see for themselves that I was all right. I was perfecting my ability to say "Fine, I'm doing just fine" and sound like I meant it because I knew that if any one of them had a hint of just how bad off I was, there would be a group of frantic women in my house within ten minutes.

Spiritual Surrender

DID YOU AND YOUR SPOUSE SHARE THE SAME SPIRITUAL BELIEF?

John grew up as a Catholic in a family with two sisters and two brothers. When I met him, he was not a practicing Catholic and organized religion did not seem to be important to him. I went to the Episcopalian church when I was very young and in high school attended the Lutheran church solely for the social aspects. I think what we lived more than spirituality was a philosophy of life, to do good, be kind, never anger the IRS, and do no wrong.

My philosophy had been derived from The Serenity Prayer, the "Desiderata," books, snappy sayings on t-shirts, and the eternal cocktail napkin. Although John and I never had any serious discussions about spirituality or religion, we lived the same kind of spiritual lives.

In the final hours before John died, his sister asked if he wanted the last rites and he nodded. I was so glad she thought to ask. I would not have asked him as he had never mentioned this in all our discussions of what the future was going to be. What I do know is that I will be with John again. To believe anything else is simply unbearable.

WHAT ATTRIBUTES DID YOUR SPOUSE BRING TO THE RELATIONSHIP, POSITIVE OR NEGATIVE?

John was such an incredibly special person that when I talk or write about him I want others to be able to see him as the person he was and not just hear a string of words. It would be easy to describe all of John's positive attributes. All you would have to do would be to look up all of the positive human traits in the dictionary and that would describe John. Loving, kind, thoughtful, funny, honorable, and cute...really, really cute. It's one thing to be loved and quite another to have a partner who makes you feel as if you're the center of his world. John did that for me. He didn't just love me quietly; he let me know I was loved and cherished every day.

I managed to sell my house several weeks before we were married, and I moved into his home. That's when the routines of our lives started, and it was like nothing I had ever experienced. John usually got up very early in the morning so he could read the entire newspaper before going to work. Five a.m. is the middle of the night for me, but I happily told him I would get up to fix his breakfast and keep him company until he went to work. He told me just to sleep—he enjoyed that quiet time before he went to work and he liked to finish the paper, so I would sleep in, and before he would leave for work, he would gently kiss me. It was so sweet. After he retired, our routine changed, of course, but he still found ways of making everything about my day special. He would bring me Frappuccinos in the morning when I woke up but wasn't out of bed yet.

The first week we were married he brought me flowers on Friday. He brought me flowers Friday for six-and-a-half years until he could no longer drive. It still takes my breath away when I think about it.

John had a wonderful sense of humor, which, fortunately, took the form of finding the quirky and sometimes dangerous things I did, if not funny, at least mildly amusing. I tried melting candles in the microwave, putting them on for ten seconds, but, unfortunately, I had set the timer for one minute and left the room. John happened to be walking through the kitchen when the door to the microwave blew open. There was a booming sound and flames shot out of the microwave. I came back into the room, told him not to worry about it, calmly walked to the stove, picked up the lid to a pot and covered the burning candles which put out the flames. The whole time John didn't move.

He looked at me, looked back at the microwave, back and forth with a look of incredulity on his face. Finally, he said "Do you think there is some alternative way we could find to accomplish that?" He wasn't angry. I think he was just dumbfounded that anyone could do anything that stupid. I'm quite sure after this I heard him talking to our insurance agent about increasing the insurance on the house, but he never complained and he never mentioned the incident. By the time of this near catastrophe, we had been married for several years, and this was not the first rodeo he had been through with me. Fortunately, he had not been around for some of my other shenanigans. He slept through the exploding eggs incident in the middle of the night, thank goodness, because it took me hours to clean up the kitchen.

John was impeccably neat and organized. I was his polar opposite. I am ADD, not in the least bit neat, and as unorganized as it is possible to be. He was incredibly tolerant. He once remarked, "It's amazing—you actually have four offices in this house—one in the den by the computer, one on your bedside table, another by the kitchen telephone, and one where we sit in the family room watching TV at night." I think the translation for this was "What are you doing with stuff piled up in all of these places?" I told him I was a very busy woman and had the important responsibility of running this house, and it required a lot of room and a lot of stuff. He smiled and replied, "Good answer."

John was generous to a fault. When my house was up for sale, he offered to buy us a new home and said that we didn't have to live in his house. I think in the back of his mind was a concern that I would not want to live in a house where he had lived with his first wife. It was one of those things that would have never occurred to me, but it demonstrates the depth of his consideration for the people around him.

John hated paying the bills and asked if I would mind taking over the chore. This request came early in our marriage before he knew I never balanced my checkbook nor did I compare my charge receipts with my credit card statement, a fact which would undoubtedly have horrified him. But I really wanted to be a good wife to him so I tried hard to stay organized and develop systems to keep track of everything. Remarkably, it worked out all right, and in all the years I did the bills, John never once asked to look at our finances, our accounts, where the money went, whether I was saving money, or any other thing to do with my spending. I knew that he only paid cash for large purchases and always paid the credit cards off each month. This was just one of the many things I learned from him that made my life much easier.

John was delighted to learn about my love of gardening. One day we were talking about an area I wanted to redo outside the glass doors to our bedroom. I described my plan to him and asked him what he thought. The next morning I woke up at 7:30 and heard John digging outside beneath a tree. He had taken all the plants out and had built a short retaining wall around the area I wanted to change. It was all ready for me to plant my garden. All the hard work had been done. He loved flowers and roses in the house, and I told him I could put in a rose garden if he wanted in the front courtyard area of our home. The next thing I knew John had arranged for the gardeners to take out all the plants, prepared the soil, and installed a complete drip system. He loved looking at the roses and having the bouquets in the house. He was such an easy man to please.

What occurred to bring you out of the denial of your situation? How did you find your way back to trusting your decisions and recapture your ability to love again?

Gradually, I realized John would not be proud of me for wallowing in my misery. I was letting everybody I loved down, worrying my daughters and friends, the people I cared so much about and who had given us so much love, support, and help. I knew I had to get it together whether I wanted to or not. I did not want to be that person whose only conversation with her friends would be about the pain I was in, the loss of John, what we had been through, or how miserable I was. I also didn't want to listen to myself complain. So I began accepting invitations to go out to lunch, for a drink, or to a movie. In truth, my daughters and grandchildren and "The Nine" saved my life. I never would have had the strength to go on without them.

It wasn't just one thing that brought me back to a state of real living. Six months after John died, one of my daughters, her family, and I moved in together. Being with part of my family and my darling grandchildren started me on the long road to healing. There is nothing like having two young children in the house; it made all the difference in the world. How can you be sad around the sound of children laughing and playing? They would crawl into my bed to hear a story at night and fall asleep. It was the best Band-Aid I could have had. Going to the market with those two sweet faces, running errands, taking the oldest to school, and picking him up gave me a purpose in life and brought me so much joy. That coupled with the adage that children say the darndest things brought the laughter back, too. We were together for two years. Although I thought about John every day during those years, life developed a rhythm of normality. I started to do some volunteer work, got back to playing golf and vacationing with my friends.

I was 64 years old, and I never really thought about being in love again because I was very content living alone. Being alone and being without John were two entirely different things. I would never get used to being without him. I missed the routine of our life, our conversations, and the laughter, always the laughter.

Over the next few years, my social life revolved around my family and friends. Being in another relationship was nothing I really considered a possibility. Two years after John died, I was diagnosed with Parkinson's disease. My reaction was relief. I knew this was going to be a piece of cake next to losing John, and I was so relieved that it was not something bad that had happened to my children or grandchildren. The diagnosis just didn't seem to mean anything to me.

Shortly after my diagnosis, I was introduced to Steve through mutual friends. Steve had lost his wife the year before. He was lonely but had not yet considered dating. To our mutual surprise, we hit it off right away. Steve fell in love almost immediately. I did not, but I thoroughly enjoyed being with him. We eventually discovered that we didn't have a real future together for various reasons, but we remained platonic friends until his death a year later.

NOW I UNDERSTAND AND BELIEVE THAT... I thought John and I would be together forever. We were not, and it nearly killed me. But what I do know now is that those seven years with John were worth a lifetime of anything else, and he left me with the best gift he could have given me: I remember what it was like to be in love.

WHAT ADVICE WOULD YOU GIVE TO YOUNG LOVERS ENTERING A NEW RELATIONSHIP?

If you ask any married, divorced, or widowed woman this question, she could write a book for you. So I've condensed my advice down to the things I think would have made a real difference in my life had I known them when I was younger.

Don't get married before you're 30. There was a time when you married whomever you were dating when you were a senior in college. So many of us were married at that time and in each other's weddings that we actually bought one style and color of bridesmaid's dress and just passed them around among everyone. You have no life experience; your knowledge base about the real world is almost zilch, and your philosophy of life, if you have one, is based on college parties and your favorite pizza place. After graduating from college, you will change and grow every year throughout your life. When you're twenty-one, you're half-baked. You need some real life experiences, work, and other relationships before marrying.

In a new relationship, spend the time learning everything you can about each other. Talk about the things that really matter to you: the important things that will shape and form your life; what your five-year and ten-year plans are. If you become more serious, discuss what you want in a marriage, what you want in a spouse, and what you want to be to that person. What kind of education do you want your children to have? How may your career changes affect your marriage?

Maintain your own friendships, interests, and hobbies. It's difficult to maintain a satisfactory relationship if your partner becomes your sole interest in life. It's your responsibility to be interesting to your partner. Auntie Mame said "Life is a banquet, and most poor suckers are starving to death."

Show your love for each other every day, and without being morbid, live each day as if it were your last day together.

Be conscious of what your partner needs; it may just be a hug on a bad day. Learn to read the signals.

Ask yourself what you can bring to this relationship to enrich it and let it continue to grow. Make great memories together.

You can walk through your life or you can plan a fulfilling life where each partner grows and learns from each other.

We are responsible for the course of our own happiness. Take the responsibility.

Epilogue to Loving John

October - 2016

For all the years after John died I could not dream about him, and it hurt. There were a lot of photographs of us, and him, but I didn't have a tape recording of his voice or a videotape of us. Somehow, the video that was taken at our wedding by friends, was lost before we ever saw it. Every day for these 7 years I have thought about not being able to see or hear him. I would have given anything to have heard his voice again.

It may sound like I could never let go, or "get on" with my life but I did. It didn't happen quickly but I did go on and I did a good job of it. But it never stopped me from loving John or wanting him back, which brings me to the miracle of yesterday.

I've moved twice since John died and each time I vowed to clean out the house to get rid of the junk that collects and seems to breed. Instead I would sit and stare at endless boxes stuffed with odds and ends I couldn't face going through.

In October of this year, 2016, I was going through the television cabinet in the living room looking for an old DVD to watch when I saw four small videotapes from our old camcorder, I honestly can't tell you how I missed seeing them through two moves although they obviously had been unpacked. Even when I found them it didn't occur to me that there might be anything but videos of our grandchildren on them. I left them sitting around for about a month before I finally took them to Costco to have them transferred to DVD so I could make copies for my children.

Now, for the shock. Yesterday I sat down to watch the DVDs. They were what I expected; our grandchildren when they were babies, plump, funny and happy. Suddenly the video changed and it almost brought me to my knees. John had taken a video of our ten day honeymoon on Kauai. There we were playing golf, laughing, driving around the island and talking. When he was taking videos of my golf shots he would describe them as if I was doing everything perfectly and then tell me what a magnificent shot it was even though the ball had only gone 10 feet. He would say, "Look how straight it went, that was great." He videotaped hours of our life on the island. I could hear him narrating in the background about whatever he was taping. He called me the "beautiful Nancy. His voice...... eight years, and I could finally hear his voice. If I closed my eyes I could make myself believe he was in the room with me. As I listened to his voice memories of those days came flooding back: the sound of Frank Sinatra, dancing at night on the patio to *Fly Me to the Moon* and *The Summer Winds*. I can feel the soft evening breeze and hear the waves pounding the rocky ledge off our patio.

Watching the videotape brought me the calming peace I had been missing for so long. I had mourned the loss of hearing John's voice. The joy I felt that day, and since, was incredible. I will never have to live another day without hearing his laughter and seeing his beautiful smile.

* * *

This story brings to mind the saying that it is better to have loved and lost than not to have loved at all. After all, loving is what we do and it is also who we become because of it.

Live Brave.

PART TWO

Emotional Responsiveness

"The first and foremost instinct of humans is neither sex nor aggression. It is to seek contact and comforting connection."

Dr. John Bowlby

CHAPTER TWO

LOOKING FOR THE CONNECTION

"The hardest—learned lesson: that people have only their kind of love to give, not our kind."

Mignon McLaughlin

Hilda

The unconditional love that I feel for Mary Catherine has had time to cultivate for over thirty years when we met and became friends.

Although over the years, I had only heard bits and pieces of her story, met some of her family members and followed her career path, nothing prepared me for the painful feelings I felt when I read the story she presented to us for our *Living Brave* questionnaire. Mary Catherine is one of the most extraordinary women that I have had the privilege of knowing and calling my friend. Aside from the fact that she is a beautiful woman, her perky and positive nature is a welcoming breath of fresh air. I know I must sound like a Hallmark movie commercial as I describe my feelings for her, but she truly is an inspiration. Allow me to introduce Mary Catherine.

MARY CATHERINE, 68

"Your circumstances can change your environment and some things are out of your control, but poor choices can dictate your life passages in a major way. Self-esteem plays a huge role."

Mary Catherine was born and raised in the deep South with traditional Christian values. She is currently married and lives in Prescott, Arizona, in a newly remodeled home in the historic district. She has two children, both married with two children each. She owns a successful management company but is retired from the day-to-day business management as her sister runs the company for her. She is very active in her church, serving on several committees. She participates in two book clubs and is an avid reader. Mary Catherine is also a volunteer with the West Yavapai Guidance Center and takes Lifelong Learning classes for seniors at Yavapai College. She enjoys hiking, yoga, and lots of travel.

Title: Trials vs. Blessings

Physical Connection

WHERE WERE YOU BORN AND RAISED, AND WHAT CAN YOU TELL US ABOUT YOUR CHILDHOOD SURROUNDINGS AND CIRCUMSTANCES?

I was born in Springhill, Louisiana, on May 20, 1948. Both of my parents were raised in southern Arkansas where the majority of my relatives lived. I had a loving childhood with a two-parent family and a large extended family of grandparents, aunts, uncles, and cousins. Both sets of my grandparents were from the same small town in southern Arkansas.

I was raised in a traditional Christian environment with my grandparents involved in the Southern Baptist Church. I was baptized at the age of eleven.

My parents moved to Jackson, Mississippi, when I was four, and we spent the next ten years there but drove to my grandparents' home in Arkansas for a weekend visit every month.

My dad was transferred with his job to Phoenix, Arizona, in 1962 when I was thirteen years old. This was a very emotional move for me as I left numerous friends, relatives, a church, and a school that I enjoyed.

TELL US OF A TIME WHEN YOU FELL DEEPLY IN LOVE—THE ATTRAC-TION/CONNECTION, THE CIRCUMSTANCES, YOUR AGE AT THE TIME, AND HOW LONG IT LASTED. WERE THERE ANY "RED FLAGS" AT THE BEGINNING OF THE RELATIONSHIP THAT YOU WERE AWARE OF BUT DID NOT ACKNOWLEDGE?

This move was an emotional disaster for me. In Mississippi I had been in junior high school, but when I moved to Arizona, the eighth grade was still grade school. I was immediately made fun of because of my Southern accent, the way I dressed, and just being the new kid in a group who had had eight years to form friendships and cliques.

Some of the kids literally followed me home from school and threw rocks at me. I could not understand what was happening and was too embarrassed to let my parents know how unhappy I was. I became isolated with no friends and no social engagement. I spent weekends at home and just tolerated school until the summer recess. I cried myself to sleep often, longing for my friends and family in the South.

I started high school in the fall and was hoping that a new school might change my circumstances, but again, kids seemed to have entered high school with friends from grade school, and I had lost a lot of self-confidence in the past several months. I usually ate lunch alone and again had no friends with whom to spend weekends with. The same kids from the grade school I had attended continued to make fun of me.

In December of my freshman year, I was eating lunch alone in the cafeteria when a very tall, dark, and handsome guy approached and asked if he could sit with me. He was a transfer student from California. He was so good looking, 6' 8" tall, and a good athlete. I was only 4'11" so there was a huge disparity in our heights. He was immediately sought after and became quite popular. Ordinarily, this would not have been my type, although at fourteen I'm not sure what my "type" was. All I knew was that he was my ticket to popularity and to ending my isolation.

In the beginning, he was so attentive and charming. I was so vulnerable at the time that I craved his attention and affection. Unlike my upbringing, he came from a chaotic, troubled background with an alcoholic, abusive father and a mother with no backbone. They did not attend church, and he was not a Christian.

I was so desperate to be his girlfriend that I succumbed to his constant pressure and eventually had sex with him, because of course, he had convinced me that was the only way I could prove my love for him.

And as you can imagine, the more intimate we became, the more possessive he became. He did not want me to have girlfriends and certainly did not want me to speak to another guy. My isolation from friends and a social environment that I had endured for a year became a different kind of isolation—one that he imposed on me.

What I thought would be a relationship that would keep me from my former isolation became exactly the same thing. Even if he went out with friends, he did not allow me to do the same thing. In the beginning, I fought against his possessiveness, which eventually led to physical abuse. Every time he was physically abusive, he would beg my forgiveness and make promises that it would never happen again. Of course, it just got worse and worse.

We dated for over two years, but in the middle of my junior year when he beat me with a tennis racket, it became so bad that I finally had to tell my parents what was going on, and I begged them to let me go back to Arkansas and live with my grandmother. I was terrified of him. You may wonder how my parents didn't know, but he always hit me in places that did not show the bruises. He was so charismatic that he had my father fooled. My dad fell prey to his athletic skills as he enjoyed going to the high school sporting events and watching him compete.

My Christian upbringing also kept me in the relationship longer than I should have stayed because I truly thought of myself as used goods. No man would ever want me because I was no longer a virgin. I had such a low self-esteem as a result of all of this.

My mother did take me to Arkansas, and I finished my junior year there. Of course, everyone at school thought I had gone away to have a baby. While I lived in Arkansas, I received countless letters from him vowing to never hit me again and telling me that he had gotten a job to buy me an engagement ring. Looking back, of course, this was all so ridiculous and naïve because we were sixteen and seventeen years old.

I did return to Arizona at the end of the school year because I missed my parents and family so much. I resisted his begging me to go back with him for several months but finally succumbed in February of my senior year.

Of course, he only kept his promise of no abuse for about a month, and it all started again. We finally agreed to split up (even he agreed) in April as we were going to separate colleges. But then I found out I was pregnant. My world crashed. Because of my Christian beliefs, I believed the only solution was marriage. We got married in May, one week after my eighteenth birthday, and had our son in January, 1967. My mother begged me not to marry him and said that she and my dad would help me raise the baby so I could continue with my college plans. I was so naïve that I thought with marriage, a baby, and my support, he would change, and we would have a loving marriage. I did love him in my own immature way at the time. When he was rational, he was very charming and attractive, and I fell in love with that side of him. The result, however, was that that side became increasingly rare with the mean, hateful side the norm. I walked on eggshells waiting for the next outburst.

The abuse continued with barbaric instances—he would hit me when I was pregnant, make me sleep on the floor with no blanket or pillow, lock me out of the house in the winter while pregnant, throw meals I cooked on the walls or in my face if they didn't meet with his approval. Right after our baby was born by cesarean section, my husband ripped up all my clothing and made me sleep on the floor. He railed if the baby cried, so I spent most nights up trying to rock and comfort my son so that he wouldn't cry and wake up my husband. I was exhausted. To go back to work, I had to go to a used clothing store and buy three or four dresses because he had ripped everything up.

The abuse continued through his numerous infidelities, lack of financial help, continuous bullying, and a move to another state where he played football on scholarship at a university. I always worked during the marriage, pregnancies, and child rearing. I was the only one with an income.

At this point and after counseling, I made the decision to leave. When he finally realized I was actually leaving, he shot himself. As his spouse, I was no-tified by the hospital that he had a self-inflected wound. He had shot himself in the stomach. If he had truly wanted to die, he would have shot himself in the head. I knew that he shot himself in the stomach to gain my sympathy and force me to stay. I had to make the agonizing decision to stick with my plan of leaving or I would have just been sucked back into a relentless nightmare, walking on egg shells, calculating every word so that he would not get angry, continual abuse, and worrying about the effects on my son.

Were there red flags? Of course, there were. I knew from the very beginning that he was not the kind of person my parents would want me to be with, but as a result of bullying and isolation, I fell prey to his advances and charms and soon got sucked into his web of abuse and possessiveness.

We were divorced about a year when my three-year-old son had to have surgery. I did notify my ex-husband, and he came to the hospital. In that vulnerable state, he talked me once again into going back to him. We never remarried; however, I got pregnant again, and we had a daughter.

He did play one season in the NFL. He would not take me or the children with him, and when I read his profile, he stated that he was single with no children. He was making good money at the time (early 1970's) of $1,000/week, yet the entire time he was gone (five months) he sent me $500.

He returned home, but I finally left him when my daughter was just an infant by sneaking out of the house with the clothes on our backs and hiding for days at the home of one of my parent's friends while he was under the influence of drugs.

After our final divorce and over the course of eighteen years, I received a total of $105 and a one-time help with a car upgrade. He did help with our children's tuition for college but sent no money on a regular basis to help with the kids. You may wonder why I didn't take him to court to get child support. I had a not-so-brilliant attorney who suggested that since he was going to go into professional football, I should ask for 10% of his gross salary instead of a specified amount. Well, his football career was short-lived due to knee injuries. He got into drug dealing and, therefore, on his tax returns reported very little income, calling himself a "self-employed wood cutter." Basically, 10% of zero is zero. As a result of his drug dealing, he spent two different sentences in federal penitentiaries.

Emotional Responsiveness

WHAT DID YOUR PARENTS MODEL IN A RELATIONSHIP FOR YOU AS A CHILD?

My parents provided a very stable environment. They were married 33 years before my father passed away at the age of 54 from lung cancer. It was not a perfect marriage, but family was important to them, and they provided a secure, loving home. I did overhear them at one time discussing divorce, but nothing came of it. They were Christians, but my grandparents provided the stronger Christian influence in my life. My parents went to church but not as regularly as my grandparents did.

WHAT WERE YOU LOOKING FOR IN THIS RELATIONSHIP?

Obviously, at the age of fourteen, I was not looking for a husband or a long-term relationship. I simply wanted to have friends in high school, and my relationship with my boyfriend then provided that acceptance.

LOOKING BACK, DID YOU AND YOUR SPOUSE SHARE THE VALUES THAT YOUR PARENTS MODELED?

No, my boyfriend/husband and I did not share the same values as my parents. My parents were Christians and were not abusive. My marriage was nothing like my parents' marriage. My mother would have never worried about what she was saying or fear physical abuse from my father.

WHAT CHANGED? WHAT OCCURRED FOR YOU TO FEEL THE LOSS OF THE RELATIONSHIP? TO WHAT EXTENT WAS IT HURTFUL, PHYSICALLY, FINANCIALLY, MENTALLY, AND EMOTIONALLY?

After my divorce and final separation, I felt like a complete loser. I was 24 years old. I had no self-confidence. I had been told I was ugly, fat, stupid, and worthless with no common sense. I had been beaten both physically and emotionally for nine years. Because I had become pregnant and had a child at eighteen, I never had the opportunity to attend college. I had always been a good student, but higher education was impossible as I had a family to support. I had no college degree, was divorced with two children, and received no child support.

Spiritual Surrender

DID YOU AND YOUR SPOUSE SHARE THE SAME SPIRITUAL BELIEF?

My spouse and I did not share the same spiritual beliefs. I was a Christian, and he would have been what I would call an agnostic. We never went to church as a couple. My beliefs were put on hold, and I was not able to express or practice those beliefs. Of course, I still believed in God and prayed constantly that the abuse would stop throughout my relationship. I didn't push to go to church. Believe me, I had a lot bigger problems to deal with on a daily basis.

WHAT ATTRIBUTES DID YOUR SPOUSE BRING TO THE RELATIONSHIP, POSITIVE OR NEGATIVE?

My spouse was very charismatic, very charming, and very handsome. That is why I fell so hard for him. He was actually humorous and fun to be with on a good day. I did truly love him. He could be very loving toward me, but then his anger would result in physical abuse, after which he would cry and apologize. It was a vicious cycle.

WHAT OCCURRED TO BRING YOU OUT OF THE DENIAL OF YOUR SITUATION? HOW DID YOU FIND YOUR WAY BACK TO TRUSTING YOUR DECISIONS AND RECAPTURE YOUR ABILITY TO LOVE AGAIN?

For years I struggled to take care of my children. I qualified for government-subsidized housing, and we lived in a government apartment for five years. I had always had good secretarial skills, so I got a job with a management company in 1973 as a secretary. I worked very hard for many years. As I began to progress in the company, my confidence level returned. I didn't date for over five years, just concentrating on my kids and trying to make ends meet. I did have tremendous emotional support from my parents. We lived near them so my kids would go to their house after school and I picked them up there after work; many evenings we stayed and had dinner with them.

I worked tirelessly and very long hours as a single mom. My job required long hours during the day and board meetings at night. I routinely worked ten to sixteen hour days. It's amazing that my children turned out as well as they did. Of course, it wasn't all smooth sailing. My son did engage in the drug culture during high school that caused much anxiety and counseling. It was very difficult as a single mom to navigate those issues.

I'm very proud to say that both of my children did survive; they both graduated from college, they are both in successful marriages, and each has a son and a daughter.

After working twenty years for the management company that I joined in 1973, I bought the company through a series of loans in 1993 and still own it today. It is a very successful business, and I enjoy a comfortable life style that affords me the opportunity to travel and enjoy retirement.

I met my current husband in 1999. He is absolutely nothing like my first husband. He was a widower whose wife had died in 1991. He has three children and nine grandchildren. He is a strong Christian man, and we share a deep faith together. We married in 2004 and moved to Prescott to enjoy our retirement. We are very involved with our children and grandchildren, as well as our church, and we enjoy playing golf together and traveling the world.

It took years to gain my self-confidence back. I would say that confidence mostly returned through my professional life. When I met my current husband, there was never a moment when I felt unsure of myself. You have to understand, however, that it had been 26 years since I had left my first husband. I, of course, did have a few relationships through the years, some not so successful, but my confidence began to return and I learned to respect myself again. It did not happen overnight. I did return to my faith and raised my children in a Christian environment. I am a strong, self-assured woman today and very comfortable in my own skin and in my marriage.

Now I understand and believe that... Your circumstances can change your environment and some things are out of your control, but poor choices can dictate your life passages in a major way. Self-esteem plays a huge role.

What advice would you give to young lovers entering a new relationship?

First of all, be true to yourself and respect yourself.

I also would strongly advise anyone to have confidence in oneself and believe in oneself before entering into a relationship. I know that is easier said than done, but it would make entering a relationship so much easier if one has self-confidence, assurance, and self-respect.

I would also advise young people to wait until they are at least in their mid-to-late twenties to even contemplate a serious relationship. A person changes so much from fifteen to twenty-five. These are years when you discover who you are, what your values are, and what you want out of life. Trying to discover these things while in a relationship with someone who is doing the same thing makes for difficult navigation.

I do not regret my past or the circumstances I went through. I have two beautiful children that I adore and four amazing grandchildren. Those circumstances strengthened who I am and formed my Christian foundation. I have accepted my past, and I think I learned from it. It has made me a strong, confident woman able to love and trust again.

As I mentioned before, my former husband became a drug dealer, and, at the current age of 69, is still dealing in drugs. He has never held a traditional job. He went on to marry four more times and has one child by each of three of those wives. He continued the abuse with his other wives. I came to know each of them and their sordid stories as a result of contact through the years with my children. He did see his children but not often. He never physically abused my children, but I think they have suffered emotionally as a result of contact with him. They have made the conscientious choice of continuing a relationship with him although they do set boundaries, and they are very aware that they are not dealing with a rational human being. I have let them make their own choices in this matter as they matured. My children have three half-sisters as a result of those marriages. It is interesting that his current wife, whom he's been with for over thirty years, has stayed with him although I see evidence of intimidation, and she has cut off all relations with her own family. They never had children together, but I am amazed that this woman has stayed with him all these years.

In closing, I would like to say that I would not change the circumstances of my life. I believe that God uses people for His purpose, and we can come out on the other side of trials in our life with enormous blessings. I have been blessed beyond measure, and I truly believe in one of my favorite scripture verses, Romans 8:28 "And we know that all things work together for good to those who love God, to those who are called according to His purpose."

* * *

They say that the wind blows evenly on all sails and that each one of us has the choice to catch the wind and direct it in the direction that we most desire. As a young girl, Mary Catherine could not have possibly understood the winds that were blowing her into a dangerous direction. But according to Dr. John Bowlby's Attachment Theory, she was most likely seeking contact and connection, as we all are in our desire for love.

As I observe Mary Catherine fully enjoying her life as a model citizen, successful business owner, involved mother and grandmother, student and volunteer in her community, my belief remains strong that the winds of fortune exists and that they are there for our sailing.

Live brave.

LOOKING FOR THE CONNECTION

"Sometimes leaving a relationship can be a wise thing to do if attempts to change a destructive situation reach insurmountable obstacles."

Jean Baker Miller & Irene Pierce Stiver, The Healing Connection

Hilda

Some individuals go through life in their tight Rubik's-Cube existence, moving within a small parameter of experiences; tightly taking little steps as to not disturb the safety of their lives or the box that keeps them bound together. Our next story-teller is not that person. Tammy is just the opposite; open and outgoing, intentional, and committed, intelligent and emotionally sensitive as she dedicates herself to the betterment of others.

We met when Tammy was a young and enthusiastic girl of 18 just entering college. Her parents were clients of mine in the salon and her younger brother was my son's age. They attend high-school together. Even back then at her youthful age, it was obvious that she would accomplish what most women could only dream of doing. During our conversations, I was impressed that she had a plan for her life. She wanted to be of service and possibly teach school. Mostly, she wanted to help others.

Because nothing breeds passion and purpose like an unforgettable painful occurrence to draw upon, Tammy experienced an agonizing relationship which eventually lit a fire within her to serve in a bigger way. She is dedicated to shining that light for others to view the possibility of a joyful future. Here is her story.

TAMMY, 48

"My father is an incredible man of integrity. His word is his word and he always stayed true to that…In that sense, my childhood is partly why I accepted my husband's lies so blindly. I just expected my husband to be like my father."

Tammy is currently the CEO of a non-profit women's resource center serving over a 1,000 women and 250 children annually in several locations throughout the state where she lives. Tammy obtained her Bachelor's Degree in Political Science & Economics, and has spent twenty-five plus years working in both corporate and non-profit administration, including several years serving internationally. Tammy's passion is helping women and children find hope in the midst of crisis and she loves serving in the non-profit community to do just that.

Title: Living the Lie

Physical Connection

WHERE WERE YOU BORN AND RAISED, AND WHAT CAN YOU TELL US ABOUT YOUR CHILDHOOD SURROUNDINGS AND CIRCUMSTANCES?

I was born in Orlando, Florida and raised across the USA. My parents were educators and teachers and their jobs took them to many parts of the U.S. from Florida to Texas, California, Arizona, and more. I consider Arizona "home" because it is where I spent junior high and high school. I come from a very loving family where faith played a central part in our lives. I have one sibling, a brother, who is four years younger and to whom I remain very close to this day.

TELL US OF A TIME WHEN YOU FELL DEEPLY IN LOVE—THE ATTRACTION/CONNECTION, THE CIRCUMSTANCES, YOUR AGE AT THE TIME, AND HOW LONG IT LASTED. WERE THERE ANY "RED FLAGS" AT THE BEGINNING OF THE RELATIONSHIP THAT YOU WERE AWARE OF BUT DID NOT ACKNOWLEDGE?

I met my future husband when I was 20 years old. He was charismatic and funny and I had never met anyone like him. He poured attention on me and made me feel like I was a prize worth pursuing. He was 8 years older and he had been through a hard time in a previous marriage which he felt was due to marrying the wrong person. Suddenly I became the right person and the savior to his broken heart. He wooed me with gifts, flowers, and extravagant gestures in which he could show off to my family and friends his attention for me – such as surprising me on a birthday by flying in from out of state, showing up at the restaurant where we were having dinner and pretending to be the waiter delivering the wine. He loved to do grand gestures like that to show off to everyone how romantic he was. He also wanted to shower my friends and family with gifts to show how generous he was. My first Christmas present after we were engaged was a car. I had grown up in a very financially-modest home. I had never had my own car before so gestures like that swept me off my feet. I wish I had understood then the difference in looking like you have financial security but living on credit, versus actually having financial security. My former husband lived on credit and was deeply in debt but I was too young to really understand the difference and to look for the signs of wise financial choices. Instead, I was dazzled by the life of wealth and travel he was dangling before me.

Were there red flags? I am amazed that I could see anything past the red flags now. In hindsight they were everywhere, but I was young, naïve, and ready to believe away any concern. Drug use and infidelity in his first marriage, drug use and pornography in his life when we met, pathological lying, twisting things to make me doubt any concerns I voiced all should have been major red flags for me. I discovered early into our marriage that many of the stories he had told me about his childhood, (owning a boat, vacation homes, travel, etc) were all stories of people he knew and he had used them as his own to build this persona about himself. None of them were true. As time went on, I noticed he would lie about everything from something as simple as where he went to lunch to more significant things like childhood memories. But he always had a way of making me doubt my own doubts and eventually I would push them away and keep trying harder in the relationship.

Emotional Responsiveness

What did your parents model in a relationship for you as a child?

My parents have a solid, loving relationship. They modeled trust, intimacy, and faithful commitment and a deep and abiding love for one another. They truly were a team throughout my life. They respect each other, consult each other on major decisions, and value each other's input. I thought everyone had relationships like they have. My father is an incredible man of integrity. His word is his word and he always stayed true to that. If he said something, it was the truth. When I was young I remember him calling a company that had inadvertently given us more of a service than we had paid for and he called to pay them the difference because it was the right thing to do. That memory struck me as a child.... to be a person of integrity and truth.

In that sense, my childhood is partly why I accepted my husband's lies so blindly. I just expected my husband to be like my father. Your word was to be trusted. It never occurred to me that my husband was lying about so much in his life.

What were you looking for in this relationship?

I was looking for "True Love", a marriage like my parents have and a faithful partner. I wanted someone who I could partner with in life to build a home and a family. I wanted a partner with whom there would be mutual respect, trust, shared values, and shared interests. Particularly important to me was shared faith. I wanted someone who shared my faith and made it central in their life like it was in mine. I wanted someone to build a true partnership with as I had seen my parent's model.

Looking back, did you and your spouse share the values that your parents modeled?

I thought we did. I thought my spouse wanted to share those values, but he was living a double life. The life he wanted to be and the choices he was actually making.

What changed? What occurred for you to feel the loss of the relationship? To what extent was it hurtful, physically, financially, mentally, and emotionally?

Pretty early on I knew something was dreadfully wrong with my marriage. But I could never put my finger on what it was and he always denied or explained away any circumstance that concerned me. He would not be where he said he was or have elaborate stories to explain away what should have been simple things like why his cell phone constantly had a "dead battery". I often had trouble reaching him or there were long absences during the day where no one was sure where he was or he arrived home in the wee hours of the morning after I had been unable to reach him with stories of customers with car trouble, etc. I was a young bride terrified he had been in an accident or injured somewhere and unable to reach him until he suddenly appeared at home at 2:00 or 3:00 in the morning with elaborate stories of what had happened. It didn't add up, but I felt guilty for not trusting him. We were newlyweds, after all. What could be wrong in the honeymoon phase of our marriage?

As the years progressed there were more significant signs of infidelity, pornography, drug use, unethical business decisions, daily lies about where he was and what he was doing, emotional distance, verbal control and abuse, emotional manipulation. Whatever I was concerned about he would talk me in circles until I was emotionally exhausted and came away sure I was wrong and he was the victim. For example, finding pornography in his car and his elaborate explanation of it belonging to a colleague and he was helping hide it from his wife. He wasn't using it, of course; he was just being a kind friend. How could I question him for that? Or finding a note in his pocket from another women and his story of her unrequited crush on him and he had hidden it to protect me since he did not return her affections. Everything he did, he did for me, he would tell me. There was even one instance where I found him at another woman's house. Again, he was doing it "for me." He had to go see her to explain why he couldn't be with her and let her down easy. Never mind that it was late at night or that he told me he would be somewhere else. All of his friends seemed to know exactly what was going on and felt sorry for me. But his response? How could I possibly be so mistrustful and treat him that way? Shame on me. Everything he did, he did for me. I was terrified of how I was living and terrified of leaving. After years of feeling like something was dreadfully wrong with ME because I was always feeling something was very wrong with us and always being told it wasn't, the strain became too much. I couldn't keep up the façade any longer and began to reach out for help and let people in on the nightmare I was living. The more I began to get help and challenge his behaviors, the more his addictions increased and he spiraled out of control.

What finally gave me the courage to ask for a temporary separation was my fear for our children and the damage his choices and my co-dependency were causing them. Friends helped me file for legal separation to protect myself and the children financially since we were in this temporary separation and his financial choices were spiraling into deeper debt. Even then, I never dreamed we would be divorced. I really thought that when faced with losing his family, he would "hit bottom' and get help. I really believed my love would "save" him. I was so very, very wrong. The separation gave him the freedom to leave and he promptly left the state to return to where his family lived. Eventually he counter-sued my legal separation by filing for divorce and after two years of legal wrangling back and forth, the divorce was granted. Even being out of state and not giving any financial support or attention to the children, he still fought me tooth and nail to keep control so that I was unable to get sole custody. Every major decision – travel, school, living, even church, had to have his approval. I remember sitting with a court appointed mediator as we worked on custody. My husband was on the phone since he was living out of state and he still talked circles around me and sold the mediator on what a loving, doting, father he was so joint custody was awarded. I felt helpless in dealing with him.

The cost? A shattered heart....loss of worth/dignity....loss of "place"....financial devastation ....emotional scars that took more than a decade to fully heal.....many years of fighting the control he still had over me by just hearing the phone ring and fearing it was him....many years of living in FEAR that he would take the children, financially ruin me....you name it, I feared it.

Spiritual Surrender

DID YOU AND YOUR SPOUSE SHARE THE SAME SPIRITUAL BELIEF?

In word only. My spouse had been raised in church and could "talk the talk" but did not truly assimilate that into his life. There was no fruit of that belief. At the time, I attributed that to his youth and poor choices. Later I realized he had never assimilated that into his life. For me, my faith IS the central thing in my life.

WHAT ATTRIBUTES DID YOUR SPOUSE BRING TO THE RELATIONSHIP, POSITIVE OR NEGATIVE?

Positive: Charismatic, persuasive, warm, friendly, smart, funny, giving. He always made people laugh; older people in particular loved his southern charm. He doted on me publically and showered all my friends and family with expensive gifts. He genuinely enjoyed giving gifts and how that made him feel. Even years after our divorce he will still send my family gifts. But it is a way that eases his guilt over the choices he made and the hurt he caused.

Negative: Controlling, demeaning, emotionally abusive. It's hard to explain how someone can begin to make you doubt yourself so completely. It happened over a long period of time....slowly beating down my self-esteem. Decisions questioned, making decisions for me because he was so much wiser, choosing my clothes for me because he had a better sense of style, decorating our house for the same reason, purchasing everything so I should feel grateful, but really it was extremely controlling. I remember being late for work because he was shining my shoes. I couldn't leave the house until he finished because no wife of his was going out looking like that. He did it out of his "love" for me, but in hindsight it was control. If he would come home and I would have had an exhausting day with a baby or toddler and maybe sat down to rest or read a magazine, I would jump up and immediately begin cleaning or preparing dinner. It was like that was our unspoken bargain. I had the "easy job" of being at home. His job was the "valuable" job so how could I even consider resting? I had it easy....I should be grateful. He was out working to provide for us so I needed to make sure everything was perfect at home to keep up my end of the bargain.

WHAT OCCURRED TO BRING YOU OUT OF THE DENIAL OF YOUR SITUA-TION? HOW DID YOU FIND YOUR WAY BACK TO TRUSTING YOUR DECI-SIONS AND RECAPTURE YOUR ABILITY TO LOVE AGAIN?

Opening up to trusted friends and allowing them to gently open my eyes to the sickness of my relationship and my own co-dependency began to help me in breaking free of the lies I was living in. My faith and my tremendous love for my children and desire to give them a healthy family also led to my finally recognizing the unhealthiness we were living in. Reading – I read everything I could get my hands on – about the situations I was dealing with and realizing I was not the first nor the last to experience this. Knowing I was not alone – that others had been through it and survived – was critical to my healing. Once I was on my own, reading, seeing a counselor, being gentle with myself as I took time to heal, spending time with friends, and eventually finding a career that allowed me to help other women who were walking the path I had walked were all parts to helping me heal. Also, learning to love myself and to be content with just myself and not feel I had to be in a relationship to be complete was so helpful.

NOW I UNDERSTAND AND BELIEVE THAT.... I wasn't imagining things. I had good reason to doubt him and the lies I was hearing. I have a valuable inner voice and I can trust that and act on it. If something doesn't feel right, it probably isn't right and I am valuable enough to question that.

I have no idea where I found them, but somewhere I found and placed on my refrigerator two quotes that I continued to read over and over again. I probably found them in one of the numerous books I have on sex addiction. Here they are:

The Bribe: The bribe is a dynamic that is seen when working with partners of sex addicts. The concept is simple: you and the partner agree to put up the appearance that everything is normal in exchange for you taking care of the children. You can tell the bribe is in a relationship when the husband's first line of defense is the checkbook. He believes he is paying you off, so what are you complaining about? If you don't like it, he will find someone who will. There are several dynamics here. He knows your abandonment issues. He tried to beat your self-esteem so low that you don't believe you could ever take care of yourself. He sees you as an object in his life providing a function. For the bribe dynamic to work, there has to be a volunteer to take the bribe. Some do this exchange willingly; especially if they live financially well, others do it because they feel trapped.

THIS WAS SO TRUE FOR ME. I felt trapped; I felt I could never provide for myself without him, much less the kids as well. He made it very clear that he was financially providing and I had a function to provide in exchange for that. My function was to keep house & raise kids and show up to look like a good family whenever he needed me to.

Verbal Reality: Addicts of any kind live in what I call "verbal reality". This means if they say it, it is true, and if they say it passionately, it is really true. The behavior and follow-through in weeks to come are not required for it to be true.

You must understand the sex addict's verbal reality; this is often how the addict manipulates you. The sex addict believes what he is saying while he is saying it, and to him that is enough to not follow through with the behavior.

Your only savior in the verbal reality is measurable behavior. The behavior is always the truth. He says "I love you" but acts out. The behavior is always the truth. He says he wants to change, but attends no meetings, makes no calls - the behavior is the truth. Don't be fooled by verbal reality and don't blame him if you buy what he says to you. In the past, your own desire to believe the best and to not make measurable behaviors the issue set up a system you were both familiar with. The system is: he does what he wants, says "I love you" or "I'll change". You believe him, nothing changes, and then you get to repeat the cycle again.

The only way to stop this is to ask what behaviors he is committed to and where he is going to check off if he did them or not. Addicts themselves buy their verbal reality so YOU cannot if you are going to recover.

This is the one I kept most on my fridge. Trying to remember if he says it, no matter how passionately, **unless the behavior follows, it is not true. The behavior NEVER followed.**

WHAT ADVICE WOULD YOU GIVE TO YOUNG LOVERS ENTERING A NEW RELATIONSHIP?

Communication is key. There must be open, truthful, and authentic communication. A person should be trustworthy. Their word must mean something. You should be able to be open with one another and not have reason to doubt what someone is telling you. You need to see him/her in an environment interacting with friends and family. How they respond in those situations is important. Is there trust? Openness? Honesty? Are there close friends that know him/her well enough that they can speak truth into their life. Is there accountability? How do they treat their family members?

I will never be in a serious relationship again without some element of counseling in it. We all have baggage in our lives from prior relationships, and counseling is important to make sure we process things individually and can enter into a new relationship without carrying some of those misperceptions with us.

* * *

As I continue to witness her substantial impact in the community and see her personal confidence regaining its strength, I am proud of her accomplishments. She encourages others and gives them hope for a future that she almost did not experience.

Live brave.

CHAPTER THREE

WHAT CHANGED

"Attachment is the great fabricator of illusions; reality can be attained only by someone who is detached."

Simone Weil

Hilda

Although I had met Jaye over the years as we traveled the same circle of spiritual studies, shared an interest in Enneagram work and I even took a class from her, I did not know the intensity of her love story. When Mary Beth and I met with her we were mesmerized with her understanding of her circumstances and her ability to manage through them. We were both taken aback by her cheerfulness and open heartedness to answering any further questions that we had. We were grateful for her willingness to educate us on a subject that is still a mystery for many of us. Here is her love story.

JAYE, 64

"Most people think that gender is a black and white category—one is either male OR female. But research shows that it is actually more of a continuum with some people being at the extremes of very male or very female and others falling in various degrees between the two poles."

As a life coach and consultant, Jaye's passion is to assist others in raising their self-awareness and move past limiting beliefs and habits to live a fuller, freer, richer, and more peaceful life. She also facilitates workshops with groups and organizations on personality type, team building, conflict resolution, and leadership development. Jaye holds a Master's Degree in Business Administration, is a certified Enneagram professional, and is a "founding mother," past president and Emeritus Director of the Arizona Enneagram Association.

Title: Tilt

Physical Connection

WHERE WERE YOU BORN AND RAISED, AND WHAT CAN YOU TELL US ABOUT YOUR CHILDHOOD SURROUNDINGS AND CIRCUMSTANCES?

I was born in Fargo, North Dakota—flat, windy, cold prairie. From high school on I felt I wanted to leave the state, joking that my guardian angel was distracted the day I was born because I was sure I had requested Key Largo, not Fargo! I am the fourth of five children, born three years after the only boy in the family, a position that benefited me because I was always trying to prove I could do anything he could do. My father was a musician who sold life insurance to support the family; my mother, a stay-at-home mom. I attended Catholic schools through high school but "fell away" after that. I was more attracted to Eastern philosophies, to spirituality more than to religion.

My first marriage at the age of 23 got me out of Fargo—way out! We went into Peace Corps Thailand and later spent seven years working in Zambia and Rwanda, Africa. The marriage didn't last, but I am grateful for the time we spent together overseas as it was mind, heart, and soul expanding. I remember returning to the U.S. from Rwanda and being totally stunned walking into a PetSmart store and seeing more food for pets in one of those new "big box" stores than had existed for people in the entire capital city of Kigali. I also got stuck in the aisle of a grocery store trying to buy yogurt and being totally overwhelmed by the number of choices. Just one carton at the corner store of Kigali would have been a treasure.

TELL US OF A TIME WHEN YOU FELL DEEPLY IN LOVE—THE ATTRAC-TION/CONNECTION, THE CIRCUMSTANCES, YOUR AGE AT THE TIME, AND HOW LONG IT LASTED. WERE THERE ANY "RED FLAGS" AT THE BE-GINNING OF THE RELATIONSHIP THAT YOU WERE AWARE OF BUT DID NOT ACKNOWLEDGE?

Once back in the U.S. and single again at the age of 40, I trained as a ballroom dance teacher at a local studio and soon partnered with someone who had been in the business for a long time to open a studio of my own. I had no dance training prior to this—I just loved to dance. So opening a studio seems a little crazy to me in hindsight, but it was a very healing choice. Music, movement, and touch were the perfect prescription. It's also where I met my next husband.

I had spent a lot of time reading and processing what happened in my first marriage, owning my part in it and letting go of what was not my fault. When I first met Larry, I wasn't immediately attracted to him despite his considerable good looks, because I sensed that he was not comfortable with himself. But, as he later explained, he had always been shy. He was married at that time but shared that the marriage had been in trouble for a long time. We became friends, and after he and his wife split up, we dated. We had much in common—a sense of adventure, a love of nature, and a spiritual orientation—and friendship grew quickly into attraction and then love. We moved in together and married about four years later.

I had not had children in my first marriage, but Larry's son and daughter, young adults when we met, became my family. His daughter married the same year we did, and she later had a son and daughter of her own. I received the unexpected experience and pleasure of being a grandmother.

Emotional Responsiveness

WHAT DID YOUR PARENTS MODEL IN A RELATIONSHIP FOR YOU AS A CHILD?

My parents modeled what *not* to do in a relationship. They argued hard, long, and often. My father was the breadwinner, and I think he felt that if he provided financially for the family that was enough. He really loved his music but couldn't support the family on that alone. He fell further and deeper into alcohol as the years passed. My parents didn't have many interests in common and they were not an affectionate couple. We weren't a demonstrative family, but I felt very loved and totally accepted by my mother and am grateful for that. I felt that if my parents had split up, it would have been better for all of us, but that would have been difficult for my mother as she had quit working outside the home when she married.

WHAT WERE YOU LOOKING FOR IN THIS RELATIONSHIP?

I was looking for love, for companionship, for a deeper connection than I had in my first marriage. And I found that. Larry and I were very compatible, very close—good friends first and then lovers. We really came closest together in nature and we hiked and camped often. Our spiritual connection deepened over time as well, and we became involved in a new thought church in Scottsdale where we met like-minded couples and enjoyed a sense of community. We eventually bought a house and partnered in making it a beautiful, warm, and welcoming home.

LOOKING BACK, DID YOU AND YOUR SPOUSE SHARE THE VALUES THAT YOUR PARENTS MODELED?

No, we were really doing everything opposite to what had been modeled by our parents. Larry's parents handled their discontent by icing each other. That to me was more deadly than my parent's arguments. And yet icing people was usually what I did when I was upset. I didn't like that about myself and wanted to change it. I recognized how my going cold and clamming up had contributed to the end of my first marriage. My desire was to talk things out as they came up so as not to repeat the past. For the most part, we succeeded in that.

WHAT CHANGED? WHAT OCCURRED FOR YOU TO FEEL THE LOSS OF THE RELATIONSHIP?

About ten years into our marriage, some distance began to creep into our relationship. I didn't understand what it was. I was beginning menopause and thought perhaps that was a factor. Overall though, the relationship was still good. But, finally, through a series of events, we realized that it was Larry who was going through a change—a ten on the Richter scale kind of change. He was no longer able to suppress or deny that he felt that his real self was female.

This did not get told to me in one fell swoop the way I just told you. Rather, it came out over a period of time. It began with me one day finding evidence of cross dressing. Going to bed that night, totally shocked, angry, and distressed, I wanted to sleep for the rest of my life. But eventually I had to wake up and deal with what was before me. The fact that I had learned his secret was so distressing to Larry that he was psychologically fragile for some time. I feared that, without my support, he might end his life as many transgender people do. That concern stayed with me through the years and contributed greatly to the way I handled what was to come.

Larry sought counseling. It seemed the cross dressing was something that only came out during times of high stress. For the following three years, there was no more evidence of cross dressing and I thought it was behind us. But, eventually, it started up again. We sought out another counselor, one who did regression therapy and who said she could address the cross dressing issue as well. But, once there, we realized we were more knowledgeable than she, and we both came away from the session feeling very low. Online Larry found an organization called Tri Ess (Society for the Second Self). We called and, blessedly, met just a few hours later with a couple dealing with the same thing. I felt as if we had been thrown a life line. We hit it off well and became friends. Larry went to a few Tri Ess meetings; I went to one. However, he didn't really resonate with most others in the group.

Then one fateful day at Costco I ran across a book called *She's Not There* by Jennifer Finney Boylan, an autobiography by a transgendered college professor. There were so many parallels to our life that I knew in my gut, "Crap, this is what we're dealing with." I shared the book with Larry, and he admitted that, yes, this felt like his experience. The Boylan's relationship felt so much like ours that I identified greatly with the book. And I believe the fact that Grace, Jenny's wife, stayed in the marriage was a considerable influence on me. At least it was one example of a marriage surviving such a monumental revelation. It meant it was possible.

Ultimately, after much struggle and counseling, Larry made the decision to transition—to go through both facial and sexual reassignment surgery (SRS)—even though he initially told me he never would. His drive to do so was incredibly strong. I was aware that he feared losing me and that if he could have chosen otherwise, he would have. It was devastating news, but I knew I couldn't stop the process. I felt as if I was standing in front of a freight train and all I could do was get out of the way. Also, I had to admit to myself that it wouldn't really work for him—or us—to continue to live a double life. I told him I would stay for the time being, but I couldn't promise I would always be there.

I mentioned a Richter scale kind of change, and I liken the transgender revelation to what I imagine an earthquake would be like for those of us who've not experienced one. We think the earth is solid, something we can rely on to hold us steady, and yet it's really not—it can give way at any time. Most of us think of gender the same way—it's something we can depend on—you're male or female, and that's one thing that's not going to change. (Dismissing, of course, some very low stats to the contrary.)

My other analogy is the old pinball machines. You go along playing the game just fine—ping, ping, ping—and then suddenly something goes wrong and ... TILT. Game over.

You need to understand that my husband was my best friend and that I hold authenticity as a high value. I could not ask him to deny his real self. What kind of relationship would that be anyway? A letter that I wrote to his family at the time still expresses it for me best. Larry grew up in the Mennonite faith, and his family is very religious. I assumed this would be very difficult news for them, and I wanted to share my perspective and also what I had learned. I wanted to help them understand. Here is an excerpt:

Dear Family,

Now that Larry has told you all his "big secret" and you have all responded, I feel it's time for me to share my perspective with you.

First of all, I know very well that this has been a huge shock for you. In anticipating your responses, I think I underestimated all of you. I know you are all struggling with this, but you have responded, for the most part, more lovingly than I expected, and I want to thank you for that.

Larry and I have been working through this for about the last two years. I would say that it is probably the hardest thing I have ever had to face, but it is also one of the greatest opportunities for personal growth that I've experienced.

It is essential in finding peace with this to understand that what Larry has is a __biological__ condition. He can no more help that he is transgendered than he can help that he has blue eyes. <u>It is not a choice.</u> Please hear that...it is not a choice.

Most people think that gender is a black and white category—one is either male OR female. But research shows that it is actually more of a continuum with some people being at the extremes of very male or very female and others falling in various degrees between the two poles. Still it is mind-boggling to hear someone who looks male from the outside say he believes he is female. It makes your head spin and the world tilt, and it brings up all kinds of feelings of right and wrong. But research also shows that the experience of gender is quite complicated and that brain gender and body gender do not always match.

The most accepted theory is that if the "hormone wash" in the brain of the developing fetus does not occur at exactly the critical period, then the brain develops differently from the body. You get a brain-body mismatch. Often young children understand who they truly are inside, but horrified parents shut them down. As transgenderism is better understood, more resources exist to help these children "match up," so to speak, before the secondary sex characteristics develop and the shaming and isolation begin.

But, of course, at the time Larry grew up, it was not well understood and certainly not acceptable. My heart aches to think of what it must be like to grow up feeling so alone, knowing you are different from others but not understanding it, feeling guilt and shame about simply being who you are. And especially to be male but feel female. It is so much more acceptable in our society to be a tomboy than to be a "sissy."

This is such a stressful condition for those who have it. There are very common threads that run through their stories. Many bury themselves in their work—you will find many are very accomplished high achievers (physicians, lawyers, engineers, professors, business owners, etc.)—others go into military or police work or other "macho" roles to disguise themselves and to try to suppress what they are. Others fall into addiction and tragically resort to suicide. But what commonly happens is that by middle age the trans person no longer has the energy to suppress who they are and it "comes out."

I can tell you that just from having shared the secret with him for the short time I have, it is **exhausting**. There is a double conversation going on in my head at all times, the real, true response and the socially acceptable one. I truly cannot even imagine what it must have been like to spend his whole life with this going on in the background. To never feel that he could simply be his real, true, authentic self and be loved just as he is...to feel always that he was an imposter...to believe that if he truly expressed himself he would be ridiculed and rejected.

My personal spiritual belief is that we are not human beings having a spiritual experience but rather spiritual beings having a human experience. I also believe that the most accurate definition of God, one that cuts across all religions, is that God is Love. I don't believe that God is judgment, blame, and shame.

I believe that one of the greatest gifts that we can give to each other and to the world is to be our true, authentic selves. I'm sure that, on some level, you all have sensed Larry's discomfort with himself. I know I did. I made up all kinds of reasons for it. I will say that it is actually refreshing to see him come into his own and to feel comfortable with himself for the first time in his life, to see him experience a happiness he never thought he'd have.

Is there also heartache? Definitely! Having to tell his loved ones and to put you—and me—through the shock, disappointment, fear—so hard. He has struggled with it tremendously. But the drive to be his true self is intense; he can't stop it, nor can I. This is common with transgendered individuals, but not all make the decision to face the wrath of the world. Some simply live a life of quiet desperation. I think it takes tremendous courage to pursue the path of authenticity and I have to say that I now admire Larry for being strong enough to face this head on.

As I said at the beginning of this letter, I have had much longer than you to adjust to this. I am not always at peace with it, even now—this is hard, I won't deny that. So I understand that you will run a strong range of emotions, not the least of which is grief—for it IS a loss—loss of a son, a brother, a father, a husband. There will be anger, sadness, resistance, depression...I know these feelings.

But it is also an opportunity to open our minds and our hearts wider and deeper than ever before, to examine long-held beliefs to see if they still serve us, to question just what love is and what it means to be human, and what really matters at the end of the day, at the end of a life. It is an opportunity to be in a relationship with a <u>real</u> person, instead of a shell.

I know you must be wondering about Larry and me. We take this day by day. I do know that we are deep friends, that I love this <u>person</u>, and that we will always have a relationship—just exactly how that will look we don't know.

That letter was written in 2009, and it is now 2016. You ask about loss—there was so much. It was like a death that went un-mourned. Trust me, no one brings you casseroles. Instead, there were lots of questions and opinions and much resistance. Sometimes I felt the energy of that resistance as a physical force. It was socially very difficult. Caitlin Jenner had not yet come along to make transgender more acceptable. That said, no one "dropped" us, except, ironically, the husband of the couple from Tri-Ess with whom we had become friends. Cross dressers distinguish themselves from transgender and those who transition can, in some cases, be seen as a threat. Most people, however, were surprisingly kind although some required a longer period of adjustment than others. Nevertheless, our couple friendships changed and either lessened or fell away completely. We met one other couple intending to stay together after the husband transitioned, but they seemed to want to keep to themselves. I became friends with a woman whose husband transitioned shortly before Larry did, and it helped me to share the experience with someone who understood it from the inside.

The rules are that, before sexual reassignment surgery, one needs to live a year as the "new" sex. I was so nervous going out into public when Larry first started living as a woman. I still remember going into Home Depot together to buy some plants and being greeted with, "Welcome, ladies." It was such a surreal feeling to have my "husband" included in that greeting—and then have that feeling mix with relief that she'd pulled it off. Stranger yet was when, at a movie, she went into the ladies' room with me for the first time. *Tilt!* But, over time, I adjusted and began caring less about what others might think.

After the requisite year of living female and getting a letter from two therapists attesting that this was indeed a case of transgender, she went through SRS and now lives her life fully as Lauryn. I guess you could say that I eventually went through a kind of transition of my own and decided that I wanted out of the marriage. I had thought I could stay because, at that stage of my life, companionship was more important than physical intimacy. Also, the idea of starting my life over in my 60s, selling our home, and splitting assets had been daunting. But my feelings had changed about all of that, and now it was my turn to speak my truth. We divorced in 2014 but continued to share the house for a time until it sold. I am now renting a little place of my own as I decide about this next phase of my life. I am dating a kind and gentle man. Lauryn is still my friend; she is family.

Spiritual Surrender

WHAT OCCURRED TO BRING YOU OUT OF THE DENIAL OF YOUR SITUATION? HOW DID YOU FIND YOUR WAY BACK TO TRUSTING YOUR DECISIONS AND RECAPTURE YOUR ABILITY TO LOVE AGAIN?

As we went through this process, I believed that there were gifts in it for me, as well as challenges. The greatest gift was the opportunity, as I said in the family letter, to open my heart bigger and wider than it had ever been before. I feel that I am a softer, more loving person for having gone through this. It also gifted me the opportunity to practice maintaining my own balance and happiness despite what is going on around me, to look beyond appearances and what others think. And the opportunity to get past my own judgments of how others would react and allow them to surprise me with their love and acceptance as Larry's family did.

As difficult a process as it was, it would have been much harder without my spiritual beliefs. I was helped beyond measure by the Enneagram of Personality Types, a deep, rich system of understanding self that I use in my work and in my life every day. It has helped me learn compassion—for myself and other—and I bless it.

Equally important was maintaining a sense of humor. I have an inclination to see humor in most situations, albeit often in an offbeat way, and would, at least in my head, amuse myself with it at times. For example, tired of answering the same questions over and over, I decided it would be handy to have an FAQ sheet to quell the curious. It was somewhat serious but also humorous. I never actually handed it out, but there was release in writing it.

I do have to say also, that when I could detach and look at it as simply a life experience, it was pretty interesting. I was reminded of how, in high school, I had said, "I just don't want to have an ordinary life." I amend that now with some humor to, "I should have been more specific."

People expected me to be angrier. I had some anger, of course, but mostly I found the whole situation sad. I felt sad that Lauryn had gone through her entire life not able to be herself, instead feeling that there was something horribly wrong with her. I felt sad that our relationship was changed and sad that I had lost my husband.

Many asked, "Aren't you angry that he got involved with you when he knew he had a secret?" Well, of course, it would have been so much better if he had shared that upfront! We wouldn't have gotten married and all of the heartbreak of coming apart could have been avoided. But I "got" that he didn't really admit it to himself. I don't think he even knew the word "transgender." Growing up how and when he did, he just tried to suppress what seemed so very wrong. He succeeded for long stretches of time. I ask myself, "What would I have done? Would I have had the courage to step out into a world so unaccepting? Would you?"

I believe that, on some level, we choose what we want to learn and experience in this lifetime. Because of that I did not feel like a victim and I didn't succumb to blame. I can only trust that this was an important experience for my soul.

Now I understand and believe that... I have long been fascinated by the concepts of nonresistance and surrender.

I truly believe they are the keys to a happy life.

I have this quote written down but no longer know who said it:

"When you can embrace all of life, Not holding on to anything beyond its time, And not avoiding it once its time has come, You will know the meaning of freedom."

And this:

"In the end what matters most is: How well did you live; How well did you love; How well did you learn to let go?"

What advice would you give to young lovers entering a new relationship?

Be honest, authentic, and compassionate with each other. Talk openly, listen deeply, laugh often, and keep your focus on what it is that you love about each other.

* * *

All of our contributors have had difficult choices to make in their love lives. Mary Beth and I discussed this particular story and could not begin to imagine the constant trepidation that must have filled the lives of both Jaye and Larry. Jaye's eloquent writing style and command for expressing her feelings openly gave us a look into a life with magnanimous choices and, as Jaye so appropriately stated in her letter to his family members; It is not a choice.

Live Brave.

WHAT CHANGED

"Civilized life, you know, is based on a huge number of illusions in which we all collaborate willingly. The trouble is we forget after a while that they are illusions, and we are deeply shocked when reality is torn down around us."

J.G.Ballard

Hilda

I think that it's natural to be drawn to others of your own heritage, culture, or circumstances. As a business owner, I enjoy the company of others who understand the challenges of owning a business. My Mexican heritage naturally draws me toward other Latinos who I feel have been raised in families similar to mine.

Upon meeting Dolores, I felt an immediate kinship. I appreciate the color of her skin; it reminds me of my father and my siblings. I like her thick and wavy hair that lends itself to any style, as long as it's short, resembling my mothers hair. I respect her commitment to the educational system from which she retired and I value her as a strong and passionate woman with a huge capacity to love. Here is her love story.

DOLORES, 68

"Be cautious of who you give your heart to. I know it's difficult to be cautious when your heart is falling in love. If you have any insecurity about your emotional health, take care of yourself, and don't think the person you love will cure everything."

Currently, Dolores is enjoying her retirement. She worked as a school administrator for thirty years and getting up in the early morning hours for those thirty years was like Chinese torture for her. She currently enjoys leisure time just doing nothing at all, visiting with family, reading, working with beads, enjoying her two dogs, and having long conversations with relatives and friends on the phone. Cooking for relatives and friends has been and still is one of her favorite activities. She has made several small trips since her retirement and plans to travel abroad in the near future. Fortunately, she feels that God has blessed her with good health and energy.

Over the years, she has suffered with depression, but her doctors have found a proper medication that seems to have the depression under control. Unfortunately, most recently, and during the writing and sharing of her story, the depression has become more prevalent from the loss of her dearest friend of forty years, a woman friend she calls her soulmate. She feels grateful that God has blessed her with wonderful friends and family who have been truly marvelous during this difficult time. She has received regular calls from all the important people in her life and frequently receives overnight guests as well, which she enjoys thoroughly.

Her goals for the future are to improve her writing skills, take drawing classes, and just enjoy the peaceful life that God has provided for her. She feels that partaking in these activities will further enrich her life.

Title: Beyond Brave

Physical Connection

WHERE WERE YOU BORN AND RAISED, AND WHAT CAN YOU TELL US ABOUT YOUR CHILDHOOD SURROUNDINGS AND CIRCUMSTANCES?

I was born and raised in El Paso, Texas, a small town where 60% of the population was Hispanic. Fortunately, this was an environment where our Mexican heritage was completely celebrated. We lived in a lower middle-class neighborhood. It was a time when we drank water from the hose while our mother watered the grass. Mulberry trees surrounded our home so all the neighborhood kids climbed the trees to pick the biggest mulberries we could find. After we ate until our stomachs were bloated, we had wars using the berries as bullets. At the end of the day we all looked purple from head to toe. We came home when it got dark but then were allowed to play an extra fifteen minutes under the main street light located catty-corner to our house. We played hide and seek in the scariest dark corners of the neighborhood. There were mostly boys my age with only one girl to play with. Both of us managed to boss around the boys quite well, thank you very much. When we played school, I was always the teacher and in charge of everyone. It made me feel quite powerful.

Our house was one of the good looking homes in the neighborhood. My dad helped Mom and made sure that it was kept beautiful; this was a joint effort that they both enjoyed.

My dad had a good job working for Flagstaff Brewing Company. Mother was a homemaker and took good care of us. We lived four blocks from the high school and four blocks from the elementary school. My mother was always very loving, and I felt close and secure around her. My two brothers are twelve and six years older than I, so I felt as if I were an only child. How my mother made me feel that way is beyond me. My dad always seemed to be working and not available. However, my mother and I always had a great time together.

TELL US OF A TIME WHEN YOU FELL DEEPLY IN LOVE—THE ATTRACTION/CONNECTION, THE CIRCUMSTANCES, YOUR AGE AT THE TIME, AND HOW LONG IT LASTED. WERE THERE ANY "RED FLAGS" AT THE BEGINNING OF THE RELATIONSHIP THAT YOU WERE AWARE OF BUT DID NOT ACKNOWLEDGE?

I was 27 years old when I fell in love with my husband who came from a Hispanic heritage as well. At that age I thought that I knew what I was doing. Yeah, right! He happened to be the brother of one of my best friends. He was 31 years old, worked for the post office, and attended the university in El Paso. He was studying to be an engineer and belonged to the Mensa organization which meant that he was extremely intelligent, another quality that attracted me to him. He was also quite good looking and could carry a great conversation on any subject. Because he worked at the post office and lived at home, he had money at all times and drove a nice car that was paid for. But besides those attributes, he fell short in the area of socializing and felt very uncomfortable in public settings. He was very much an introvert and didn't know how to dance, two negatives that I chose to ignore.

My parents were always quite social, attending local dances and a variety of friends' house parties to play Canasta. They traveled and, of course, hosted parties and barbecues at their home for every occasion.

My husband's family life was not ideal. His father had always been abusive with the entire family. His sister told me that sometimes as children they would be in the living room when their father would just walk by and slap them. He also abused liquor and was particularly abusive when he drank. The children saw their dad hitting their mom on various occasions. At times when his mom served his dad a meal that he didn't like, he would throw the plate at her or at the wall. I chose to ignore all of this. I also chose to ignore that his mom and dad slept in separate bedrooms, something that was quite unusual in Hispanic families. My future husband's wonderful good looks and intellectual talk swept me off my feet. We dated for three years and then married. The post office offered him a promotion and a transfer to Phoenix to fill a management position. Several days after our honeymoon, we made the move to Phoenix.

I did notice that he was extremely close to his mother in a rather unhealthy way. For example, he was used to giving his mother a hefty amount of his check every month, which was okay until he insisted on following this tradition after we were married.

After our move to Phoenix, I realized that he was apart from his mother for the first time, so he wanted to visit her every weekend. As this went on for several weekends a month, I chose not to accompany him. He also called his mother three or four times daily, which, at the time, resulted in a $300 dollar-a-month phone bill.

We arrived in Phoenix not knowing anyone and the first years were very difficult for me. I felt lonely, unloved, and underappreciated. Shortly after we married he became more abusive than usual. A big red flag before we were married was his very bad temper. Almost anything made him angry and violent. As an example, my dear cousin Luis came to visit me and we went for a few drinks at a neighborhood bar. I was truly enjoying this special moment with Luis when suddenly my husband stormed in through the door. He took one look at me and my cousin and stormed out, expecting me to follow. I did not. He went straight to my apartment and trashed it, knocking over bookshelves, breaking things, and retrieving all gifts that he had given me. We didn't speak for three weeks until he contacted me. He expected an apology and an explanation. I told him that the man was my cousin and I had done nothing wrong. He never apologized. But I ridiculously thought that after we were married he would chill out a bit, but he did not. In fact he became worse and became physically abusive. He would get angry at almost anything and would start to cuss and throw things around. Several times he punched me on my head where bruises wouldn't show while calling me a whore, stupid, and a liar. I didn't fight back. I still don't know why I didn't try to defend myself or fight back. To this day, I continue to wonder why.

At this point, now living in Phoenix, I had not yet looked for work. Needless to say I felt it was time for me to get a teaching job. I was depressed, weepy, and unsure of myself, but I did manage to borrow the one car we had and apply in several school districts in the valley. I was a university graduate with a degree, but unfortunately had waited for two years to start looking. To my surprise several districts offered me a contract. I chose Phoenix Elementary School District. After a few months of working and sharing our car I purchased my own car. It felt wonderful to have my own transportation; it gave me a feeling of independence. The more I worked, the more empowered I felt. I knew it was time for me to leave, but it took me three full years to gain the courage. I purposely took birth control pills as I knew that if I became pregnant I would never be rid of him. At the end of three years in this abusive relationship I left him and filed for divorce. I went home to El Paso and lived with my older brother. Two months after I arrived in El Paso my father died. He took his own life by driving into a train. This was a double whammy for me from which it took me a long time to recover.

Emotional Responsiveness

WHAT DID YOUR PARENTS MODEL IN A RELATIONSHIP FOR YOU AS A CHILD?

When I was young, I could tell my parents were truly in love. They had their disagreements and arguments, but generally they were a happy couple. I never saw my dad abuse my mother verbally or physically. They went dancing, took trips to various cities in Mexico, had people over regularly to play Canasta and had customary barbecues in our back yard. A sure barbecue was on the Fourth of July. That was a must! All of their friends and compadres (friends that had baptized me and my brothers) were invited for a big feast. They would all arrive at 5 in the afternoon. Next on the agenda were hors d`oeuvres, beer and wine. There was always plenty of beer since dad worked for the local brewery.

After great jokes and wonderful, intelligent political conversation, the entire party would make their way to the city park that was just three blocks from our house. There we enjoyed fireworks for two hours and patriotic music from local bands. After the great attraction, the crowd would find their way back to our house and the feast began. My mom would be in charge of bringing all the side dishes outside while my father cooked burgers, chicken, and hotdogs and roasted jalapenos on the grill. My dad would also take us (regularly) to Furr's cafeteria for lunch on Wednesdays (his day off), to the movies and any seasonal activities going on in El Paso. One of our favorite things to do was going to the UT Miners games (our local university team). Christmas and all the yearly holidays were spent in our house where the entire family and friends would congregate. My mother was a fabulous cook.

In the end, the whole family was in shock when my mother, only 57 years of age, died unexpectedly of a brain tumor. Life was never the same after that. Dad never recovered! I am sure that is the reason my dad decided to take his own life.

WHAT WERE YOU LOOKING FOR IN THIS RELATIONSHIP?

I guess all I wanted in a relationship was a responsible, loving person that would come home every day and just be at peace. That was not to be. I imagined that in a relationship one could trust each other, support each other, and learn all kinds of things from each other. I thought the person I married would be a good father and a good role model. I wanted a person who could be affectionate and caring; a person who had aspirations of bettering themselves. And a person who would take care of me emotionally, physically and aspire to be a better person. I wanted someone who would have a moral compass and just enjoy life. After my husband graduated as an engineer he never pursued a career in engineering. He remained at the post office until he retired.

LOOKING BACK, DID YOU AND YOUR SPOUSE SHARE THE VALUES THAT YOUR PARENTS MODELED?

Absolutely not! He did not have a happy and healthy childhood as I did. The modeling he received at home was physical abuse, drunkenness, and treating women as low class people. This was completely opposite to my upbringing experience. Consequently, I don't think he was capable of having the values that were modeled for me. His upbringing was different; he had an abusive father and an indulgent mother who fulfilled all his wishes and did everything he commanded.

WHAT CHANGED? WHAT OCCURRED FOR YOU TO FEEL THE LOSS OF THE RELATIONSHIP? TO WHAT EXTENT WAS IT HURTFUL, PHYSICALLY, FINANCIALLY, MENTALLY, AND EMOTIONALLY?

Eventually what changed for me was that I was truly unhappy and depressed. I felt like a failure, and I knew that this man would never change. It seemed that he was incapable of change. He was so used to having his way and doing what he wanted that he was unable to think of anyone else's needs. This turned out to be true, for he was married three other times after our marriage ended. It was very difficult for me to admit that I had made a mistake, and that only I could fix it. I knew that if I stayed in this relationship I would eventually die. I think the early death of my mother was so tragic for me that it sent me into a deep depression. When my dad died and I was divorced, I felt overwhelmed with loss. When I first married, my depression had lifted only to have it come back with a vengeance a few months after the honeymoon. I think that my depression kept me from leaving him early on in the relationship. Financially, even though I had a job, I still had to move in with my brother for a year before I was able to move into my own apartment. I remember I was so very depressed that I did not sleep for a year. I would sleep one or two hours a day. I only thank God that I did not have a nervous breakdown during that time (I was a perfect candidate for it). Eventually I managed to recapture the feeling that I was in control of my own life.

Spiritual Surrender

DID YOU AND YOUR SPOUSE SHARE THE SAME SPIRITUAL BELIEF?

Both my ex-husband and I were raised in the Catholic Church.

Unfortunately we never attended church while married. For that I blame myself as I didn't demand that we attend church regularly. Religion was not a big part of our lives in our marriage.

WHAT ATTRIBUTES DID YOUR SPOUSE BRING TO THE RELATIONSHIP, POSITIVE OR NEGATIVE?

My husband had a steady job that he took seriously. He was intelligent and articulate. He suffered from manic/depression and purposely did not take the meds prescribed for him. He thought that he could deal with it and overcome his condition himself. Mr. Macho, not an unusual behavior in Hispanic males. After the arguments that we had, he would shower me with clothes, perfume, flowers, etc. These gifts had little meaning for me. He had a bad temper that could flare up anytime. I was loving toward him and could show affection and often spoiled him with his favorite meals. I always tried to look well dressed and groomed. When in an uncomfortable social situation I always advised or suggested the proper thing for him to do. I kept a very clean apartment. I worked hard to keep a nice home for him. I was also very responsible when it came to my job.

WHAT OCCURRED TO BRING YOU OUT OF THE DENIAL OF YOUR SITUATION? HOW DID YOU FIND YOUR WAY BACK TO TRUSTING YOUR DECISIONS AND RECAPTURE YOUR ABILITY TO LOVE AGAIN?

I think that my shame, sheer survival, and feeling secure that I could survive without him gave me the courage to move out. And indeed I did move out and filed for divorce. This decision also came with a great deal of shame that I failed in my marriage. I think that throughout all of our difficulties, I had stopped loving him. I had no therapy or professional help that I should have had. I did share everything with my wonderful friend who I met in college. She was married and had five children but somehow had time to listen to all my problems, and for that I will always be grateful and indebted to her. A few months after leaving I knew I had made the right decision.

NOW I UNDERSTAND AND BELIEVE THAT... That life is a process of eventful journeys filled with joy, sadness, hope, sorrows, desires, awakenings, and fulfillment of events. How we react to all these states of mind makes all the difference in the world. One thing that I feel is true is that different feelings can accompany each event stated above. It is up to us to determine and take responsibility for all experiences that we have. The winter of our lives also allows us to look back and forgive ourselves, take a more positive look toward the future and accept what has been and what will be in the future.

WHAT ADVICE WOULD YOU GIVE TO YOUNG LOVERS ENTERING A NEW RELATIONSHIP?

My advice would be one of caution. Be cautious of who you give your heart to. I know it's difficult to be cautious when your heart is falling in love. If you have any insecurity about your emotional health, take care of yourself and don't think the person you love will cure everything. Try to find out everything about his family of origin. Try to have a healthy exchange of what you need in a relationship. Show all your colors, try not to hide what you may think are your weaknesses. And most importantly... be yourself.

* * *

In their book *Wise Aging*, Rabbi Rachel Cowan and Dr. Linda Thal followed Erik Erikson's pioneering work on *"the concept that life has eight stages and proposed that each stage has a specific psychological task that must be accomplished for healthy development, he identified the eighth stage's task as finding 'integrity' in our life's journey. Here we integrate our life history, weaving together stories, finding threads of connections and discovering the meaning and propose of our life in the whole."* As I read these words I couldn't help but think of Dolores. She shares her stories and threads them together with her family and close connections. She is proud of her heritage, as she should be, for she is a woman filled with love. This past year she lost a dear friend and I watched her struggle with the meaning and purpose of her life. But she is on the mend...to continue loving those who need her close to them.

Live brave.

PART THREE

SPIRITUAL SURRENDER

"Meditation is like mining veins of gold from within your own being. The more you mine them, the more you follow them down into your own being, the more you discover that those veins of gold in you are also in every other person. Out of that, a greater compassion or intimacy for others naturally evolves. I've seen that happen time and time again for people."

Dean Ornish, M.D.

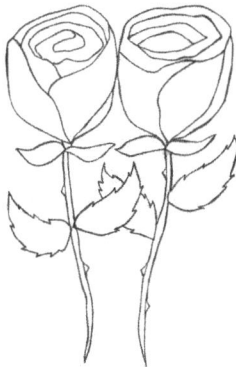

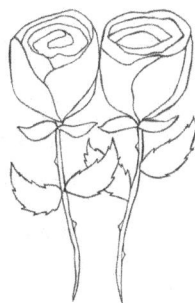

CHAPTER FOUR

THE ATTRIBUTES OF A RELATIONSHIP

"In the end, all things point to God..."

M. Scott Peck, M.D.

Hilda

When I make the statement that I have been friends with someone for over thirty years, I don't say it lightly. Somewhere inside of me, I feel the bond that has kept me tethered to that person. When I think of Lee, my mind conjures up the image of her singing and playing her guitar in my home surrounded by a welcoming audience. And for the same number of years she has been a loyal client in my salon. I have had the privilege of witnessing her transform into a super star and I have prayed for her along the way.

Our relationship began while we were both in therapy working through tough times. Our therapist introduced us and said that we could weave together a friendship. And indeed, for many years we have shared a compassionate heart for one another and encouraged each other through our rough times of loving. Here is my friend Lee.

Lee, 66

"Never allow the challenges of life to make you lose hope and become bitter or beaten. There is always hope. There are always options."

Lee is an author and award-winning singer-songwriter, combining jazz and storytelling into compelling music she calls "Cowgirl Jazz."

Title: When the Music Stopped: Finding My Voice Again

Physical Connection

WHERE WERE YOU BORN AND RAISED, AND WHAT CAN YOU TELL US ABOUT YOUR CHILDHOOD SURROUNDINGS AND CIRCUMSTANCES?

I grew up in Phoenix, Arizona, in an upper middle-class family with a mom, dad, and five kids. My twin Sis and I were the youngest.

TELL US OF A TIME WHEN YOU FELL DEEPLY IN LOVE—THE ATTRACTION/CONNECTION, THE CIRCUMSTANCES, YOUR AGE AT THE TIME, AND HOW LONG IT LASTED. WERE THERE ANY "RED FLAGS" AT THE BEGINNING OF THE RELATIONSHIP THAT YOU WERE AWARE OF BUT DID NOT ACKNOWLEDGE?

I fell in love at age 26 to a handsome, creative and very intelligent stained-glass artist who had grown up in our circle of friends. I was always attracted to his creativity and his photographic memory. He also had an amazing sense of humor and was a great conversationalist. I believe he appreciated my creativity as well. I was a dance major at Arizona State University in addition to singing at night. I had been singing in the coffee houses since age 14, so on our first date when he asked me what my dream was, I told him it was to be a full-fledged professional singer. He said, "Well, let's see if we can make that happen!"

In a previous relationship there was not the emotional support that I wanted and needed to thrive as a creative artist. So I knew that with his emotional support I could be successful. We were married for twenty years while we both worked as artists.

A "red flag" was that his distant father had died of a debilitating illness that was never diagnosed. Later we found out that he had died of Huntington's disease. Sadly, he had lied about the doctors' opinions that he had Huntington's disease. At the time there was no definitive test, but later it came out that three different doctors had given their opinions that he had the disease. He actually told us that the doctors said they did NOT think he had Huntington's. His brother came forward after the father's death and said that the autopsy revealed Huntington's and that he had not told us the truth. Maybe it was his dad's attempt to protect his son that made him lie.

Emotional Responsiveness

WHAT DID YOUR PARENTS MODEL IN A RELATIONSHIP FOR YOU AS A CHILD?

They modeled loyalty, humor, adventure, and respect for each other. They had a good working relationship. They also modeled avoidance of conflict. I have had to learn how to "fight fair," and how important conflict resolution is to any intimate relationship.

WHAT WERE YOU LOOKING FOR IN THIS RELATIONSHIP?

I was looking for someone who would be supportive of my music and be a fun companion. He was also a creative person who shared my adventurous spirit. We were a couple of kids in love who wanted an adventurous life.

LOOKING BACK, DID YOU AND YOUR SPOUSE SHARE THE VALUES THAT YOUR PARENTS MODELED?

In my early years, my parents had a traditional relationship in that my dad was the breadwinner, a lawyer, and mom took care of the kids. Later in life, my dad retired from law and became a professional speaker. They worked together building a successful business and my mom was very supportive of this new creative life. As a family we were all involved—sending out books and tapes and doing mass mailings, being entrepreneurs. It was a real adventure. My creative relationship modeled the second half of my parents' lives.

WHAT CHANGED? WHAT OCCURRED FOR YOU TO FEEL THE LOSS OF THE RELATIONSHIP? TO WHAT EXTENT WAS IT HURTFUL, PHYSICALLY, FINANCIALLY, MENTALLY, AND EMOTIONALLY?

My husband started having health problems while we were living and working as artists in San Francisco. I became the primary breadwinner as his health declined. Because his income was no longer dependable, we moved back to

Arizona so I could join my dad as sales and marketing director of his public speaking business. I put my music on hold in order to keep up with the medical bills and a single income. As I learned the business of public speaking, however, I used my music as a hook and wrote songs for the events that we produced. I also used music in my speeches to add uniqueness.

It was difficult being the sole breadwinner, and it became more difficult with doctors not diagnosing properly. My husband's symptoms became more dramatic: outbursts of anger, inability to sleep, and tremors. He was misdiagnosed with depression and the stress of our problems started affecting my own health. I became a caretaker in the last ten years of our marriage. My husband was pretty much reduced to watching TV on the couch. He was able to walk around and talk but was unable to work or drive. Ultimately, he was diagnosed with Huntington's disease, a neurological disease that has no cure. HD is a fatal genetic disorder that causes the progressive breakdown of nerve cells in the brain. It is similar to Lou Gehrig's disease or ALS as it too deteriorates a person's physical abilities during their prime working years. As the disease advances, uncoordinated, jerky body movements become more apparent along with a decline in mental abilities and behavioral and psychiatric problems.

Aside from the outbursts of anger from time to time, my husband seemed to be able to think, understand, and communicate thoughts normally. His physical abilities were gradually impeded and coordinated movement became very difficult. By now it had been about 25 years from when his symptoms became apparent, but eventually full-time care was required in the later stages of his disease.

Spiritual Surrender

Did you and your spouse share the same spiritual belief?

Yes, we attended a non-denomination Science of Mind Church for about ten years. I believe it helped us cope with the tragic decline of his health. We both believed in God and believed God was the source of all creativity. In addition, we eventually sought professional therapeutic counseling to help us cope and work toward a better life while we were trying to figure out what we could do to help our relationship amidst his health challenges.

WHAT ATTRIBUTES DID YOUR SPOUSE BRING TO THE RELATIONSHIP, POSITIVE OR NEGATIVE?

He was courageous and philosophical. He never complained and was an inspiration to all who knew him. We had so much fun being artists together when we were thriving—he was a tremendous support to me in my creative growth. Unfortunately, as his health declined and he became more desperate, he would have outbursts of anger that could be frightening. He would throw things when he became angry and break things. Most of the time I would leave the room when he had outbursts like that—but the last time he threw something I called 911. The police came and he had to answer for his behavior. I did not press charges, but he never did it again. I knew he was frustrated when unable to hold a job, and he became hopeless as his health declined more and more.

WHAT OCCURRED TO BRING YOU OUT OF THE DENIAL OF YOUR SITUATION? HOW DID YOU FIND YOUR WAY BACK TO TRUSTING YOUR DECISIONS AND RECAPTURE YOUR ABILITY TO LOVE AGAIN?

When he was finally diagnosed with HD (after showing symptoms for ten years) and my own health was declining as my caretaking role took over my life, I realized I would have to go on with my life. We had talked about this several times during the ten years his symptoms began to manifest more seriously. I had said things like, "If this turns out to be a long-term terminal illness, I will probably have to go on with my life." He would say, "Well, I would expect you to." When the diagnosis was made definitively, I knew that I would have to go on with my life. It did not happen right away because we had to get him set up with disability and medical insurance. We divorced and lived together another year before he was eligible for this financial help. Once he was set up with disability and medical insurance, he moved to northern Arizona where his brother and mother lived. I visited him monthly and took him out to lunch. He was not happy that we divorced and his life had taken a different turn. Even after we had talked about it several times, when the time actually came he was not happy about it. But he never acted resentful and was always loving and grateful that we continued to see each other. After a few years, his brother set him up in a supervisory care facility in Phoenix where I was able to take him to lunch more frequently. His mother and his best friend never forgave me for divorcing him, but his brother understood and was compassionate. I understood all of the emotions involved and just did what I had to do to get on with my life. It took a lot of courage and hard work and therapeutic support, but I am grateful I did this to create a new life for myself.

I liked being married so I hoped I would marry again. Eventually, I joined Sierra Singles, the ski club, and continued in therapy to try to heal my heart and get my health back. Even though initially I was mad at God and didn't understand why this had happened to us, after a couple years, I decided it would be better to have God in my life.

I continued getting therapeutic help and building my own health back again. My therapist said I needed to find my "Spiritual Home," so I visited a few churches. I was sitting in a non-denominational church one day feeling proud that I had asked a not-very-nice man not to call me unless he could be a better friend. I was feeling peaceful and proud of myself. Suddenly, a man crawled over me from the aisle and turned and smiled like he'd found his long lost friend. I was so taken aback that I stuck my hand out and said, "Hello, my name is Lee. What's yours?" He told me and was very attentive. He asked me out to lunch—I was not available for lunch but said I was available for dinner. He met me at the door that night with flowers. He ended the night giving me two CD's that he loved of the music and songs of Enya. To repay his generosity, I sang a couple of my original songs for him with my guitar. He asked me out again, was very compassionate about what had happened in my previous marriage, and said he thought I was very brave to go on with my life. He was respectful, kind, and sent a very strong message that he wanted our relationship to work.

It turned out that he was very financially successful, but I wanted love and not a "workaholic," so I had to find out if he and I resonated in that way. We did. We have been together since 1999.

I could not have dreamed of the creative lifestyle I have now with a home in Jackson Hole, WY, and a home in Paradise Valley, AZ. He flies me here, there, and everywhere in a Cessna Citation Jet, and I have been able to rise to great heights in my music business, including being awarded Best Western Album of the Year by the Academy of Western Artists. I am currently finishing the recording and production of my eighth CD, *Let Me Be the One,* an all-jazz CD about love in its many dimensions. We are very in sync in our desire to be the very best people we can be and enjoy going to church together and living our spirituality every day.

My relationship with my new man is very different from my other marriage as he is a very different person from my former husband. He is a thinker and planner, a visionary, and a wonderful force for good in this world in many ways. For about fifteen years, we had a foundation called "Earth Friends Conservation Fund" and we financially supported over 100 conservation groups in the American West.

NOW I UNDERSTAND AND BELIEVE THAT... I have learned to be open to all the ways this "fresh start" has been different from my other relationship and, while we have challenges, I could never have dreamed that I could have such an amazing and fabulous new life and love! God is good!

WHAT ADVICE WOULD YOU GIVE TO YOUNG LOVERS ENTERING A NEW RELATIONSHIP?

Never allow the challenges of life to make you lose hope and become bitter or beaten. There is always hope. There are always options. You must keep your health good beyond everything because that way you will prevail. Also, believe that God has great plans for you because it is true. Reach out for help—others have gone through life's challenges too. Allow God to work in your life and be open to change.

I chose the title, "When the Music Stopped: Finding My Voice Again," because, for a time, it did feel like the music in my life had stopped. I call the experience with my previous husband "My Mount Everest," because it demanded everything I had to survive, pick myself up, and make a new life. He bravely lasted another eighteen years after we divorced—12 of it in a supervisory care facility unable to walk, talk, or move a muscle. It was not easy "finding my voice again." I thought I might never fall in love again, but I did. I thought I might never sing again, but I have.

My former husband passed away this year—I visited him every year and sang to him. I needed the help of a couple of friends just to be able to do it, but he appreciated it so much...I know. He was a great man and I don't regret anything. But, with the help of my wonderful new man and the new life we have created together, I have definitely found my voice again and I'm blessed to be creating the music I've always dreamed of.

* * *

Recently I read a new book that I will add to my favorites; *How to Love Yourself (and sometimes other people) Spiritual Advice for Modern Relationships*, by Lodro Rinzler and Meggan Watterson. From the perspective of the authors one must first feel worthy of love, and not just the love that comes from others, but the love that we must give to ourselves. As we see the value that we can bring to others, as we acknowledge the gifts and talents that have been birthed within us, and as we yearn to increase our lives, tough choices are made. For years, loving oneself has taken a bad rap. Self-love has been viewed as self-indulgent. And yes, we do have much of that kind of self-centeredness in our world. But we also have the love that goes unexpressed and never developed, because someone chooses not to love themselves first.

From *How to Love Yourself*, *"When you are confident in who you are, in your own ability to befriend and love yourself, that radiates out into the world. The most attractive thing is when someone is confident in who they are and is willing to share it with the world. Radiate your splendor as part of loving yourself."*

Live brave.

The Attributes of a Relationship

"Nothing is a waste of time if you use the experience wisely."

Auguste Rodin

Hilda

While working on my pastoral counseling degree, I was required to counsel clients seeking a spiritual perspective on their personal challenges. Almost twenty years have past since Debra and I met, and we have remained in each others lives from the time when she walked into my office. Although our professional time together came to an end, over the years, Debra and I have stayed in touch. I have been invited to celebrate the passages of her ever-evolving life. Beautiful and determined is how I describe this woman and that is also how she lives her days. From her exquisite taste in fashion to her tastefully decorated home, her eye for beauty is commendable. Always striving to challenge herself and improve the quality of her happiness and for those around her, she is a wise and unstoppable woman.

DEBRA, 52

"Never give up on love! Call me a dreamer or a romantic at heart. After going through what I had endured, many people would have gone running from any future relationships, but I did the opposite. I ran right into a new one!"

Debra was born and raised on the East Coast, but is a 33 year resident of Phoenix, Arizona. Happily married with two daughters and five four-legged children, she graduated summa cum laude with a Bachelors of Arts Degree in Journalism with an emphasis in Public Relations just shy of her 50th birthday. She has been published in local news periodicals and magazines in the Phoenix area and serves on various philanthropic boards. While a homebody at heart, she loves to travel, shop, hike, and is a closet interior decorator. Most importantly, Debra is a dreamer and vows to never stop dreaming.

Title: Curve Ball

Physical Connection

WHERE WERE YOU BORN AND RAISED, AND WHAT CAN YOU TELL US
ABOUT YOUR CHILDHOOD SURROUNDINGS AND CIRCUMSTANCES?

I was born and raised in a small industrial town just outside of Pittsburgh, Pennsylvania. My parents were first and second generation Italian immigrants with a strong work ethic and Roman Catholic faith. Faith, family and work were the three main pillars of our daily lives. We were a working-class family, but to be honest, I do not recall wanting for much. When I was first born, we lived in a two-bedroom housing project, which was originally built by the government to house temporary steel workers. I shared a bedroom with my younger brother until I was in the third grade at which time we moved into our new home in the country. A 3 bedroom/1 bath, 1300 square foot home with a big green grassy front and back lawn unlike the postage stamp size yard we had at the project or "Terrace" as it was called. My mother still lives in this home today and when I go back to visit, my former bedroom actually looks more like a closet to me than a bedroom. The world in which I grew up does not exist today...a simpler time...although I'm sure almost every generation would say the same. Nearly everyone in my world was catholic, a Kennedy democrat and connected in some way with one of the many local steel mills which ran up and down the local Ohio River. We NEVER missed a Sunday mass....Catholic guilt was the order of the day. It was a fear-driven way of life; not uncommon for Italian Americans. Unending lectures from my mother and grandmother about remaining a virgin until marriage were imbedded in my brain. Strangely enough, I don't believe my brother was subjected to the same lectures. While I push back and decry that we were living in different times, the guilt had been laid and was firmly in place. As a teenager, my bedroom walls did not have posters of David Cassidy or Bobby Sherman like most other teenage girls....I had posters of jet airplanes and photos of exotic far-away places. My simple dream was to be a flight attendant and travel the world. Looking back, my true goal was to just "get out of Dodge" and that is exactly what I did.

TELL US OF A TIME WHEN YOU FELL DEEPLY IN LOVE; THE ATTRACTION/ CONNECTION, CIRCUMSTANCES AND YOUR AGE AT THE TIME AND HOW LONG IT LASTED. WERE THERE ANY "RED FLAGS" AT THE BEGINNING OF THE RELATIONSHIP THAT YOU WERE AWARE OF BUT DID NOT ACKNOWLEDGE? IF THERE WERE "RED FLAGS" WHAT WERE THEY?

Without giving away the ending of my story....I've been truly in love and intimate with only two men in my entire life and married them both. I was painfully shy around the opposite sex. While I was told I was an attractive girl/ woman, I never had a boyfriend in high school. Did not have my first date and kiss until after I graduated from high school. I went out on a few dates here and there but never truly had a "boyfriend". I was only 20 years old when I bravely announced I was moving from Pittsburgh to beautiful Phoenix, Arizona. After attending Secretarial School (yes, there used to actually be schools for secretaries), I found myself a job in a local travel agency. It was through this agency that I was able to take a familiarization trip to Scottsdale, Arizona. This was it! Big blue sky country! Such a stark difference from the typical dreary overcast days in the Pittsburgh area. I was not going to waste anymore time...this was where I wanted to be. So without a job waiting for me, a place to live or knowing a single living soul, I packed up my Oldsmobile Cutlass Supreme and my mother and I drove across the country. Granted this was by no means a covered wagon, but by today's standards, we did it without cell phones or GPS...simply a paper map to guide us. Looking back, I don't know how we did it.

I found a place to live and a job as a secretary in a Big 8 Accounting Firm within weeks. As much as I wanted to stay in the travel industry, believe it or not, I could actually make more money as a secretary rather than a travel agent. Now that I was on my own, I had to make every dollar count. My mother returned to Pittsburgh and I was truly on my own. It was at the end of my first month in Phoenix when someone at my new job had casually mentioned that Sunday nights were really "hopping" at Lunt Avenue Marble Club in Scottsdale. Lunt Avenue was a chain restaurant/bar in the local Phoenix/Scottsdale area. I had been there before so I felt safe. So that weekend I mustered up the courage to go out by myself. Nervously trying to fit in with a drink in my hand (drinking age in Arizona was 18 at the time), a handsome older man came up to me and started a conversation. To be honest, I can't remember if he asked me to dance or if I wanted a drink, but he approached me and we began a conversation. He turned out to be 14 years my senior, a native of the Dominican Republic and a major league baseball player who was in the Scottsdale area for spring training. He was wearing his National Championship ring he earned from a few years prior and while in the twilight of his playing career was still in great physical shape. I was awestruck and as an avid sports fan, I recognized his name. I couldn't believe someone of his stature was actually paying attention to me. I think it's safe to say the attraction was electric on both ends. Were there red flags? EVERYWHERE!!! Unfortunately, I just barreled through every one of those flags at my own peril. We were the classic case of a May-December relationship with absolutely nothing in common except for our attraction to one another. I was young and naïve; he was older and recently burned by a nasty divorce. I was just beginning my life and career and his was coming to a close. I was a devout Catholic and he was a Baptist (born again Christian). I was born and raised in a middle class American home and he was born dirt poor in a third world country later becoming a millionaire, only to lose most of his fortune to divorce and the IRS. It was a recipe for disaster.

Emotional Responsiveness

WHAT DID YOUR PARENTS MODEL IN A RELATIONSHIP FOR YOU AS A CHILD?

My parents were married 53 years when my father passed away from lung cancer. As a child, I always thought my mother was too subservient to my father. I actually remember my father saying things like "I am the king of this castle". I would just roll my eyes and proclaim that my marriage would be different. The truth is that they had a very strong and loving relationship. Their respective families knew of each other since the time they were children...they grew up in the same small town, went to the same schools, churches and had the same traditions. They were a perfect match. My mother's calm and loving demeanor was able to quash my father's fiery temper and my father was able to provide a very stable and comfortable life for my mother and the children. His sense of humor was a family staple and his ability to tell a story was legendary.

WHAT WERE YOU LOOKING FOR IN THIS RELATIONSHIP? LOOKING BACK, DID YOU AND YOUR SPOUSE SHARE THE VALUES THAT YOUR PARENTS MODELED?

Not at all. My parents were truly in love when they met and married. I'm not sure I can say the same for me and my first husband. That old "Catholic guilt" played a big role in my relationship. It was not long after we first met that we became intimate. I was so consumed with guilt that I literally vowed to God that I would make it right by marrying this man. I harken back to the Academy Award winning movie *Moonstruck* for clearer reference. I love this movie... it always brings me back to my roots. I can relate to the scene where Loretta Casterini (Cher) runs to the local Catholic Church to pray and confess her sin of "sleeping with the brother of my fiancé." What I did was really not that much different. To say our two-year dating path was rocky was putting it mildly. I feel confident in saying that any experienced women in my shoes would never have stayed with this man. He was emotionally unavailable; struggling to find a new career when all he had known was baseball his entire life; struggling with English as a second language, having ongoing fights with his ex-wife who had taken away his parental rights of his two young children (major red flag!!!) and ultimately leaving the country and moving back to the Dominican Republic. We actually broke up for about 6 months while he was living in the Dominican Republic. I was physically ill. I could barely function. Every time the phone rang, I prayed it was him calling and coming back to me. I was finally beginning to face life without him and move on when I received a post card in the mail from him informing me that he was thinking of me. This started up the relationship again. A month later, I was on an airplane visiting him in the Dominican Republic. Four months later, we were married in the Dominican Republic where we lived for the first year of our marriage.

Living in the Dominican was difficult. In recent years, Punta Cana has become a popular tourist and cruise stop destination in the Dominican....I did not live in a tourist spot! We lived in the capital city of Santo Domingo. Granted we lived in a very nice town house where I had a maid named Isabel. Isabel washed our clothes by hand and dried them outside on a line....she was a hard worker who could not speak a word of English. Ironically, I would have traded Isabel in a minute if I could have had such American basics as cable television, a telephone and reliable electricity! I quickly learned, and still remember the Spanish phrase "se fue la luz"...the lights went/are out. I had trouble adjusting to the culture, the language, the food....just about everything including my new husband.

What changed? What occurred for you to feel the loss of the relationship? To what extent was it hurtful, physically, financially, mentally, and emotionally?

I would say it is a pretty bad omen when on your wedding night, the groom turns on the television and watches a basketball game rather than make love to his new wife. I cried myself to sleep that night. The next eight years were not that much different. Yes, there were a few good moments, but mostly pain and anguish. We were married in March and I became pregnant in November. Our beautiful daughter was born the following August back in the good old U.S. of A. Living in the Dominican Republic was an extremely trying experience. So when I found out I was pregnant, I declared that I needed to be back on U.S. soil. He was able to get back into baseball as a coach in the minor leagues. This is by no means a glamorous position since working in the minor leagues as a player or coach means travelling to small towns on small budgets six months out of the year. Needless to say, I was on my own most of the time. I learned to be self-sufficient as a spouse and parent. I took care of all the bills, parented and worked full time as an Executive Secretary for a major financial institution. I truly believed he loved our daughter as a baby and child, but really did not know how to be a good parent. He would be gone for weeks and months and never phone....again; this was before cell phones and easy access. It was a very lonely existence. I'm sure he would tell you that he did not call me because he did not want to fight. It was a vicious cycle. One example that I can laugh about today was not so funny at the time. For whatever the reason, my Italian temper would flair and I would begin to raise my voice and yell at him...he would then begin to start making a sign of the cross and in Spanish begin to ask the devil to leave my body! Are you kidding me?!!! I would not advise this as a way to calm someone down who is angry! God help me! Again, enter my Catholic faith. While it helped to sustain me, it also helped me to endure my suffering. Up until this point, no one in my immediate family had ever filed for divorce and I was not going to be the first. I would continue to endure this unhealthy relationship even if it killed me. After 10 years, it almost did.

Spiritual Surrender

DID YOU AND YOUR SPOUSE SHARE THE SAME SPIRITUAL BELIEF?

As previously stated, no, we did not. I did, however, demand that our daughter be baptized and raised Catholic. She even attended Catholic school as a child. My ex-husband would later admit that the day our daughter was baptized Catholic was one of the worst days of his life. He not only was not Catholic, but was anti-Catholic. He feared the Catholic Church...with all of those statues! We had so many fights about religion; I could not even begin to count the number. If we ever were to go to church together, I had to give in and go to one of his Baptist or non-denominational churches. It was always me giving in to him; he would never go into a Catholic church. To this day, I try to keep an open mind, but find myself very defensive around evangelicals fearing the same persecution.

WHAT ATTRIBUTES DID YOUR SPOUSE BRING TO THE RELATIONSHIP, POSITIVE OR NEGATIVE?

My ex-husband came to our relationship with a lot of baggage. I came to the relationship with unrealistic expectations. I think more than our age difference, our cultural and religious differences were the ultimate nails in the coffin. Religious differences are hard enough, but when you also have underlying basic cultural differences, it is nearly impossible to overcome. My husband was raised in a third world country where basic survival was at the forefront. He was one of eight children. His family was so poor that they had to "give away" the two youngest siblings as children to another family to raise as their own, a concept that is almost impossible to grasp as an American. While later in life he became one of the first proclaimed millionaire pitchers in major league baseball, he could not escape his upbringing. He simply was not programmed to care about things like Hallmark greeting cards for sentimentality; calling in to touch base on a regular basis when he was travelling around the country and the world; or acknowledging your partner as an equal. I liken it to the old phrase, "You are what you eat". Metaphorically, the "food" that you are fed as a child such as love, respect, acceptance and security are crucial building blocks into whom you become as an adult. His parents were actually very lovely people and were married for many, many years. His father has passed away, but his mother is still alive and lives here in the U.S. She still does not speak English, but has tried to reach out to our daughter over the years in her native Spanish. I find it very confusing that she continues to reach out to our daughter while her son does not.

What occurred to bring you out of the denial of your situation? What were some of the ways in which you found to heal your heart? How did you find your way back to trusting your decisions and recapturing your ability to love again?

Crippling and debilitating panic attacks were ironically my savior. After nearly 10 years of enduring this unhealthy relationship, my nervous system finally had had enough. I went from being a strong and independent woman to someone who could not work, drive, or stop my body from visibly shaking. In the old days, it would be called a nervous breakdown. It was terrifying. I had never heard of panic attacks. The reason for these attacks should have been crystal clear, but I was floating down that river in Egypt "de Nile". I finally found a psychologist who specializes in anxiety disorders and began discussing my life and just as a "side note", I mentioned that my marriage had some issues....such issues were at the core my anxiety. Besides our religious, cultural and age differences, a big problem for us was financial....the millions were gone. It was extremely stressful making ends meet on a monthly basis. At one point near the end of the marriage, he could not find a "paying" job in baseball, so he joined a team of former major league baseball players who toured the world as ambassadors for major league baseball. Great gig if you don't need an income as all travel and expenses were paid for, but there was no compensation paid. He did that for nearly a year while I stayed at home, worked, took care of our daughter and paid the bills. This was one of the straws that broke the proverbial camel's back. After months of working with a counselor and some added medication, I came to realize that I needed to end this marriage/relationship. It was one of the hardest things I've ever had to do. *"Feel the Fear and Do It Anyway"*....a book by Susan Jeffers was also a life saving book and vehicle that helped me through this troubled time in my life. My husband claimed he did not want the divorce, but I know deep down he knew it had to end. Unfortunately, he could not deal with his emotions and became MIA for years choosing to have no relationship with his daughter. He would tell you that I kept our daughter from him, but that simply is not the case and he knows it.

WHAT ADVICE WOULD YOU GIVE TO YOUNG LOVERS ENTERING A NEW RELATIONSHIP?

Never give up on love! Call me a dreamer or a romantic at heart. After going through what I had endured, many people would have gone running from any future relationships, but I did the opposite. I ran right into a new one! I met my second husband while I was going through my divorce, which turned into a two year protracted battle over child support. This new relationship was everything my old one was not. This new man in my life was a blue-eyed All-American type, college-educated, responsible and from the same mid-western area of the country that I was from. We worked in the same office building for years....me on the 3rd floor and he on the 13th floor....it was a mutual acquaintance who introduced us. While he was not Catholic, he was not anti-Catholic; he really wasn't anything, just a good man with a good heart. He later converted to Catholicism after the birth of our daughter. He also later adopted my older daughter and she now calls him dad.

My Italian family jokes that he is the "Tom Hogan" (Consiglieri from the Godfather) of our family....he even resembles Robert Duvall! We have been married now for nearly 19 years and together for over 21 years. He has been nothing but loving and supportive of me since day one. It was also through his encouragement and support that I was able to go back to college in my forties to ascertain my Bachelors of Arts Degree in Journalism from ASU's Walter Cronkite School of Journalism. While our backgrounds are more similar than my ex's, we still have very different personalities. I am the more emotional and romantic party in the relationship and he is more grounded and level-headed....it makes for a good balance. I believe there are some basic foundations that really need to be in line for a long-term relationship to work, but subtle personality differences make for a good balance.

NOW I UNDERSTAND AND BELIEVE THAT... After my divorce, my father would say to me, "all those wasted years". I would say back to my dad, "they were not wasted years. They were valuable life lessons. I would not be the person I am today without having gone through my life experiences." I truly believe that if I had not gone through the hardships of my previous relationship, I might not have valued my new one as much. A simple daily phone call to touch base and check in is viewed as a sign of love and devotion to me that may have been overlooked or taken for granted had I not gone through my previous relationship/experience. We are stronger than we realize. The old adage is true...what doesn't kill you, makes you stronger...and I might add wiser. The truth is even if life throws you a curve ball, you can still hit a homerun!

* * *

This was the story of a young woman with a strong will, a desire for love and the fortitude to make changes when the time was ready. Wisdom takes time and much can happen along the way. But what one gathers along the way is so much more than wasted years. In her own words: *The old adage is true...what doesn't kill you, makes you stronger...and I might add wiser. The truth is even if life throws you a curve ball, you can still hit a homerun!* Bravo! My darling friend!

Live brave.

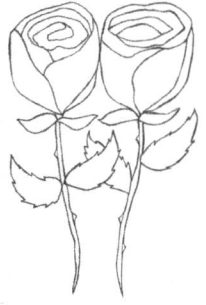

CHAPTER FIVE

HEALING AND TRUSTING AGAIN

"Even the best possible relationships proceed through periods of connection to disconnection to reconnection. But reconnection is never merely going back to some good old place. When this process occurs, each person and the relationship itself inevitably move on to a new level, to bring more than they were before."

Jean Baker Miller, M.D.

Mary Beth

I met David shortly after my Father passed away. I was very eager to meet him for he had recently published a book, *I Didn't Know What To Say,* written for those of us who struggle with what to say to someone who has recently experienced the passing away of a loved one. I think we can all admit that sometimes it is very difficult to know how to express our sympathy and concern. David delivers sound and comforting advice in his book based on his own loss, particularly the passing of a spouse.

David is soft-spoken and articulate in conversation and exceptionally open and honest regarding his painful experience. In meeting with him, Hilda and I were impressed with his ability to have "picked up the pieces of his broken heart" after the devastating death of not only his first wife, but his second wife as well. We were also inspired by his courage to write and speak nationally about the effects of such great loss in an effort to help others.

In his answers to our *Living Brave* questions, David tells his story with sincerity and raw emotion and we believe you will appreciate his sharing and his message of hope.

DAVID, 67

"Facing the grieving process a second time was harder than the first time for a few reasons. First, I already knew how much I would hurt in grieving."

David is the father of eight, grandfather of 28, is a recognized and sought-after national speaker and published writer: *Grit* newspaper, *Christian Herald* magazine, Brown Gold magazine, *The Gospel Herald* magazine, and has been a regular contributor to *Union Gospel Press* publications. Knapp has served as an administrator and professor at two junior colleges and currently is a regional public relations director for an international religious non-profit, New Tribes Mission. With a deep desire to empower people to be better friends to the grieving and to encourage the heartbroken to go through the process of finding relief and regaining a winning attitude for the next chapter or phase of life, David has recently published a book, *I Didn't Know What to Say: Being a Better Friend to Those Who Experience Loss.*

In line with his life values, Dr. Knapp serves on the advisory board for an international non-profit organization, Kidz at Heart. He has been very active in churches in the Mesa and Scottsdale, Arizona areas. He now resides in Mesa, Arizona with his wife Crystal, founder and editor of *Reach Up* magazine. In his limited free time, in addition to spending time with family, he enjoys reading and fishing.

Title: It Must Have Been Love

Physical Connection

WHERE WERE YOU BORN AND RAISED, AND WHAT CAN YOU TELL US ABOUT YOUR CHILDHOOD SURROUNDINGS AND CIRCUMSTANCES?

No one really thinks of southern Iowa when the term "poverty stricken" is mentioned. Ringgold County is one of two counties in Iowa that has been given that distinction. Those of us who lived there thought it was funny, however. We all lived at about the same level and so did not consider ourselves as "poverty stricken." In fact, we thought life was not so bad.

The first born of any family can often be given special attention. I was that kid. My dad took me everywhere he could in our rural community. Our farm was the typical one with livestock and crops, along with a large garden. I liked that life as a kid. We attended a small church where everyone knew everything about everyone else.

Our family bubble burst the day my dad was killed in a farming accident. Winter had only delivered half her force that sunny February day that changed our lives forever. I was 12 years old and expected to grow up that day...and I did. On the day of that accident, Mom was a young 30-year-old pregnant mother living in a home with no indoor plumbing and a pot belly stove that burned coal or wood for heat. My youngest brother, child number five, was born one week after my dad's funeral. My mom's grief seemed to cause our lives to stop. She spent a lot of time in bed. She only got up to do minimum care for her other four small children. Our finances crashed as well.

The farm had to be sold and everything along with it. We moved to a small town, population 127, and began a new life.

Two years later, Mom married a 50-year-old man who had never been married or had any siblings as a boy. The family adjustments were multiplied for us all. My mom had three more babies in the next couple of years (a set of twins included). As the eldest, I carried a lot of the burden of the work load and helped with some of the adjustments through my high school years. Sadly, this marriage began to break down and only lasted ten years. By the time their divorce was final, I was out of the home and already married.

TELL US OF A TIME WHEN YOU FELL DEEPLY IN LOVE—THE ATTRAC-
TION/CONNECTION, THE CIRCUMSTANCES, YOUR AGE AT THE TIME,
AND HOW LONG IT LASTED. WERE THERE ANY "RED FLAGS" AT THE BE-
GINNING OF THE RELATIONSHIP THAT YOU WERE AWARE OF BUT DID
NOT ACKNOWLEDGE?

"Till death do us part," I repeated. Those words seemed to echo throughout
the huge college chapel following my promise and then my bride's commitment. The witnesses of our wedding, family and friends, stood by smiling. Our
parents sat with proud looks on their faces. In all honesty, however, I only
viewed those words as a symbol of commitment. I did not really think I would
experience that part of those important words—let alone do it twice.

Ruth and I had never been happier than we were that delightful day in July.
The memories of how we met flashed through our minds. It was indeed amazing that from over 9,000 college kids at the Christian conference, we happened to sit together for a meal and really hit it off. We were both glad that I
looked for her at the second meal that began a regular event for the five days
of the conference.

Our wedding crowned three years of getting acquainted through writing
letters and occasional long distance phone calls. Ruth's dormitory for nursing students at the Washington Hospital Center in DC was a long way from
where I was in Kansas City. Looking back, this strengthened our relationship
because it forced both of us to express our hearts, feelings, and beliefs on paper
without the distraction of the physical area. That was great for my growth,
both emotionally with her and spiritually with the Lord.

The proof of the depth of our relationship revealed itself in the ensuing years
of life. We were not only committed to each other but we understood each
other. We did, indeed, marry our best friend. To keep our growth together on
a "roll" we spent every one of our wedding anniversaries—alone—discussing
the "state of our union."

We were best friends and enjoyed life and raising kids together. Cancer challenged all of that. However, our strong bond held us together for the seven
years Ruth battled the dreaded disease. Twenty years of marriage seemed so
short when the end seemed so close. The day she died, I hurt more than I
could ever imagine a human aching.

During my grieving process, I had gotten some great counsel to "grieve well" in order to be able to love again. So, I "leaned into" the grieving process and learned all I could from the pain and emotional surprises it afforded. I'm glad I did.

My role at the college as professor and president kept my days filled along with caring for four active teens. Later that year, a widow lady came to the school who absolutely swept me off my feet. I mean, I don't know what I thought about love at first sight before that, but the fact that it happened to me was for sure. I thought all those feelings had died. What a beautiful lady!

The next year Judith and I found ourselves in a large church in Edmonton, Alberta, Canada, with six sons on one side and two daughters and Judith's sister on the other. Judith's four boys were not so sure about Mom remarrying until we all had a chance to get well-acquainted. Again, the room echoed our vows, "Till death do us part."

These words had much deeper meaning to both of us. We had both experienced this hard truth to the fullest. However, even with that, we viewed the reality of it happening again as being a lifetime away.

Falling in love again was fun. There, I said it. A lot of the unknowns about life and love had been answered for both of us. All we needed to do was plug each other into the equation. Of course, we had to establish a new identity. Our new identity was a new "US." It was not like our parents' relationship. It was not like our previous marriage relationships. It was a unique, new relationship that required learning and growing together. So, we did that.

Though there were no "red flags," there was the weighty process of blending eight teenagers. It became twice the task either of us had imagined. Yes, the volume was an issue. When you bring two families together, they bring their baggage along. That means twice as many problems. The growth and mistakes of our kids only drove us to the Lord and to each other. We learned early on to talk about everything, no matter how hard the subject. We reviewed the development of each of our kids every three to six months. We experienced joys and challenges in our successful blending of families from two different countries and cultures.

After fifteen years of marriage, Judith's health began to decline inexplicably.

After five years of not knowing what was wrong with her, the pancreatic cancer was discovered. Her last three months of life were spent saying goodbye to our eight children and their spouses, along with the 24 grandkids. Then, I was alone again.

Many times during our last few months together, Judith would insist that I get married again. Of course, that was not on my mind then, so I dismissed it. But, way too soon, I faced that possibility.

Facing the grieving process a second time was harder than the first time for a few reasons. First, I already knew how much I would hurt in grieving. Second, because Judith and I had hurt deeply before we were married, we were able to love more deeply. Third, I was now physically alone more than the first time with all the kids out of the house. The silence was stifling. I "leaned into" the pain of grief knowing relief would eventually emerge.

Now I faced the challenge of finding a lady who had the characteristics and qualities I knew I was looking for. With both Ruth and Judith, I was engrossed in a school with many people around and many opportunities to meet new folks. This time, I was older (meaning I did not have a lifetime to search) and had limited social encounters.

I reverted to looking for a new "friend" the modern way...the internet. I signed up on Christian Mingle. After months of vain searches, I expanded my search farther and farther from my home. Then, there she was. I looked at Crystal's profile several times before I got my nerve up to actually contact her.

Crystal's profile revealed many attributes that singled her out from most of those I viewed. In addition to being gorgeous, she had a background in Christian ministry and was the editor of a magazine. Since I was planning to write a book and also to continue in my Christian ministry, it looked like a possible fit.

We communicated electronically for a while, and I began to sense a tender heart in her, which I liked. After a few weeks, we set up a phone call and then a Skype session. Things still looked promising to me, so I asked to meet her near her town.

A meeting for lunch turned into a three-day visit (her friends found accommodations for me). We enjoyed our time together. Later, Crystal admitted that some of our talks seemed like a job interview, which I guess was true. So, for the next several months, I drove from Phoenix to Los Angeles to visit her and her family every two weeks.

Again, falling in love was a lot of fun. The day came when I bowed on one knee in front of her and her family and asked her to marry me. SHE SAID YES!

Crystal has brought a lot of hope, encouragement, and delight into my life. Even one of my grandkids observed to his mom, "Grandpa sure does laugh a lot with her." And I do.

We are now in our third year of marriage and it still feels like we are newly-weds.

Emotional Responsiveness

WHAT DID YOUR PARENTS MODEL IN A RELATIONSHIP FOR YOU AS A CHILD?

In a sense, I had two sets of parents to watch carry out their roles in the home. My mom and dad had limited contact in our home around us kids because dad was out doing farm work so much. I did pick up a high respect for my dad from the way mom would talk about him and respect him when he was in the house. However, in the year before dad died, I observed some frustration between them in their attempts to communicate and understand each other.

My other set of parents was my mom and my stepdad. Again, I saw my mom show love and respect for my stepdad at the outset of their relationship. However, within a couple of years, that began to falter. She seemed to decrease in her ability to respect him because he was not living up to a certain standard she had for him. He felt that. Also, I saw my stepdad begin to pull away from her. He had the idea that after they were married, certain traits about her would change. They did not.

From these examples in my life I observed some things about how NOT to have a good relationship. I also had a strong Bible-based education and knew from the Bible that a solid, loving relationship in marriage was possible when certain acceptance, politeness, and loving principles were practiced by both.

WHAT WERE YOU LOOKING FOR IN THIS RELATIONSHIP?

My expectations for a relationship with a spouse revolved around my teaching and understanding of what the Bible communicates about the marriage bond. I valued truth, openness, a common basis of Biblical teaching, unity, love and respect. Many of these could be defined as simple "people skills;" however, a basic characteristic of commitment and integrity needed to be in the mix. Differences of personality were not as much of a concern to me if those things were present in the relationship. This was true for all three of my successful searches for a spouse.

LOOKING BACK, DID YOU AND YOUR SPOUSE SHARE THE VALUES THAT YOUR PARENTS MODELED?

The values I have shared with all three of my wives have come from our faith and trust in the message of the Bible. Ruth's parents and Crystal's parents followed these principles well, and the other parental examples in our lives gave us some "don't do it this way" messages.

WHAT CHANGED? WHAT OCCURRED FOR YOU TO FEEL THE LOSS OF THE RELATIONSHIP? TO WHAT EXTENT WAS IT HURTFUL, PHYSICALLY, FINANCIALLY, MENTALLY, AND EMOTIONALLY?

One of the unexpected blows I experienced in the grieving process after each of my wives died was the heartache of lost love. It was one thing to lose someone you know to death, but it went deeper as I missed my lover. It was like I had a hole in my soul that could not be filled. I even had to tell myself out loud, "She is gone!" So, at first, I put out a picture of her in every room of the house for months after her death. Then, slowly, I began to put them away as the emotional pain began to subside.

I was also shocked that there were so many financial and legal things to deal with following a death. Some things were not cleared up for nearly a year later.

Spiritual Surrender

DID YOU AND YOUR SPOUSE SHARE THE SAME SPIRITUAL BELIEF?

For me and each of my three wives, our spiritual beliefs were the foundation for our entire relationship. Our belief in our personal relationship with Jesus Christ was the common core value that formed and held together our marriages. Even when human, personal differences came up our basis was back to

God. When struggles of life and raising kids emerged, we clung to each other and our relationship with God. Then when cancer entered the picture, our basis on God kept us together to the end.

WHAT ATTRIBUTES DID YOUR SPOUSE BRING TO THE RELATIONSHIP, POSITIVE OR NEGATIVE?

On our anniversary each year, Ruth and I would go off alone and talk about the "state" of our relationship including growth and difficulties. Sure enough, Ruth asked how I had been during the throes of the hardest days that winter. When Ruth did not have the energy to give much attention to me because she was so exhausted from the chemotherapy, I began to feel a bit "unloved." I hesitantly, yet openly, shared with her how I had struggled and how God met me. Through my study of the Bible, I was reminded that God showed "unconditional love" to us and that when I kept serving and loving Ruth, even if I did not feel like it, that was love. God said to me, "It's okay." She simply said, "I thought so. It's okay with me too."

The following six years were filled with days and weeks of hope and disappointment. We faced treatments and then recurrences, over and over. Her breast cancer spread to her bones which the doctors chased around her body with radiation. In the end, it spread to her spinal column and then to her brain.

The most memorable time happened again during our "state of our union" talk that next July. Following a special day on the eastern shore of Lake Michigan, we sat talking. During a warm embrace, Ruth softly said, "I have never felt so at one with you."

Judith had been in a challenging marriage before her first husband died. During those times, she had learned steadfastness and loyalty to what is right. This gave her an uncommon ability to love unconditionally. She brought that trait into our marriage. It became a strong basis for the successful blending of our eight kids and our relationship as a couple.

Crystal had never been married before we got together. She had developed a strong sense of who she was and that her basis of happiness in life was to come from her connection with God. This she brought into our relationship which created a lot of peace from the very beginning in our home.

WHAT OCCURRED TO BRING YOU OUT OF THE DENIAL OF YOUR SITUA-

TION? WHAT WERE SOME OF THE WAYS IN WHICH YOU FOUND TO HEAL YOUR HEART? HOW DID YOU FIND YOUR WAY BACK TO TRUSTING YOUR DECISIONS AND RECAPTURING YOUR ABILITY TO LOVE AGAIN?

Three short months after our last "state of the union" session, I watched Ruth take her last breath. I didn't know a human could hurt so much. Within days, I became aware of this hole in my soul that seemed permanent.

Losing a spouse has many aspects to it that are not always understood by many. Indeed, there is the death and physical loss of that person, leaving a void in your life. There is also a loss of intimacy in communication. I had no one to tell even small things to that Ruth would appreciate hearing. My biggest loss, however, was the loss of the relationship. It seemed that, in addition to grief due to the death of a friend, I had lost the close relationship we had. Love songs were next to impossible for me to listen to.

NOW I UNDERSTAND AND BELIEVE THAT... Identifying and grieving the various aspects of a loss is vital in the healing process.

WHAT ADVICE WOULD YOU GIVE TO YOUNG LOVERS ENTERING A NEW RELATIONSHIP?

A. Learn to accept your lover the way he or she is; don't think you can change that person.
B. Apply normal "people skills" to your relationship with your mate. Don't be someone who takes them for granted as a person.
C. Always use truth and honesty as the basis of your relationship.
D. Don't expect your lover to fulfill every emotional and spiritual need you will ever have.

* * *

For those whose loved ones have passed, David's story is an inspiration to open one's heart to "love again" while holding the departed loved one's memory close. Live bravely ... in love.

Live Brave

THE TWO-NIGHT STAND

A Novelette by Hilda

To look at Sylvia is to know her—her skin, a beautiful golden brown; her hair, long, thick and shiny; a mouth that knows only to smile, and black, round eyes as peaceful as the sound of a flute playing softly at afternoon tea. A slim and petite size four, Sylvia is also strong and secure from years of dedicated exercise and a healthy life style. With a personality overflowing with optimism, she projects the unmistakable quality of a woman who has embraced wisdom in her mid-fifties.

A client for more than twenty years, our time together in the salon passes quickly. Since Sylvia is unusually sociable for an accountant, our conversations over the years have been about work, family, social and political agendas, spirituality, and our one-and-only sons who were both born in the same hospital just a few days apart thirty-six years ago. Both Sylvia and I were raised Catholic, grew up with traditional Mexican customs, and have been married and divorced. Her marriage lasted thirty years and although she has been divorced for several years, she has no desire to marry or even date again. With much in common, we never lack for subject matter to talk about.

On this particular day as she entered the salon, I could tell that something was weighing heavily on her. Normally outgoing and cheerful, she said nothing and barely made eye contact with me. Her only greeting was a slight tap on my arm as she moved past me to the shampoo area where she sat down to wait her turn. I felt myself becoming apprehensive. In all our years together, even through her divorce, I had never seen her so withdrawn.

After her shampoo and our discussion about any changes to her haircut, I told her that I could see that something was troubling her and wondered if she wanted to talk about it. She held her breath, sat motionless for a few moments, and then drew in enough air to release the tears cupped in her eyes. As her head dropped, her tears poured onto the cutting cape. I grabbed tissue from a counter behind me and handed them to her as fast as I could. As rapidly as the tears had come, Sylvia now quickly composed herself and looked at me with a reassuring smile.

She began her story. "I did something very foolish thirty six years ago...very foolish, and now it has come back to haunt me. The worst part is that it involves my son. It could change his life drastically, and he knows nothing about it."

There were no clients left in the salon and my assistants had gone home early. We were alone and could talk without interruption.

Sylvia continued. "Many years ago when I was nineteen and a freshman at Arizona State University working on my degree, I worked evenings at Goldwater's department store in downtown Phoenix. As you remember, Hilda, it was the most upscale department store in our city at the time and acquiring employment there was a great opportunity for a young girl. My position at the store was called a rover, which meant that I would help wherever I was needed most for that particular evening. I had been at Goldwater's for several months and had learned to work in most departments when the store supervisor called me into her office and assigned me to the men's department for the next three months of the holiday season. I would work every evening, five days a week, for Mr. Angelo, the department manager. Most rovers were afraid of him because he was extremely organized and demanded that the dressing rooms and displays be orderly at all times. I welcomed the opportunity to learn from Mr. Angelo, but, mostly, I was excited to be working with all the cute guys coming in to shop. I had dated very little during high school and had met no one worth dating at the university since moving to Phoenix from Los Angeles.

"The month of October passed quickly. The days were getting shorter, the holidays closer, and the temporary holiday staff had been hired. The holiday rush was on, and the store vibrated with a non-stop, hectic pace. Mr. Angelo, another rover, and I kept our department running smoothly. At times we worked for eight hours straight until we closed out our department...leaving it completely re-organized and ready for the morning crew for the next day.

"On Monday, the first week in November, Mr. Angelo was in a terrible car accident. A drunk driver had run a red light and hit Mr. Angelo's car on the driver's side. He was rushed to the hospital with a broken leg and arm, severe bruising, and a whiplash. His family was unsure when he would return to the store but thought that he would be out at least a month. The day manager of the men's department worked a bit later until I arrived for the evening shift, but it was impossible for anyone else to help during this time of year. I was given the temporary responsibility of managing the department, so, along with another rover and occasional holiday staffer, I ran the department as well as I could.

"The following Monday, I was notified that Mr. Angelo was well enough to leave the hospital and that he would be recuperating at home. That same evening, I was also told that all rovers were busy in other departments and that I would have to work the shift alone. As soon as they could get all store temps placed though, they would try to send me some help. Ironically, that evening was the busiest evening of the year. I was running in and out of dressing rooms, exchanging sizes, and working the cash register when I called the office and pleaded, 'PLEASE SEND HELP!' I thought I would die in the department and no one would ever find me under the piles of pants, shirts, jackets, underwear, and pajamas. It was a mess. If Mr. Angelo saw this now, he would have a heart attack and die right on the spot. A few minutes later, still working alone, I called again and asked for *help*. This time I even started to cry on the phone...

"A man who was purchasing several pairs of slacks and some shirts was waiting for me at the cash register as I ran out of the dressing rooms. As calmly as I could, remembering that Goldwater's takes pride in their high level of service, I took a deep breath and began checking the merchandise. (This was before scanners, so the price of every item had to be manually entered into the cash register.)

"A young man who was shopping for the first time without his mother was waiting for help in the dressing room and was calling my name. Other men were forming a line at the register. It was a nightmare in process, and the evening had just begun. I called out to the young man in the dressing room to give me a few more minutes, and as I completed the sale, I asked the client if there was anything else that I could do for him. Of course, he wanted something else—separate gift boxes for all of the merchandise!

"From behind me, I heard a man's voice say, 'I'll get those for you.'

"As I looked down to my right underneath the counter, I saw the back of a man's head as he bent down to pull out the gift boxes. In an even quieter voice, he said, 'Nice legs.' Instantly, a blush rushed from my legs to my face. I prayed that the customer had not heard this man's comment, whoever he was.

"As he stood up and placed the gift boxes into the bag with the rest of the customer's purchases, I saw his face for the first time. He was a giant—at least six feet three inches tall, if not taller, and extremely attractive. His reddish-blonde hair was cut short, military style. His hazel eyes were large, his lips full, and his nose strong, but not big. His smile was warm and friendly, and his manner appeared to be that of a well-bred gentleman. The way he wore the stunning black suit (clearly a Goldwater's brand) with his shoes perfectly cleaned and polished told me without question that he was in the military.

"He introduced himself to me as Luke O'Ryan, the temp who was there to help me for the evening. Relieved to have him with me, I decided not to mention his comment about my legs. Frankly, he did not appear the type to make such a comment. He appeared to be much too well-mannered for such mischievousness. Goldwater's dress code was very strict. Men had to wear a black or navy blue suit and tie. Women wore either a black or navy blue dress, and although miniskirts were the style in the sixties, our dresses had to touch our knees. I may have cheated a bit with the length of the dress that I was wearing that evening, so he might have noticed too much leg showing. No one had ever made a comment about my legs in my entire life. I was a little embarrassed, but at the same time, I felt complimented. During that busy evening, Luke and I barely had time to talk to each other. At the end of the shift, all I cared about was that the night was over, and I was grateful for the help.

"For the next two weeks, Luke and I worked together. He knew much more about men's apparel than I. He knew where everything was located in the entire store, and his height was a plus in reaching all the high places. Overall, he was neat, fast, organized, and had a great sense of humor. Not only did he keep the staff laughing but the customers found him entertaining. He had a confidence about him that was noticeable. He was not at all narcissistic, but exuded a natural assurance of himself.

"What I learned about Luke's personal life was that he was home on medical leave from Vietnam. He had sustained an injury to his left hip from a shell fragment of an exploding artillery round. After his hospitalization abroad, he was sent home to await his orders for returning to Vietnam. A high-energy, constantly-in-motion kind of man, he had decided to stay busy and work as a temp at the store until he heard back from the Army. He had worked at Goldwater's during high school until he left for West Point Military Academy at the age of nineteen. Luke was now twenty-five years old and a Captain. Following in his father's footsteps, he was dedicated to his service in the military and believed that serving his country was not an option but a necessity. I also learned that he was not married, nor did he have a girlfriend. He was very cute, laughed most of the time, and I was really enjoying him.

"Two days before Thanksgiving, Luke asked if I would join him for Thanksgiving dinner at his parent's home. I was unable to be with my family in California because the store would be open for the busiest day of the year, the day after Thanksgiving—Black Friday. Since I could not afford to fly home for a one-day visit, I accepted his invitation.

"As you know, Hilda, my family did not have much money when I was growing up. Both my parents worked the melon fields around the San Bernardino-Riverside area just east of Los Angeles. For extra money, my mother cleaned houses and my father did yard work on weekends. I did not grow up with nice things, nor did I have the opportunity to develop an eye for fashion. Working at Goldwater's had given me *some* sense of style—enough to know that I had a long way to go in learning what looked good with what! That's probably why I enjoyed working in the men's department. Men are much less complicated and easier to please, or at least I thought so back then. Nevertheless, it took everything my family had to send me to the university, and buying a wardrobe was not in the budget. Fortunately, I shared an apartment with my cousins who lived in South Phoenix. With the exception of the two dresses that I wore to work, I did not have anything nice to wear for Thanksgiving dinner. My cousin Lucia came to my rescue by lending me an outfit that she had made in high school for a project in home economics. She assured me that it would be perfect for the occasion.

"Thinking back, I must have looked like a clown. The outfit was a forest green, crushed velvet miniskirt and vest. Underneath the vest, I wore a white Peter Pan collar blouse with long sleeves, which Lucia accessorized with lots of inexpensive gold chains that draped at different lengths from my neck to my waistband. Three-inch hoop earrings complemented my gold chains, and I teased up my hair at least three inches for that 'fluff on top of the head' look that was so popular back then. My cousin also insisted that I wear a pair of very high black platform shoes, white stockings, and a wide black belt to accentuate my small waist."

In the salon, Sylvia and I sat and laughed uncontrollably as she described her Thanksgiving outfit. Knowing her as a sophisticated and stylish shopper, I could not imagine that she would have worn such a get-up. I had long finished her haircut and blow dry, and we now sat facing each other as Sylvia continued her story.

"When Luke arrived in his 1965 maroon Chevelle SuperSport convertible, he commented on how nice I looked. He was wearing a pair of khaki slacks with a white cotton shirt, a navy blue pullover sweater, and brown loafers.

"As we pulled up to his parents' home, I was taken aback by the size of the house. It looked like a picture-perfect postcard of one of those Hollywood mansions of the rich and famous. It was a red brick ranch style home with a shake shingle roof. The windows were oversized and accentuated by white shutters. A perfectly manicured lawn with lush, flawlessly groomed landscape and tall trees surrounded the house. Large pots, overflowing with colorful flowers, emphasized the grand entrance to the front door, and the biggest and most elaborate holiday wreath hung there with the words *Welcome and Happy Holidays*.

"The house was located in the prestigious North Central Phoenix Corridor. I had heard mention of the area at work when the employees would say that Mrs. So-and-So lived in the North Central Corridor, and now I could see for myself that this was certainly where the wealthy lived.

"As we parked in front of the four-car garage, a woman rushed out from the side door to greet us. Making a quick assessment of the way she was dressed, I was certain that I looked absolutely ridiculous and that I needed to make some changes quickly. As swiftly as I could, I took off the cheap gold chains and pulled off the loop earrings. While smoothing my hair down several inches from the top, I wondered how I was going to take off my white hose without being noticed. The woman came close to the car, called Luke's name, and threw her arms out to hug him as he stepped out of the car. She kissed his cheeks and began to cry, obviously very glad to see him.

"I had a few seconds to get my hose off and was trying to get my shoes back on when Luke brought her to my side of the car. He introduced me as his friend from work and told me that this was his Aunt Rebecca, his mother's younger sister. She and her husband and four children had just arrived from Minnesota and would be staying for a week to enjoy the warm November weather and to spend time with Luke while he waited for his orders.

"Inside the house, I felt even more uncomfortable about my attire. Luke's mother, a lovely, genteel woman, the epitome of a conservative mother dressed in traditional clothing, greeted me warmly with a welcoming smile, never looking away from my eyes down to my outfit. I thought that if she let herself look at what I was wearing, she would laugh out loud and cause everyone else to go into hysterics. His father, a tall, lanky, easy-going man greeted me with an appropriate, 'Luke has spoken highly of you, Sylvia. Welcome to our home. We are delighted that you chose to join us.' The rest of the family was just as pleasant—two aunts and their husbands, six children between them, Luke's younger brother, Thomas, and Luke's best friend Ben, who lived just a couple of doors down the street. In all, there were sixteen of us who sat at the dinner table. I had never seen a table large enough to accommodate that many before.

"As I watched everyone taking their places at the table, it was obvious that this refined family knew what they were going to do with all of the utensils that were arranged on the placemats. I had no clue what fork or spoon I would begin with, and why were there so many different sizes of forks to choose from anyway? Composing myself, I remembered that I was a quick study. Simply by paying close attention to what others were doing, eating slowly, staying calm, and smiling a lot, I would follow along and do just fine. It was at this point that I felt I should have never accepted Luke's invitation. What was I thinking anyway? I certainly came from the wrong side of the tracks or at least lacked the experience of formal dining protocol.

"In spite of my insecurities, dinner was absolutely delightful. The entire family included me in their conversations, asked me questions about my family in California and why I had decided to move to Arizona, and, before I knew it, what I thought was going to be an embarrassing dining experience was over. Next, Luke and I were invited to Ben's home, just two doors away, for dessert. Luke and Ben had grown up together since the age of five when Luke's parents had moved into the neighborhood. Ben had joined the Air Force reserves and had completed his service. He now worked with his father in the insurance business.

"At Ben's home, we had another great family experience. Dessert was served around the football game in the family room. I was amazed that both men and women watched the game and that the women were actually interested. It was then that I learned that Luke and Ben had both played football in high school and that Luke had gone on to play at West Point.

"By the time the football games ended and Luke and I walked back to his parent's home for yet another dessert, it was late. Both of us had to be at work by five the next morning ready for Black Friday. Luke took me home, walked me to my front door, gave me a hug, and thanked me for spending the day with him, his family, and his friends. He said I was wonderful and that everyone enjoyed meeting me. Aside from thinking how much I enjoyed being with him, I wondered if he had any feelings beyond friendship toward me. Nevertheless, I was glad that I had accepted his invitation, and I was *really* happy to take off that outfit!

"The next two weeks at work were absolutely crazy. Mr. Angelo was back managing the department but moving slowly. Luke had been assigned to another area, and every evening we had a different temp working with us in the men's department. The shopping frenzy was in full swing, but the good news was that I was on winter break from the university and my studies. Although Luke came by the department to say hello every evening, I never saw him, nor did we talk, outside of work.

"Five days before Christmas, Luke did not come by to see me; however, sometime during the rush of that evening, he called me. He had not come to work that day because he had heard from the Army...he was leaving for Vietnam in three days. His voice sounded strong and confident as he shared his news.

"Then in a timorous voice, he asked, 'Sylvia, will you have dinner with me tomorrow evening, and will you consider spending the night with me?'

"There were people all around me, and I could see Mr. Angelo walking toward me with an armful of clothing to be put away. I had never spent the night with a man before. I wondered if he meant that I would sleep with him. My mind began thinking of the lectures from my mother as I was growing up. 'Sleeping with a man without marriage is dangerous. It can only lead to no good. Why would he buy the cow if he can have the milk for free?'

'Yes, I will have dinner with you tomorrow, but I have never spent the night with a man before. What should I bring?'

'Just your toothbrush. I'll take care of the rest. I will come by your apartment tomorrow evening at seven. I realize that I am asking you to take time off from work. Is that all right with you?'

"I thought it strange that he would be concerned about my taking time off from work. The bigger concern for me was spending the night with him. As I hung up the phone, I became nervous and excited, like a child anticipating a surprise. The rest of the evening I couldn't stop thinking about us being together in that way. I had been attracted to him from the first time I looked at his face, but he had never given me any sign of interest. Even after Thanksgiving dinner when he had dropped me off at the apartment, he had just hugged me. I wondered what had changed.

"By the time Luke arrived at my front door at exactly seven, I was a nervous wreck. I chose to wear the same black dress that I wore to work—the one that I was wearing the evening we met. I wondered if he would still think I had nice legs, but the truth was that it was the nicer of the two dresses that I owned. As I opened the door, we smiled at each other. Then he reached for me and hugged me tight. He was wearing a beautiful dark gray suit with a white silk turtleneck pullover. He looked absolutely handsome.

"I had never been to the Biltmore Resort in Phoenix before. As it turned out, it would be an evening of many firsts for me. We drove up to valet parking, and the young man who opened my door welcomed me by addressing me as Ma'am and called Luke by name. They obviously knew each other, and as I learned later during dinner, Luke's family had been regulars there for Sunday brunches and dinners for many years, as well as the hotel his father used when business associates came to town.

"Hilda, I remember everything about dinner that evening, including what I ate. I won't bore you with all of that, but it was delicious. The service was incredible, and I didn't even worry about what fork I was going to use first.

"Most everyone working in the dining room knew Luke and came by with best wishes on his return to service. It was obvious that he and his family were well known and well liked. I remember feeling rather uncomfortable with myself because I felt a degree of smugness being seen with him. Anyway, being with him felt amazingly wonderful.

"During dinner, I became intoxicated with our conversation. The stories of his childhood adventures with his best friend, Ben, the tenderness with which he talked about his mother, the respect he felt toward his father, who owned a very successful investment company, and the love he felt for his younger brother, Thomas, filled me with admiration, not only for him, but for his family. I shared stories of my family and their struggles as they moved from Mexico to California and proudly became American citizens. We both felt grateful to have such close and loving families who taught us the value of family and friends and the blessings of living in this country. I found it interesting that although we were so different culturally and economically our dreams and desires for the future were exactly the same. We never discussed Vietnam. I had no idea what it was like for him other than the little I knew about his injury. Our dinner was finally over, and once again I became excited as I anticipated our first kiss. At that point, my mind could not think beyond the kiss.

"The Biltmore had been elegantly decorated for the Christmas holidays. People were milling around everywhere, and a festive atmosphere filled the hotel. As we walked through the lobby and out the back doors to the gardens en route to our room, Luke put his arm around me and brought me in close to his body. Any chill that I might have felt on this cool, crisp evening disappeared as each step took on a kind of melodic rhythm. With every stride, I became more and more at ease being held so closely by him.

"As we entered the room, it was obvious that the room had been prepared for us. Lights were dim and candles flickered everywhere. Soft music was playing, a bottle of wine was chilling in an ice bucket on a table, the bed covers had been pulled down, and several red roses lay on the nightstand beside the bed.

"Pouring the wine and handing me a glass, Luke raised his glass and toasted to *'Everything beautiful.'* Initially, I thought it unusual, but then I remembered his family. Their home, their lives, the way they talked to each other, how they had raised him and his brother, and how they viewed the world...it was all so beautiful. I could understand his outlook about his life and his surroundings. It reflected everywhere and I was standing in the middle of it all, dizzy with anticipation of a future with him.

"It has been almost forty years since that memorable evening, but I can still hear his voice in my mind. 'Sylvia, go in and wait for me in the shower. I will be in there to wash your back in a moment.' Obediently, but not as if I had lost control, I walked into a candle-lit room, undressed, and stepped into a warm spray of water to await my backwash. Within moments, my back facing the door, I heard it open and felt his hands on my shoulders. Gently, with big circles moving across my shoulders and down to my waist, with a bar of soap and a soft washcloth in his large hands, he washed every inch of me and soothed away any trepidation that I had held in my body earlier that evening. We never said a word to each other. Quietly, with only the sound of the water and the music that I could hear coming from the bedroom, I allowed myself to enjoy yet another first.

"After turning off the water, Luke took a white, terrycloth robe, wrapped me in it, lifted me up into his arms and carried me to the bed where he laid me on my back facing him. Sitting on the edge of the bed, he opened my robe to my waist, never taking his eyes away from my eyes. We smiled at each other as he reached for one of the roses on the nightstand. Pulling the first petal from the rose, he placed it at the base of my throat, in that little hollow place right where the collarbones meet at the center. Speaking for the first time since before our shower, he said in a whisper, 'This petal is for your beautiful hair that I have wanted to touch since the day I saw you standing in front of the cash register...with your back to me.' He took the next petal, placed it touching the first petal and went down my chest, 'This petal is for your beautiful eyes that call me to be inside of you. Petal three is for having such *nice legs*.' And on he went until rose petals touched each other going all the way down to my navel."

Sylvia began to cry, remembering such a tender experience so many years ago. I actually wanted to cry with her. I wanted to cry for all of the women, including myself, who had not had such a gentle experience...their first time.

"As he placed the last petal on my navel, Luke said softly, 'I know this is your first time, and I promise to be gentle. This petal is for *everything beautiful* that we are both about to experience together.' He then drew in a full, deep breath and, starting at my belly, blew the petals with a strong gust of air, scattering them across my breasts and shoulders. The coolness of his breath and the whimsical gesture made me laugh out loud. While I was still laughing, his hands moved quickly up to my face and as he cupped my cheeks and mouth gently...he kissed me. And he kissed me all night long.

"That evening I discovered parts of my body that I didn't know existed inside of me. Initially, I heard the sounds of someone crying painfully but then realized that it was the sound of ecstasy coming from within me. I felt my heart pound as if it would leave my chest and I wished that I could lock that feeling into my chamber forever. I saw myself as a grown woman, so I could gladly put my childish bashfulness aside. The smell of sweat thrilled me. I lost my serious and calculating mind to uncontrollable desires of wild passion and begged for more. To merely say that the evening was unforgettable would render it benign. But I do not have the words to describe it any other way.

"It must have been early in the morning when we finally succumbed to exhaustion and fell asleep in each other's embrace. I remember thinking that I couldn't wait to awaken to see him again. I slept in a deep sleep of gentle waves and tender breathing that kept me buried in the scent of our love making.

"But in the morning when I woke, he was gone. A note written on the hotel's stationary told me that he did not want to wake me, but that he had to leave.

"I spent Christmas with my parents in California. It was a short vacation and within two days I was back to work at Goldwater's. The after-Christmas sales were going on, Mr. Angelo was back to his old, fast-pace self again, and every day I thought of Luke. But I did not hear from him. I listened to the reports of the fighting in Vietnam and watched the anti-war movement on television. I prayed for Luke and waited to hear from him. With our conversation at dinner, the roses, our lovemaking, and the rush in the morning of leaving and saying goodbye, he never said that he would stay in touch. When thoughts of being used by him appeared in my mind, I would push them away, saying to myself that it must have been an oversight on his part. Of course, he meant to give me an address where he could be reached or the phone number to his parents' home or even Ben's number in case I needed to talk to someone. But I never heard from him.

"The year passed, and the war continued. I was in my second year at the university. I left Goldwater's and took a job in an accounting firm. Though it was only a part-time position, I was paid more money working shorter hours and no longer worked evenings. There was still no word from Luke. At times, I would drive to the North Central area and go by his parents' home and Ben's home just two doors away, but I never saw anyone. I didn't have the nerve to ring either of the doorbells and ask how Luke was. Maybe they wouldn't even remember me. Although, how could they ever forget my forest green crushed velvet outfit?

"In the second year of working at the accounting firm, I began dating Horace Smith, the owner. Actually, I didn't realize that we were dating. Most of the time that we spent together was in the office in meetings and dinners with clients, and because I had been given the task of assisting him with many of his personal clients, I assumed that we were working. Although he was a very nice, quiet, thoughtful man, he was a small, scholarly-looking gentleman, fifteen years older than I—not exactly the kind of man who attracted me. He had been married for several years when his wife passed away of breast cancer. They had no children.

"I know it sounds terribly naïve, but I had no idea that he was interested in me personally. I simply thought that he was preparing me to take over some responsibilities at the office. Anyway, I was very surprised the day Horace called me into his office and asked if I would consider marrying him.

"It had been two years since I had heard from Luke. I didn't know if he was still alive or if he ever thought of us being together. By now it was clear that if he cared for me, he would have already made contact. As much as my heart ached and as much as I wished that my life included him, I said yes to the marriage proposal.

"I planned a small wedding with family and friends within three months. That would give me plenty of time to get our families together, and I made sure that the wedding would take place in the summer time when business was slower. I would be on summer vacation from classes, so Horace and I could go on a nice honeymoon to Hawaii. Since I had never traveled beyond Arizona and California, Horace even insisted that I make reservations at the most expensive resort in Maui. As the plans came together, my cousins began to tease me about sleeping with my fiancé before marrying him. They would say, 'You have to try a pair of shoes on before you take them home. What if you get them home and they don't fit?' I kept insisting that we didn't have that kind of relationship, to which they would say, 'If you're going to be married to him, you're going to have to have sex with him.'

"Thus far in our relationship, Horace had barely kissed me. He courted me with flowers and greeting cards and an occasional box of chocolates from See's Candies. He enjoyed the symphony, opera, and historical documentaries. I felt as if I was getting an education when I began joining him for such events. A well-read, financially sound, serious thinker and hard-working man—I had only to gain from marrying him. The kissing and the sex would work themselves into our lives eventually.

"The week before our wedding day, my cousins got the best of me. I asked Horace if I could spend the night with him at his home. Although he resisted, stating that he wanted to wait until the honeymoon, I persisted and spent the night. Methodical by nature, Horace had a system for everything, including going to bed at a certain time, making sure that everything was left orderly and in its assigned place, laying out his clothes to wear the next day and, of course, making love. He was gentle, reserved, and quick. There were no roses, backwashes, wine, or candles, and there was a wedding in a week.

"The next morning when I arrived at work, there was a message for me to call Mr. O'Ryan. At first I thought that it could be Luke's father. Maybe he had some news. But how did he find me without Luke's help? I immediately called the number, and it was Luke who said the words: 'Sylvia, Mr. Angelo gave me your phone number. I'm so glad you called me back. Thomas was killed in a car accident last week. He was hit by a drunk driver and died instantly. It is horrible! You can imagine how my family is taking all of this. I'm in town for only two days. Can I see you this evening? I need to see you and talk with you.'

"My thoughts rushed in like waves crashing on cliff rocks during a turbulent storm. The thought of seeing him again made my body ache. At the same time, I felt myself gripped with the pain that he was feeling for losing his brother. How terrible to lose a loved one in such a senseless manner. I couldn't imagine how his parents were holding up.

"We met at the Biltmore for dinner. We ate, drank a bottle of wine, cried about Thomas and his parents, and talked until we were the last ones in the dining room. I never asked him why he never wrote or called. I also did not tell him that in less than a week I would be married to a man that I hardly knew. Instead, it was me who asked, 'Do you want to spend the night together?' He didn't hesitate.

"That was the foolish thing I did thirty-six years ago. Foolish and wonderful. Wonderful and foolish. As if only moments had passed since we had last been with each other, our lovemaking was as natural as being hungry for food and then eating. Our time together fed me as if I would never experience hunger again. My hands touched every inch of his muscular body. I devoured his lips and ran my hands through his short military haircut and grabbed his face and brought him to me over and over again. I would never forget the taste of his neck and the scent of his chest. We held on tight to each other through the night and I tried not to fall asleep, but in the morning, once again, I awoke to an empty bed. A rose and a note were on the nightstand. *I didn't want to wake you. You are Everything Beautiful. Thank you. Love, Luke.*"

Sylvia and I sat in silence for a long while as she caught her breath, sat back in the chair and looked at her hands. I needed a bit of silence myself as I sat ever so still and tried to imagine what it took for her to share such an intimate experience with me. She had always been such a private person...up until now. We sat in silence.

Sylvia began again.

"The morning of my wedding day, while I was dressing in my tiny apartment bedroom, it was my mother who noticed the blanket of guilt and doubt that covered my face. She began with the simple statement, 'You don't have to do anything that you don't want to do.'

"She took me off guard. I had absolute respect for her, but I answered her quickly and defensively, 'Of course, I'm certain I want to do this. I'm almost twenty-three years old, old enough to know what I want.'

"That's when I broke down in tears. My mother held me in her arms, and I could not say another word. My thoughts were drawn back to when I was a child. The kids in my neighborhood, in the barrio where we grew up, played outside all of the time. We played hide and seek at night. There was one boy that I liked. He was the only Anglo who dared to come into our neighborhood to play. The rest of the kids in our school were afraid of us...like we were somehow dangerous. We were Mexican and our parents worked the fields. Our parents didn't speak English, but we were learning it as fast as we could in school. All we wanted was to be part of this neighborhood. Our parents wanted to belong to the country, but we were too young to understand why it was so important to live in the United States.

"That Anglo, his name was Darrell and he liked me too, but his parents would not allow him to like a Mexican girl. You remember, Hilda, how it was for us back then? We were ostracized, and yet the farmers, ranchers, and business owners would beg the Mexicans to come and work in the States. Anyway, when Darrell's parents found out that he was playing with a bunch of Mexican kids and that he liked me, they forbade him to play with us. I remember thinking how unfair it was that we couldn't just play together...we were young kids. How could it hurt anyone?

"From that time forward, I wanted to marry an Anglo. That way I would fit in and belong to the country. I would have an Anglo's last name, and no one would question my right to be here. I know that was unrealistic thinking, but this is what I thought about when Horace asked me to marry him.

"As I tried to convince my mother that I was simply nervous, she said again, 'You don't have to do anything that you don't want to do with all of your heart. Your father and I will be happy with any decision that you make right this very minute. Marriage is a big commitment. Think about it, Sylvia.' Three hours later the ceremony ended, and I was Sylvia Smith."

"Six months later, six months pregnant, I received a call from Ben. His news hit me like a wrecking ball bringing down an entire building with the first strike. Luke had been shot several times in his upper body and had also taken a shot to his forehead during an enemy attack in a village north of Hue, Vietnam. Chest and shoulder wounds would heal. The major concern was the hit to the head. Because the frontal lobes are the part of the brain that store memory, if he lived, he would not remember anything about his past...if he lived. Luke had been taken to a military hospital in Honolulu, Hawaii, where he would remain hospitalized until he could travel to Walter Reed Army Hospital in Washington, D.C. Ben promised that he would call and keep me informed. I asked Ben why he had my phone number. He answered that Luke had given it to him on his last visit to the States six months earlier when Thomas had passed away. Luke had asked Ben to call me and let me know if anything ever happened to him. I did not tell Ben that I was married and pregnant.

"I prayed continuously for Luke's life to be spared. I would never see Luke again, and Ben's words stuck in that place where *my* memories would be stored forever. 'If he lives, he will not remember anything from his past.' I knew that included me. I tried desperately to keep myself happy for the sake of the baby that I felt moving around in my belly. I continued to work in the office, and after the Christmas holidays, I dropped out of school to prepare the house for the baby. Mostly, I prayed that Luke would live and that he would be able to see the world again as *everything beautiful.*

"My marriage to Horace was calm and uncomplicated. We were polite and respectful to each other. We continued to work well together at the office, and I appreciated having a large and lovely home. There was plenty of money to do anything that I wanted, but neither of us spent outrageously. We lived comfortably, and I was able to see my family often in California. With my new last name, Smith, I felt free and safe as if I belonged in this country. Life moved quickly, and I did not hear from Ben again.

"Horace and I were unprepared for the day that our baby boy was born. He was actually two weeks early, and we had not decided on a name. We had no idea if it would be a boy or a girl, but my doctor and his nurses at the office had guessed it to be a girl, based on the way I carried and the shape of my belly. The nurses assured me that they were rarely wrong about such matters. They suggested that I buy pink.

"The labor was long and difficult. As tiny as I am, it was not easy delivering a nine-pound boy. When the nurse brought him in, all cleaned up and wrapped in a blue cotton blanket, I began to cry uncontrollably. I assured Horace that they were tears of joy. In his usual controlled manner, he excused himself from the room and said that he would give me time to be alone with the boy.

"As I unwrapped and examined every inch of his little body, I both cried and smiled, marveling at this little person. He was perfect but still no name.

"I fell asleep holding him close to me. I don't know how long we had been asleep when I awoke to the sound of a nurse's voice. 'Just a reminder, Mrs. Smith. We have to have a name before you can take this little one home.'

"Luke," I answered. "We will name him Luke."

"Horace liked the name and never asked why I had chosen it. We took our baby home, and our lives began again...calm and uncomplicated. A year passed quickly and still I did not hear from Ben. I assumed the worst—that Luke had died and Ben did not want to call me with the news. At times I would tell myself to erase any memory of him or to give up any hope that I would ever see him again. I would try to forget what it was like when we first made love— tender and rich with all the excitement of surprise that only first-time lovers can appreciate. Remembering our lovemaking the second time together as we had fallen asleep tightly wrapped around each other's bodies. The note that he had left behind with the rose with the words, *I didn't want to wake you. You are Everything Beautiful. Thank you. Love, Luke.*'

"How could I ever forget those moments that my body still remembered and ached for? I would argue with myself that it would take time, lots of time, to forget our short but meaningful relationship. And then, there was the guilt— the never-ending feeling of having done something terribly wrong. And the fact that my son now carried his name made it seem even more immoral. At times, I regretted having given him the name, yet other times I cherished the thoughts it brought me.

"In my heart, I know that I was a good wife to Horace. I treated him respect- fully in every way. Within months of having the baby, we hired a wonderful woman from Mexico to help with Luke and the house, and I went back to work at the office. My schedule began early morning so that I could be home to prepare the evening meal. I ran our home just the way Horace expected it to be run—organized, immaculate, maintained inside and out, and he loved coming home to my meals and a very happy baby. I entertained for friends and for business, and we thrived financially. As much as he could, Horace would show me that he was satisfied with our life together. Every Friday night he still brought home flowers and a box of See's Candies with a sweet card. It was his way of expressing his feelings. Ours was not a sexual partnership. Horace didn't care about that part of our relationship. I reconciled myself to knowing that he was happy, the baby was healthy and cheerful, and I could find my pleasure being an important part of their lives.

"Three years after the birth of Luke, while attending a large financial seminar, I spotted Ben in the crowd. Quickly moving through people, I made my way to him, hoping that we could talk privately. He was surrounded by a group of men and women and seemed to be engrossed in conversation when he spotted me. It had been five years since I had met him at the Thanksgiving dinner and over three years since we had talked on the phone with the news about Luke's injuries. He looked just as handsome as he did the day I met him. As he walked toward me, he opened his arms and, as soon as he was close enough, hugged me tightly. As he held me, I could feel his chest moving rapidly. We began to sob and held on even tighter. Finally, Ben collected himself to tell me the story.

"Both embarrassed and apologetic for not contacting me for over three years, he informed me that Luke was alive and living in Hawaii with his wife Suzanne. She had been a nurse in the hospital in Honolulu where Luke recuperated for almost a year. Luke's physical body had healed, and he could do all of the normal things that a big, strong man is capable of, but, as the doctors had predicted, Luke had lost all of his memory from his past. He had also been diagnosed with Post Traumatic Stress Syndrome and, consequently, suffered with panic and anxiety disorder.

"Holding my hands, Ben went on to tell me that several times he and Luke's parents had gone to Honolulu to be with him. With the help of the doctors, an incredible staff of therapists, diet, exercise, and medication, they had reconstructed Luke's health, his family, and his friendships, and Luke was now living a fairly normal life with Suzanne in Honolulu. The biggest challenge was keeping him as calm as possible.

"My prayers had been answered. Luke was alive."

Two hours had passed, and Sylvia and I were still sitting in my little hair salon/ studio. Evening was beginning to fall over the city. Sylvia's eyes were closed and her head tilted slightly back. She breathed long and deep, and I could almost see her thoughts filling her mind. We sat quietly a bit longer.

"Do you want to continue, Sylvia, or do you want to stop for now?" I asked softly.

"If you have the time, Hilda, I would like to finish the story."

"Yes, continue. I want to hear it all."

Getting up from my chair, I made us each a cup of chamomile tea with a little honey. As I sat down, Sylvia continued.

"Six months after my conversation with Ben and the update about Luke's condition, Christmas rolled around again. Little Luke and I had gone Christmas shopping at our favorite store—Goldwater's. Luke was now three-and-a-half years old. Tall for his age, very polite, well spoken, like all children who are raised speaking mostly to adults, Luke met no strangers.

"We began our shopping in the men's department where we bought Horace a sweater and visited with Mr. Angelo, who was still managing the department. We had remained close and had a standing joke that if I ever wanted to come back and work with him, the door was always open.

"Holding hands, Luke and I walked on to continue our shopping. As we stepped onto the escalator, Luke complained that he was too old to hold hands. After giving him that 'mother look' and that slight tug to his hand that only a mother can master, we continued holding hands. As the escalator carried us upward, I began to see a familiar head of reddish blonde hair come into view at the top of the escalator. Then I saw the forehead with a tiny scar mid-center, unforgettable hazel eyes, a strong nose, and those lips...those beautiful, full lips. It was Luke!

"Standing in his full six-foot-three-inch stature, arms crossed at his chest, staring ahead, he looked right at me and never changed his expression. He had no idea who I was. The escalator dropped us off less than five feet in front of him, yet he looked at me as a stranger looks at someone who has just come into view. Still holding my son's hand, I moved closer to him, and as I reached out my right hand and said hello, he was taken by surprise, took a step back, and shook his head sideways, communicating 'no.' He did not reach out his hand for mine.

"As I withdrew my hand, I smiled at him, and told him that it was okay. 'We used to work together a while back. Actually, we worked here in this department store several years ago,' I said to him.

"Obviously upset by my statement, he looked upward as if he were trying to reach inside of his forehead for a thought or memory that would confirm my story. Then, without warning, my baby boy released my hand, took a step toward him, and with his right hand, took the tall man's large hand in his little three-and-a-half-year-old size hand and, shaking it, said, 'Hi, my name is Luke.' That being said, he ran away toward a toy display that he had evidently spotted on our way up the escalator.

"Stunned, Luke stared at me harder and still shaking his head, stammered and stuttered and asked, 'Why...is...his...name...Luke?'"

"It just is," I said. "It's nothing. I promise. It's coincidental. I'm sorry that I frightened you. I'm so sorry."

"Luke's body began to turn, looking around behind him. I saw a Japanese woman walk up beside him and take his arm in hers. She asked him if he was all right. He was visibly anxious. I felt terrible. I didn't mean to upset him. I shouldn't have said anything. I should have just kept on walking and never made an attempt to connect with him. I couldn't stop myself, and now it was too late.

"With a sweet smile, she bowed her head slightly and said, 'My husband is not feeling well today. We must leave now,' and they walked away.

"I stood unable to move and watched, as arm and arm, they moved farther away from me. I was still staring when I saw him stop, turn around, and look intently into my eyes. I knew then that he recognized me. There was no question in my mind that he knew who I was, but he turned back around and walked away with his wife.

"And that was the last time that I saw Luke O'Ryan. Thirty-three years ago at the top of the escalator on the second floor of Goldwater's. Until this week, I thought that I would never see or hear from him again."

"Sylvia, what happened this week?" I asked hurriedly, as my heart was still pounding from the experience that she had just described.

"Two days ago I received a call from Ben. It has been thirty-three and a half years since I last saw him. He had some news for me...again. Luke's parents have passed away. With Thomas also gone, Luke is heir to a large inheritance. His parents left plenty of money to care for him for the rest of his life, but Luke has never touched the money. He and Suzanne have lived comfortably, yet minimally, in Honolulu, and because her parents were also extremely wealthy, together they have accumulated a fortune. Luke and Suzanne did not have any children.

"Hilda, Luke has Lou Gehrig's disease and is dying. He has less than six months to live."

Sylvia stopped talking. The sound of our crying filled the studio. We pulled our chairs closer together and held hands and wiped our faces as tears ran down our cheeks. We gazed at each other as if we could feel each other's painful hearts. Almost forty years had passed since they had first met and aside from two nights together, their lives had been separated by circumstances and events that were finally coming to an end.

Our tears stopped, and we sat in silence. I had absolutely no judgment about the choices Sylvia had made. I looked at her and saw a woman who had worked hard all of her life. She had been a good daughter, a devoted wife, a loving mother, a loyal friend, and a great client to me.

Almost four years ago, she had divorced Horace after being married for thirty-two years. She never discussed it in detail and never said one unkind word about him. She simply said that the marriage had run its course. She left his business intact and did not ask for any money that was due her for all of the years they had worked the business together. She had acquired a position with a large company as a senior accountant, moved into a townhouse, and enjoyed living alone. She and her son, who lived in Washington, D.C. and worked at the Pentagon, had an exceptionally close relationship, visiting each other often. At the age of thirty-six, he had yet to marry.

"Aside from Ben wanting you to know that Luke is dying, what does the money have to do with you...and with your son?"

"Luke remembered. That day at Goldwater's, on the second floor at the top of the escalator, he recognized me. I knew that he had. I felt it in my heart. He called Ben that same day and told him that he had a son. He felt that Luke was his son. He recognized me, and he remembered that we had been together. Luke did not want Suzanne to know about his remembering and his feelings about having a son. And, at that point, thirty-three years ago, he asked Ben to please remember for him...in case he forgot again."

Sylvia continued, "Ben was with Luke just last week in Honolulu. During their visit, Luke asked Ben to find me and ask me if Luke is his son. He wants to know for many reasons. The first is that he wants to see his son again. He wants to know him and talk to him, and he wants to know that part of him will live on when he dies. And, if after a DNA test proves him to be his biological son, he wants to leave him all of his inheritance."

"Oh...my...God," I said, stretching each word with astonishment.

Amazingly, Sylvia appeared to be much more relaxed at this moment than she was when she first walked in the front door of the salon. She was certainly more relaxed than I was at this very moment.

"Have you decided what you are going to do?" I asked.

Taking her time to sip her tea and looking out the window as a young couple walked by holding hands, she continued, "When I came in here earlier, I didn't know what I was going to do, but now I know. It was wonderful...telling the story. Somehow, bringing it up from inside of me, I can now see it more clearly. I have never told this story to anyone before. It has disturbed me, encouraged me, wounded me deeply; yet, oddly, it has kept me hopeful and grateful for having loved another so intensely. Perhaps it has taught me patience, and I have been less judgmental of others who have remained hopeful, even when there was none in sight. But it is time to end the story. When Luke dies, he will take the story with him, and you and I will let it become a story that you once heard in your salon. It will leave behind a sweet memory like flowers that have withered and died, having served their purpose, now nourishment for the next crop to show off their beautiful faces. Maybe they will be roses.

"My son loves his father. Their relationship is based on respect, trust, and complete unconditional love. Horace attended every sporting event, coached Luke through tough times, watched him with the pride of a father, celebrated his decision to join the Army, and was with him every step of the way through the passage from childhood to manhood. There is nothing that needs to come between that bond now."

We sat for a bit longer and enjoyed the silence again that filled the space in the salon. Tomorrow would come soon enough, and there would be more stories to hear.

As Sylvia stood to leave, she remembered that just that day, she had received recent photos of Luke in his formal Army uniform. Quickly, she took them out to show him off. I smiled as I saw a very happy young man. His thick, reddish-blonde hair, hazel eyes, strong nose and full lips smiled back at me as I guessed him to be at least six-feet-three-inches tall.

PART FOUR

Physical Connection

"Believe in a love that is being stored up for you
like an inheritance, and have faith that in this love
there is a strength and a blessing so large that you
can travel as far as you wish without having to step
outside it."

Rainer Maria Rilke, Letters to a Young Poet

COMMITTED COUPLES. . .
THE REWARDS OF LONG-LASTING
PARTNERSHIP

The following stories will highlight couples who
have defined a committed life of companionship,
compatibility, and trust and who have success-
fully moved through the trials of relationship challenges. They are currently enjoying the rewards of
a devoted, long-lasting, and loving partnership.
We are grateful for their efforts in answering the
questions that we posed and we appreciate their
honesty as they opened their lives and shared their
personal stories.

CHAPTER SIX

AT THE BEGINNING

"I have no doubt, however, that when it comes to our sense of love, belonging, and worthiness, we are most radically shaped by our families of origin—what we hear, what we are told, and perhaps most importantly, how we observe our parents engaging with the world."

Brene Brown, Ph.D., Daring Greatly

Hilda

I have rarely been at a loss for words to describe any feeling that I have ever experienced. It's my nature to be talkative. Perhaps that is why I write.

My feelings for Linda are indescribable. Over twenty years ago I began my counseling, coaching relationship with her. To say that she has saved my life, that she has altered my personal and professional path, and that she keeps me centered on my purpose and meaning for my life, would be an understatement. More than any other human being, she has positively affected the outcome of my future. I unconditionally love her. And I love her husband Richard because he loves her also. They are an amazing couple.

Here is their love story.

Linda, 70

> *"Just a few weeks after making that decision not to date, out of the blue Richard called me and asked me to go to a play. I was irritated! I didn't know him well and here I was being tested right off the bat after making my new decision."*

Hilda

Linda is an international workshop leader, professional life coach, and co-author of the book *Full Heart Satisfied Belly*. She is a certified Enneagram teacher and has been using the Enneagram as a primary tool in her work for over 25 years. She has over 35 years' experience working with individuals, businesses, and the government to enhance life and increase productivity. Her professional training is in Transpersonal Psychology and Imagery. She has been in private practice in Colorado, Maryland, and, currently, in Scottsdale, Arizona. In addition, she was a professional speaker on the national speaking circuit for 10 years. Her primary message is the importance of recognizing the connection between the mind, emotions, and success.

For the past eleven years, she has been under contract with Maricopa County Superior Court in Phoenix, Arizona where she facilitates executive coaching and judicial observation with Superior Court judicial officers.

Married 30 years to Richard

Title: Love waits on Welcome, not on time

Physical Connection

WHERE WERE YOU BORN AND RAISED, AND WHAT CAN YOU TELL US ABOUT YOUR CHILDHOOD SURROUNDINGS AND CIRCUMSTANCES?

I was born and raised in a small Colorado mountain town where it was said that "they rolled the sidewalks up at night!" I rode my bike everywhere, we never locked our doors and we knew everyone in the town. I was born right after World War II and my parents were struggling financially to make ends meet. We lived in a two-room house in the back yard of my Aunt's house.

My father worked several part time jobs but his aspiration was to be a writer. However there was no quiet space in the house for focused attention, so he moved an old shed down from the site of my Grandfather's gold mine and set up a desk and his typewriter in the shed in the back yard for his writing office.

I had no sense of deprivation or poverty. My mother was a highly creative and artistic woman and made me doll clothes and tiny furniture to play with. We had a sand box outside where we built roads and buildings and I was quite happy. There was no television in those days in my town so I was not exposed to any vision of how it should be any different than it was at our house in our little town.

My parents were both outdoors people. I climbed my first mountain when I was 2. They liked to hike and fish in the most remote places and would carry a cast iron skillet in their backpack to cook the fish they caught for dinner! It was a very grounded and wholesome way to live.

I was the second of two children, my brother being 6 years older. My father was an exceptionally good writer and quickly began selling his stories to the New York Times. His first two fiction books were published shortly thereafter. My parents purchased some lots in town and proceeded to build a log house. They literally built it themselves! The only thing that was subcontracted was digging the foundation. They worked together shaving the logs, sawing and nailing. Every morning my father would go to his writing office and write all morning. Then we would have lunch and walk the few blocks to the building site where they would start working on the house. They put up an old bed and I would take my nap listening to them hammering and nailing. It took them about 18 months to complete the house and we moved in when I was 6. After living in such small quarters, it felt like a mansion!

My parents lived in that house for the next 40 years until they died. They paid cash for everything, including the house. They never had a mortgage, a car payment or a credit card!

My father continued his writing career and had more than 150 Western books published with about 10 movies made from his books. He also did a lot of writing for Disney Studios. His books came out in sequence as did the subsequent movies such as Lassie and Zorro. He wrote episodes for the TV shows; High Chaparral and Bonanza and many others. My father became the town celebrity and one of the most prominent citizens. My mother was an artist and an amazing gardener. My parents were both highly intelligent and followed current world events. They were each other's best friend. I only saw them have one argument and it was over how to build the stairs inside the house!

My parents had similar backgrounds and values. They had each lost their primary parent at an early age and were strongly bonded to one another. Even though I seldom saw them fight, they did have cold wars. Those were the times when it was very quiet in the house and few words were spoken. We all read in the evening and listened to the radio, so I didn't consciously pick up on the tension that was sometimes between them. I have no idea how they worked out their conflicts and differences.

One way my father expressed his anger was at my brother. Even though both my parents were somewhat non-conformist, my brother was 50% more a non-conformist than they were. He was the "Fonzie" in our town, cool to the other teenagers but a rebel in my father's eye. The constant war between my brother and father was a draining energy on the family.

Another thing that was a subtle, but profound influence on me was that my parents were not overly affectionate with us. Also, everyone in my family was Mental or Mind types on the Enneagram. I was the only Heart type and I always longed for more affection and emotional connection.

Another aspect of my father's behavior that affected me deeply was his inability to have eye contact with me. He would wander around the house imagining the plot to one of his stories and pat me on the head as he passed. If we were out and he met someone who might have some traits he could use in his next story he would give them eye contact with great interest. Then he would go back to looking past me with a vacant look on his face or being totally within himself while he put the pieces of his plot together! I now know that that was his insecurity and self-containment but it took many years for me to figure out why I was so insecure in my relationships when I came from what seemed like such a stable and reliable family.

I was raised with a lot of adults who were powerful or famous and I was often the only child present. It was on the set of one of my Dad's movies that I first saw an adult (a female actress) throw a fit and act like a child. I was astounded to see an adult act like that! One of the gifts that my childhood gave me was not being intimidated by supposedly powerful people and that has served me well in my career and later when I was dating.

HOW OLD WERE YOU WHEN YOU HAD YOUR FIRST CRUSH RELATIONSHIP, AND HOW DID IT EVENTUALLY DEVELOP OR END?

My first crush with a boy was when I was in 7th grade and I got twitter pated with one of the high school basketball players. I would practically swoon when he ran by me at games! However, he never noticed me as I was several years younger and had thick glasses and braces on my teeth. I was not in his league! Oddly enough, two years later when the braces were off and I had developed, that same boy chased me all over to go out with him and I would have nothing to do with him! By that time the crush was over and I thought he was arrogant!

CURRENTLY, HOW DO YOU RATE YOUR PHYSICAL AND MENTAL HEALTH, AND HOW DOES IT AFFECT YOUR RELATIONSHIP?

I have generally been a healthy character throughout my life. Now at 70 I can see how my energy is no longer endless and my bones are more delicate. I actually cracked a rib in a very minor bike accident last year and that was startling!

I have learned through the years to express my own emotions in ways that are safe and most of the time, direct. As I grow older, being well rested and not over doing in any way are the two major key components to my being balanced. That is always important but currently it is essential! I have rearranged our life significantly in order to reduce financial and emotional stress. As my husband is now dealing with MCI (Mild Cognitive Impairment) I am beginning the journey of being his primary caretaker. No one knows exactly how that diagnosis will proceed so we have to take it one day at a time. I have reduced my work to three days a week. And I get support through Mayo Clinic, the Alzheimer's Association as well as friends and colleagues.

All of this affects my relationship. My husband is 13 years older than I am and it is no surprise that we would eventually be faced with some on-going physical condition we would have to deal with. None of it is easy and yet if I stay in gratitude for what he still can do and we can share together, it is much easier. The most important thing is for me to stay balanced physically and emotionally since I now carry the load of our relationship as well as all the mechanics of our living.

ARE YOU PHYSICALLY CONNECTED TO YOUR PARTNER? IF SO, HOW DO YOU KEEP THAT CONNECTION ALIVE? HOW IMPORTANT IS PHYSICAL CONNECTION TO YOUR RELATIONSHIP?

We are still physically connected, even at what could be considered advance ages! We still cuddle, tickle, laugh, kiss and enjoy sex. It is an important part of our relationship. I believe having good communication is what is vital to a physical connection. Being able to express your anger in a healthy way that is not destructive keeps passion alive. Pushing emotions down, or under the carpet is sure to dilute physical trust and intimacy. My husband often says that being married to me means nothing gets swept under the carpet!

Emotional Responsiveness

WHAT DID YOUR PARENTS MODEL FOR YOU AS A CHILD ABOUT MAR-RIAGE? HOW DID YOU CONNECT WITH YOUR MOTHER? DESCRIBE YOUR RELATIONSHIP WITH YOUR FATHER.

I was an excellent student in high school. I was in student council in high school and was chosen for Girl's State. I only needed a few credits to graduate my senior year. However, during my junior year of high school I started dating a boy at school who was the son of the town drunk. He was the pick of the litter of his 8 brothers and sisters in his Mexican/Italian family. My parents were not pleased with my choice. He was handsome and smart and, of course, I thought I loved him. And I did, as best as any 15 year-old girl is capable. Being starved for affection, I was willing to roll the dice and have sex at 16 if that's what it took to be loved. I got pregnant in 1963 and that caused a big scandal! My parents offered to take me to get an abortion, or help me raise the baby and not to consider marriage as a viable option. They pointed out how different this boy's values were than mine. They supported me in my choice but cautioned me not to believe that marriage was the best choice. Still, that was the only acceptable choice I saw at 16 and so we married. My first daughter was born when I was barely 17 years old!

The marriage was doomed from the start. My parents were right about our different values and how our views of the world were so diverse. My husband was an angry young man and felt trapped. He was a profound introvert and didn't want to do much of anything but watch television. At times he became violent with me. I hid that from my parents and friends. In the 1960's the only people I knew who were divorced were actresses in Hollywood so I didn't even consider divorce as an option.

I now know that I coped with my dysfunctional marriage by having babies. I loved babies and some of my fondest memories are of my children when they were infants. So, I got pregnant four more times in my first marriage. Unfortunately, I had the RH blood factor and three of my babies didn't make it to term. My second daughter only survived by emergency transfusions and barely survived. Finally, the doctor said I was putting myself in danger by getting pregnant so I talked my husband into adopting a baby boy. By that time I knew the marriage was in trouble but my only joy was being a mother and I didn't want to give that up.

Shortly after we adopted my son, we moved from my little town to the big city of Denver. It was there that my first marriage began to unravel. I realized that no one there knew my history or cared if I was married or not. I discovered I had been playing a role of happy mother and wife to prove to all those small town people that my marriage was not just because I was pregnant. My husband got a good job where he wore a suit and tie for the first time and learned about computers. He had an affair. I filed for divorce and then discovered I couldn't get a job that paid enough for a babysitter for three children. I made a decision to stay in the marriage until I could get an education. I went to college when I was 24 and it took me 6 years to get through 4 years of school while I worked part time and was a full time mom. Many times I studied all night and started the next day with 2 hours of sleep! Coffee and cigarettes kept me awake! When it was time for my Masters in Psychology I got depressed and went to see a psychiatrists. He said, "lady you don't need a psychiatrist, you need a lawyer!" After 14 years of marriage, at the age of 30, I finally divorced.

I can summarize the next 10 years of my life by saying that I didn't leave a stone unturned when it came to dating! I made up for all those young years when I had been married and had very little fun. I had a lot of dysfunctional relationships until I started into my own personal growth work. It was there I got the connection between my father and mother's marriage and their hidden dysfunctions. As I worked on myself by going to therapy and groups, my relationships began to improve. I moved from wanting to marry everyone I dated to having him or her want to marry me! I now could see both sides of the pattern. Finally, I decided to take a break from dating for a year! By that time I was in private practice in Denver, Colorado, taught relationship workshops and was a professional speaker.

WHAT WERE YOU LOOKING FOR WHEN YOU DECIDED TO MARRY YOUR PARTNER, AND WHAT DID YOU KNOW FOR SURE ABOUT YOURSELF?

Just a few weeks after making that decision not to date, out of the blue Richard called me and asked me to go to a play. I was irritated! I didn't know him well and here I was being tested right off the bat after making my new decision. He was an attractive man so I figured if I didn't call him back for a few days he would find someone else to go to the play with him. After several days I finally called him back. When he told me he hadn't gotten a date, I was very clear with him that I was willing to go to the play but that I didn't consider it a date.

I was tired the night of the play and considered cancelling but reluctantly went and met him in front of the theater. It turned out to be a fun evening and I was surprised to find out that he was a nice guy and easy to talk to. At that point I didn't waiver on dating but since we had a good time together I did agree to spend some more time with him as a friend. Over the next few months I saw him about once a week as a friend. We never kissed or held hands. Maybe hugged good-bye but it was purely platonic.

WHAT SIGNIFICANT MEMORIES DO YOU HAVE AS YOU WERE GETTING TO KNOW EACH OTHER? WHAT DO YOU REMEMBER MOST ABOUT THE FIRST TIME YOU MET?

That all changed the day he came to help me move. It was the move from hell for a lot of reasons. It was hot, tempers were short and we only had the truck for a short period of time. Everyone was stressed out except Richard. He kept his composure and calmly solved issues that seemed insurmountable. Like moving my hot tub over a 6-foot fence for instance. I was impressed and my head turned. When he left I kissed him good -bye and it was clearly not as a friend. The next day we went with some friends to the mountains and started our love affair!

My daughters watched all this happen and later told me they knew we would get married. I didn't know it then, but it wasn't too long before that became apparent.

However, I did have some concerns. I was not going to make another foolish marriage decision! He had been single for so long that I wondered if he could be faithful. I watched how he processed and how he was with his friends. Even though he hated conflict I saw he could get angry. Those were all good signs. He had a good relationship with his family and had learned the deeper reasons he had avoided marriage up until then.

He was a man of many talents. Not your typical engineer. He had an artistic side and played the drums. He was into personal growth and we went to workshops together. We both went to Mile Hi Church in Denver and were metaphysical. We had similar values and our childhoods had been very much alike. We were both younger children with one older sibling. When I met his sister I discovered we had the same bedspread on our beds and the same books on our shelf!

I knew it felt right but I meditated on making the choice to marry him.

After we got engaged I got fearful and sorted out what I would do if it didn't work out. When I realized the worst that could happen would be I would be divorced again, my stress was relieved. I had learned how to manage my life, I was financially independent and had a reliable career.

So I married for the second time at the age of 42. By then my children were all out of the house, my youngest being 19. Since then we have had four grandchildren and two step-grandchildren that now range in age from 15 to 25. My ex-husband has not chosen to play an active role in his children's or grandchildren's lives since the divorce so Richard is the only Papa that they know.

SURELY THERE WERE CHALLENGES ALONG THE WAY IN YOUR RELATIONSHIP. HOW HAVE YOU LEARNED TO WORK EFFECTIVELY WITH THOSE CHALLENGES?

Two days after we married we moved from Denver to Maryland for a job Richard had taken as an aerospace engineer at Godard NASA. He worked on the solar panels for the Hubble Telescope. That first year of marriage was probably the hardest. I left Colorado for the first time and left my kids, parents, friends, my office and clients in one fell swoop. Even though I was speaking all over the country and maintaining my private practice by phone and commuting back to Denver at least once a month, it was still hard. My whole life had changed and I was now in partnership instead of being in charge of everything. I traveled so much that when I came home my house didn't seem like mine. Richard would forget to call me when I was traveling and get defensive when I was hurt and angry and felt abandoned. He gave up knowing what city I was in and that made me feel like he didn't care. He got terrified when we had a heated argument, thinking I would leave him. We went into couple's therapy after we were married just a few months. It settled us down and helped us realize the impact of all the changes we had gone through. We learned how to stay connected as a couple instead of just being two self-reliant individuals. Before long we met other couples in the DC area through our church and had a new set of friends. They are forever friends who we are still close to almost 30 years later!

Since then we have gone through a move from Maryland to Arizona, countless health issues, the death of both my parents and his father, many real estate investments and financial ups and downs. Our latest challenge with Richard's memory loss is just one of the many things we have dealt with. Anyone who gets married and expects it to be all fun and games will be disappointed.

What advice would you have for young lovers?

My advice is to do your emotional work as best you can so you will attract someone on your level. Be willing and prepared to continue to do the emotional work once you are married. I often say, and believe, that the work really begins once you are married if you want a vital and alive relationship.

And last but not least, keep your sense of humor. Laughter is still the best medicine and can help you keep your perspective!

* * *

RICHARD, 83

"I had never been married and I was 50 years old when someone invited me to a personal growth workshop. It was one of those several day intense events. I didn't know when I signed up that this would be the beginning of the biggest change in my life."

Richard received a BA in Mechanical Engineering from Northeastern University in Boston, Massachusetts. He worked in the field of engineering for a variety of companies but spent the majority of his career in the aerospace industry. He worked one on one with the astronauts developing flight instrumentation on many missions. He was on a team of engineers that developed the crew quarters for sky lab which later was displayed at the Air and Space Museum in Washington DC. He was chosen as a neutral bouncy diver simulating weightlessness on orbit. His career took him to many foreign countries including Saudi Arabia and the Netherlands. For the last 10 years of his career in aerospace he worked for NASA on the Hubble Telescope Project and solar energy development. His last assignment with NASA was a launch off the coast of Japan. He retired from aerospace engineering in 1997.

Married 30 years to Linda

Title: Love waits on Welcome, not on time

Physical Connection

WHERE WERE YOU BORN AND RAISED, AND WHAT CAN YOU TELL US ABOUT YOUR CHILDHOOD SURROUNDINGS AND CIRCUMSTANCES?

My father was a professor of Forrest Zoology at the New York State College of Forestry at Syracuse University. My sister Wilma was three years older than me and for several summers when we were young our family spent the entire summer in the Huntington Wildlife Preserve for our father's research. During that time we lived in a small mountain cabin on Deer Lake which was three miles from any civilization. Our toys and games were self-made. We hiked, collected plants and flowers and swam. Watching our father perform taxidermy on the forest animals to be used in his classes fascinated my sister and me.

In the early years we slept on pine boughs and went to sleep hearing loons and the sound of fish splashing on the lake.

That was all before the beginning of World War II and I have fond memories of our family being very close and happily sharing this unique experience.

However, everything changed when my father went to war. The days of the Huntington Forrest trips were over. My mother, sister and I lived in Syracuse and listened to the reports of the war on the radio hoping to hear that where our father was located was safe. Everything was rationed. We had a garden out of town where the townspeople went to grow vegetables. It was called a Victory Garden and we walked there every day pulling a wagon.

My mother stepped up to become the head of the household and for the first time in her married life, was no longer in her husband's shadow.

It was 5 years before my father came home after the war. He had become a Bird Colonel and was commander of Camp Picket Virginia. He was used to being in charge and unquestioned. My mother had been in charge of our household for the last 5 years. A power and control dynamic began that was never understood or worked out in their relationship. To make matters worse, I later found out that my mother had an affair while my father was gone and had told him about it! My parents argued a lot now and there was tension in the air that I didn't understand and it felt very uncomfortable! Many years later I discovered that I had made a decision based on my parent's unhappiness which was, if that's what marriage is, I want no part of it!!

HOW OLD WERE YOU WHEN YOU HAD YOUR FIRST CRUSH RELATIONSHIP, AND HOW DID IT EVENTUALLY DEVELOP OR END?

My first real "crush" was when I was in college and I actually cared enough about Bernie to consider asking her to get married. By that time my mother had been chronically ill for some time (probably from the stress in the marriage) and Bernie also had some health issues. I told my Dad I was seriously interested in Bernie and he told me to forget her or I would be burdened in the same way he was with my mother. And so I walked away. I later found out that Bernie's problem was an ulcer! But by that time I was long gone.

For the next 35 years I continued to live out my fear of marriage by having serial relationships but always bailing out or sabotaging the relationship if it began to get serious. I was always looking for the "right one" and was totally unaware that my parent's unhappy marriage had any influence on the way I was living my life. I was successful in my career and kept busy with many hobbies and fun activities. But underneath it all, I was lonely, sad and disconnected.

I had never been married and I was 50 years old when someone invited me to a personal growth workshop. It was one of those several day intense events. I didn't know when I signed up that this would be the beginning of the biggest change in my life. During the workshop I discovered the impact of my decision to avoid getting deeply involved with a woman. It wasn't about not finding the right one. It was the fear I had of losing myself like my mother did in her marriage. I was also terrified of conflict so as soon as any disagreements cropped up in my relationship, I would unconsciously start plotting my escape. Until then all of this had been subconsciously directing my life!

At that workshop there was a closed eye exercise I will never forget. The setting was being on a boat that represented my life. I was simply a passenger and suddenly the captain died and I had to take over steering and directing the boat or figuratively, my life. I grabbed the wheel of the boat for the first time and my life was never the same again! That was the right experience for me at the right time! I began to take responsibility for my life and my choices. I continued with a number of other workshops after that experience and learned more and more about myself. I had an on again, off again relationship of 5 years with a woman which I was now trying to make work with all my new insights. I gave it a good shot but eventually it became apparent that the best thing to do was end that relationship. This time I knew what I was doing and I made a conscious choice.

A few months later I won tickets to a play and now, being in between relationships, I asked a couple of woman to go but they weren't available. I saw Linda, who I had met a few times at church and decided to ask her even though I hardly knew her. I left her a voice mail and didn't hear from her for several days. When she called me back she immediately asked me if I had found someone to go with me to the play.

I said, "No, I hadn't" and there was a long pause. Finally she said, "Okay, I will go with you to the play as a friend, but not as a date. I am not looking for a relationship at this time! I will meet you at the play."

I was a little put out by her attitude and regretted even asking her, but I figured it was too late to cancel. I went without any intention of trying to impress her and dropped my first date persona. For the first time with a woman I was just being my authentic self.

Surprisingly, we had an amazingly good time! I found myself talking freely and enjoyed a real exchange. I realized I liked this interesting woman who was obviously not trying to impress me either. After that play we became friends and I looked forward to spending time with her. We could talk about anything. I had never had an experience with a woman that was so mutually authentic.

That friendship continued for several months and then I volunteered to help her move. That day a romantic spark was lit! Looking back the key events that made all that possible were me taking responsibility for my life at that early workshop and dropping my dating persona on our first date.

A turning point in my relationship with Linda was when we went on a trip to Quebec, Canada. We drove there from Vermont and had no accommodations reserved. Neither of us had been there before. We were both excited and open to adventure. I discovered that Linda was the most flexible and trusting woman I had ever dated. She went with the flow as we created it. She was more interested in history than she was shopping.

We had the time of our lives and it was then that I realized that I could not imagine my life without Linda.

For the first time in my life the fear of marriage was less than the fear of losing her. We were able to process disagreements and go on with our relationship. I felt like we could conquer anything together. I asked her to marry me in 1989 and our wedding invitation said "Love waits on welcome, not on time" from the Course in Miracles.

We have now been married 30 years.

SURELY THERE WERE CHALLENGES ALONG THE WAY IN YOUR RELATIONSHIP. HOW HAVE YOU LEARNED TO WORK EFFECTIVELY WITH THOSE CHALLENGES?

Of course there were some challenges. I got married when I was 56!

It surprised me that someone really wanted to know where I was and what I was doing. It took a while to understand that she just needed to feel connected. At first an argument was really scary based on my childhood experience, but eventually I learned to speak my word, my feelings and even my anger. Oddly enough, Linda encouraged me to tell her my truth even when it wasn't harmonious or pleasant!

ARE YOU PHYSICALLY CONNECTED TO YOUR PARTNER? IF SO, HOW DO YOU KEEP THAT CONNECTION ALIVE? HOW IMPORTANT IS PHYSICAL CONNECTION TO YOUR RELATIONSHIP?

Our physical connection is very important to me. It has always been a conduit that keeps us steady. Our sexual life is less intense and frequent but still feels just as intimate and joyful and a verification of the life force of our union. I'm grateful to still be sexually active at the age of 83!

CURRENTLY, HOW DO YOU RATE YOUR PHYSICAL AND MENTAL HEALTH, AND HOW DOES IT AFFECT YOUR RELATIONSHIP?

I've also had a number of physical challenges through our marriage. I had a heart condition from the beginning and eventually had by- pass surgery. I had an emergency intestinal tumor that had to be removed. I've had prostate surgery and a few other operations along the line. Linda has been completely supportive and there for me every step of the way.

Now I have a new challenge called memory loss or beginning dementia.

It was diagnosed 5 years ago and has been gradually getting worse each year. No one knows if it will progress or how fast that might be. It is both scary and frustrating and it bothers me how much Linda has to pick up in our relationship to keep us balanced. I'm grateful she is 13 years younger but it makes me sad when I think I am letting her down!

We participate in groups about how to cope with this diagnosis and it helps to know other men and couples who have the same challenge.

WHAT ADVICE WOULD YOU HAVE FOR YOUNG LOVERS?

My advice to young lovers is that finding your best partner is not like buying a car. The ads are not always accurate nor is the appearance the most important aspect. It's more like getting ready to go on a remote Canadian canoe trip. You want to pick someone who you genuinely like as a person, can help you carry the supplies, paddle the boat, enjoy the journey and laugh along the way!

AT THE BEGINNING

"When we were children, we used to think that when we were grown up we would no longer be vulnerable. But to grow up is to accept vulnerability. To be alive is to be vulnerable."

Madeline L'Engle

Hilda

Several years ago I met Terri as a client at the salon. Although we only see each other for her appointments and she is almost twenty years younger than I, we have developed a kinship with each other of mutual love and respect. Our conversations are about family, children, work and spiritual matters, which I cherish. Her family, including her husband and 3 sons, has filled me with hope for younger couples raising teenagers with high values and strong principles. Serious by nature and yet playful in heart, Terri is a favorite.

As you will read, Drew is more playful, which I think keeps the fun in their family life. I like that he wrote: As a parent to three active boys, our commitment to exercise and the importance of staying physically fit is really important to us. We want to have the energy and stamina to keep up the pace of play.

Here is their love story.

DREW, 49

"My wife is graceful under pressure. She is a calming influence in our family during times of chaos and strife. I am the most stressed when I am worried about the health of one of my kids or my wife. Period!! She is better at not borrowing trouble."

Drew was born on the east coast but moved around a lot as a kid. He attended high school and college in southern California so considers himself a Californian.

He married his college sweetheart, moved to northern California after college for a few years and has lived in Arizona since 1993.

He graduated from Claremont McKenna College with a degree in Accounting and Economics and played football for CMC.

Professionally, he started in public accounting right out of college for a few years and then went to work in the mortgage banking business. Currently he works for a private equity firm that focuses on real estate investment management. He and his wife have three boys, ages 17, 14, and 12.

Married 26 years to Terri

Title: I married my college sweetheart

Physical Connection

WHERE WERE YOU BORN AND RAISED, AND WHAT CAN YOU TELL US ABOUT YOUR CHILDHOOD SURROUNDINGS AND CIRCUMSTANCES?

I was born on the east coast but moved around a lot as a kid. My father was in sales and sales management and he moved around for work. We lived in Rome, Italy for a couple of years where I attended kindergarten and first grade. I finished elementary school in Northern Virginia. I come from a mostly middle-class Italian/American family. I have two younger siblings...one brother 4 years younger and one sister 5 years younger. I mostly remember being left on my own a lot as a child. By the time I was in middle school I had lived in at least 10 different cities. We moved to St Louis, MO in the middle of sixth grade. I recall that this was very traumatic for me because I had finally established some roots and friendships living in Virginia. I really hated living in St. Louis. I was undersized in middle school and bullied frequently. We moved to Southern California during the summer before 9th grade. It was a fresh start at the right time for me. I had a good high school experience and remained in Southern California to attend college.

HOW OLD WERE YOU WHEN YOU HAD YOUR FIRST CRUSH RELATIONSHIP, AND HOW DID IT EVENTUALLY DEVELOP OR END?

I had my first crush in the 7th grade with my next door neighbor. It never really began since I moved to California shortly thereafter. I dated some in middle school and high school but nothing too serious until my senior year and even that didn't continue when I moved away to college.

CURRENTLY, HOW DO YOU RATE YOUR PHYSICAL AND MENTAL HEALTH, AND HOW DOES IT AFFECT YOUR RELATIONSHIP?

I am in good physical condition. I exercise at least 5-6 times a week. I am an ex-college athlete with a few nagging issues that will require surgery to fix but the pain is mostly manageable. I feel like I have good mental health. I have been dealing with moderate anger management issues for years. I think it is probably the one area that impacts all of my relationships the most. My wife reminds me that our kids are not little adults and that I need to change my expectations. I like it when things are in order and predictable and raising three teenage boys is neither orderly nor predictable. So my anger probably stems from losing patience and control over the situation. We handle it the best we can, but this issue absolutely is something that affects our relationship and our harmony, both as a couple and as a family. I also tend to blow things out of proportion a little. We are still working on this aspect. Even after 26 years of marriage there are still things that we need to work on. This one is on me and so I continue to try to work on it. Breathing exercises help....but I forget to do them when I get angry. It helps that both my wife and I are committed to fitness and exercising together. We enjoy being together at the gym and staying fit together is very important to our relationship.

ARE YOU PHYSICALLY CONNECTED TO YOUR PARTNER? IF SO, HOW DO YOU KEEP THAT CONNECTION ALIVE? HOW IMPORTANT IS PHYSICAL CONNECTION TO YOUR RELATIONSHIP?

Yes, very much so. We try to commit time for date nights and we exercise together regularly. Even if we are not exercising together we feel connected through staying in shape. We encourage each other to stay active. To me physical connection is critically important to having and maintaining a healthy relationship. There are other aspects which are equally important; communication, spirituality, and honor. Terri and I participated in a Gary Smalley workshop on marriage and relationships before kids and he passed around a Stradivarius violin to the crowd to show how you should treat your spouse, like a priceless violin. I remember that. So I think that besides communication and spirituality, honor is a biggie, too.

Emotional Responsiveness

WHAT DID YOUR PARENTS MODEL FOR YOU AS A CHILD ABOUT MAR-
RIAGE? HOW DID YOU CONNECT WITH YOUR MOTHER? DESCRIBE YOUR
RELATIONSHIP WITH YOUR FATHER.

My parents modeled loyalty through difficult times and in much of my childhood they shouldered the burden of making a living together. They also modeled independence. We moved away from the larger extended family early in
my childhood so I did not experience the same dynamic that my wife has with
her family which I now am very grateful to share. We didn't have many family traditions, unlike my wife's family which has lots of traditions. My wife
and I have tried to start our own family traditions together as well as remain
connected to the larger extended family. I don't have much of an emotional
connection with my mother or father. My relationship with my father is not
as strong as I would like, at least not in the traditional sense. I moved away
from home right after high school graduation and have been independent ever
since. While I see my parents a couple of times each year, it's usually only for
a few days at a time. I am extremely independent and have not relied on my
parents for much support, emotional or financial, over the years.

WHAT WERE YOU LOOKING FOR WHEN YOU DECIDED TO MARRY YOUR
PARTNER, AND WHAT DID YOU KNOW FOR SURE ABOUT YOURSELF?

I was looking for a life partner who would always be there for me in good
times and bad. I was very young when I started dating my wife, only 19, but
even then I knew that I wanted to share my life with her. We became engaged
during our senior year and were married one year later. I knew that I would
be a loyal and faithful friend to her and that I would always be there for her.

WHAT SIGNIFICANT MEMORIES DO YOU HAVE AS YOU WERE GETTING TO
KNOW EACH OTHER? WHAT DO YOU REMEMBER MOST ABOUT THE FIRST
TIME YOU MET?

During the second semester of my sophomore year my wife moved back to
Arizona to attend ASU. We had only been dating for a few months but I was
devastated. My wife on the other hand was not as serious about the relationship. I remember feeling hopeless because she was the first person I ever made
a serious commitment to and to whom I said I love you and she was moving

away. Things worked out though as they often do with us. Since then we have been best friends and have never really been apart.

Our first meeting was by chance and fairly uneventful and without much fanfare. Not a love at first sight scenario. We were in line at a movie on campus. She was with some other people who I knew and I was on a date. I was going to get popcorn and asked her if she wanted any. I did not introduce myself and I'm not sure she knew who I was. I did not see her again until the following year. She was friends with another girl who I was interested in. I started to think about her differently after spending some time with another one of her close friends and so I asked my roommate to set us up for a dance called Screw Your Roommate. It was October 9th 1986. Things worked out for us, as they often do.

SURELY THERE WERE CHALLENGES ALONG THE WAY IN YOUR RELATIONSHIP. HOW HAVE YOU LEARNED TO WORK EFFECTIVELY WITH THOSE CHALLENGES?

Communication and honesty. Openness about fears and worries. We have had a few bumps and bruises along the way but nothing serious or worth getting troubled over. Usual growing pains like new jobs, old jobs, new houses, kids coming on the scene, etc. All life challenges that we met head on together. We have always maintained openness and honesty in our communication but we tackle life's challenges differently. I am more of a worrier and look at things in black and white. My wife, on the other hand, is much more able to let things play out and can see the brighter side of things. I think it is because of these differences that we've been able to weather some of the more significant challenges. I am not sure how things would have fared if we handled adversity the same way.

Spiritual Significance

DO YOU AND YOUR PARTNER SHARE THE SAME SPIRITUAL BELIEF, AND IF NOT, HOW DO YOU FIND YOUR WAY THROUGH IT? IF YOU RAISED CHILDREN TOGETHER, HOW WERE THEY RAISED SPIRITUALLY?

Yes. We are both Christian and share a deep faith in and love for a living God. We were raised differently but ended up on the same path together. While I was raised Catholic, we went to church only on Easter and Christmas. My wife, on the other hand, comes from a traditional Lutheran family who was very involved in their church community.

Today we are similarly very active in our church community continuing that tradition. We attend a Lutheran Church and the boys attend regularly and participate in a lot of church-related activities, including being active members of the youth group and attending many events hosted by our church. Additionally, my two older boys attend Brophy College Preparatory School and are very active there as well. One thing that I enjoy the most at our church are the history lessons. No particular reason....I just do.

WHAT ATTRIBUTES HAS YOUR PARTNER BROUGHT TO THIS RELATIONSHIP THAT HAVE NURTURED AND SUSTAINED IT?

My wife is committed to being an active participant in our church and our broader faith-based community. My wife is graceful under pressure. She is a calming influence in our family during times of chaos and strife. I am the most stressed when I am worried about the health of one of my kids or my wife. Period!! She is better at not borrowing trouble. I am the one who gets on the internet and becomes fearful not faithful. She is the other way around. We have had several situations over the years that were very serious and stressful. Fortunately they worked out. I worked for a big bank that failed publicly while I was a senior executive at that bank. I lost my job as a result, but I was not nearly as stressed as I was during the health issues that have come our way over the years.

My wife is a good listener and a great friend to many people. These are just a few of her attributes that I am grateful for and wish I would share.

LOOKING BACK AT YOUR MANY YEARS TOGETHER, WHICH ARE OF YOUR LIVES HAS BROUGHT YOU CLOSER TOGETHER?

Our commitment to family and spending time together has brought us closer. Events such as traveling as a family, vacationing, going out to dinner, etc., are all really special to us. Our commitment to our faith and faith community and to practicing our faith out in the open and to sharing our faith with others is really important. It has brought us closer together and has helped us weather some storms. As a parent to three active boys, our commitment to exercise and the importance of staying physically fit is really important to us. We want to have the energy and stamina to keep up the pace of play.

WHAT ADVICE WOULD YOU HAVE FOR YOUNG LOVERS?

I am not good at giving advice – Stay off Facebook!

* * *

Terri, 49

"There are lots of theories and experts about how to have a good marriage, but each couple has to find what works for them and their circumstances and 'couple personality.'"

Terri grew up in Alaska and Arizona and went to college at Scripps College in Claremont, California. She met her husband Drew in college and became engaged during their senior year. They married on April 14, 1990, and moved to Sacramento where she attended McGeorge School of Law. They moved to Arizona in 1993, and Terri joined a law firm while Drew opened a branch for a California bank. Five years later she left the firm to take an in-house position with a health care organization. Their three sons were born between 1999 and 2004. A year and a half after the third son was born, Terri took some time to focus on the boys, stay at home and put her career on the back burner. Once the youngest was in pre-Kindergarten every day, she started her own firm out of their home mostly on a part time basis. In 2015 one of her clients asked her to join their firm as Associate General Counsel and they decided that the time was right for her to accept the opportunity and closed her individual practice. Currently she works full time, but is fortunate to have two days a week when she works from home.

Married 26 years to Drew

Title: It's all about family

Physical Connection

WHERE WERE YOU BORN AND RAISED, AND WHAT CAN YOU TELL US ABOUT YOUR CHILDHOOD SURROUNDINGS AND CIRCUMSTANCES?

I was born in Stillwater, Oklahoma, during my Dad's last year of veterinary school. Apparently my parents were so low on money that my dad made my mom wait until midnight to leave for the hospital to give birth because he was concerned he would be charged for two days! And this was on Christmas Eve—my poor mom!

We moved to Anchorage, Alaska when I was two years old, with my big sister and little dog, driving the long bumpy road from the mid-west to Alaska. We moved to Arizona when I was in 5th grade where my younger sister was born and my family still resides. I was raised with grandparents and many aunts and uncles and cousins nearby or often visiting for holidays and family reunions or events. Drew did not see his extended family often and moved around a lot, so he was not initially used to the amount of time I spent with my family. Fortunately, he become accustomed to it and determined this was how he wanted to raise his family; staying primarily in one place, focusing on family time, and with many family traditions.

How old were you when you had your first crush relationship, and how did it eventually develop or end?

In kindergarten, I announced to everyone that I was going to marry Jonathan, a boy in my class. Apparently, Jonathan and I were quite serious about our plans and discussed when we'd get married and have a family in quite practical and serious terms, but our teachers were concerned because we liked to hold hands and give each other a "peck on the cheek" to say hello and goodbye. I don't recall the ending of this romance, but I do recall seeing him several years later (after we'd gone to separate schools), and when my mom reminded me who he was, I was so embarrassed! Looks like I was practical about raising a family pretty early – and I'm still that way today.

Currently, how do you rate your physical and mental health, and how does it affect your relationship?

My physical health is very good; I practice yoga, walk and hike regularly and I eat a fairly balanced diet. Drew is also very athletic and has always stayed in good shape. My mental or emotional health is pretty good, or at least much better than it was a year ago after losing my dear older sister following a terrible car accident. Drew was my single biggest support and he shouldered the majority of the responsibility for our home and boys during this difficult time of grief and loss. Not once has he complained or suggested I should "get over it" and, instead, he has patiently listened, and stepped in to care for our family when I could not. He also supported my parents and sisters' families during this difficult time for all of us. This was not an easy time for any of us, but Drew was incredibly strong and giving and I will always be grateful for how he stood by me during this tragedy....certainly living our vows to be there for one another in good times and in bad.

When I get out of sync with exercise, I feel it emotionally. I have long believed that you can't have optimal emotional health without working on your physical health as well. I think one of the things that keeps Drew and me in mostly good emotional health with our marriage is our commitment to physical exercise.

ARE YOU PHYSICALLY CONNECTED TO YOUR PARTNER? IF SO, HOW DO YOU KEEP THAT CONNECTION ALIVE? HOW IMPORTANT IS PHYSICAL CONNECTION TO YOUR RELATIONSHIP?

I recall being very physically attracted to Drew immediately after meeting him. The energy of attraction has always existed between us, and still does, but it has been tempered by the addition of three boys (and pets, a house, etc.!) to our lives, and the stress and fatigue this naturally brings. While the joy of our family is tremendous, family life can certainly take a toll on the romantic aspects of being a couple, at least while the children are young and need a lot of care and support, day and night! Parenting is rewarding, but so exhausting too (which makes sleep sometimes more attractive than anything else!) I truly believe that someday, when the boys are living on their own, we will return to that powerful physical attraction that existed originally and maybe even surpass it! We do our best to keep our connection alive by having fairly regular date nights, weekend trips together, remaining interested in each other's separate interests, and exercising together.

Emotional Responsiveness

WHAT DID YOUR PARENTS MODEL FOR YOU AS A CHILD ABOUT MARRIAGE? HOW DID YOU CONNECT WITH YOUR MOTHER? DESCRIBE YOUR RELATIONSHIP WITH YOUR FATHER.

My parents modeled a very traditional relationship of husband and wife, with the husband being the clear leader and my mom being very giving and placing her needs and desires second to what my dad wanted. I used to perceive this as a weakness in my mom and I never liked it when she would do what my dad wanted, even if she disagreed, or when she would make excuses for my dad's behavior (working a lot of hours or being hard on my sister and me). Now, however, I realize, after being in my own marriage and having children that she was doing the best she knew how to do for her children and husband and how she and my dad worked that out was not for me to judge. No two people have the same relationship as another couple and respecting differences, even if you do not understand another's choices, is essential to a lasting marriage. My mom was giving in such a selfless way, and she was and still is a very giving and thoughtful mom who does a lot of little things to let her family know she cares. She is an example of how it doesn't take large gifts to express love – sometimes a well-placed sticky note and cookie or a well-timed call is the best encouragement and love you could hope for! I thought I was so different from my mom, believing in a woman's right to work and have a voice and be a full partner in a marriage. After becoming a wife and mother and seeing her be an amazing grandma, I hope to be more like my mom in so many ways. My dad worked a lot and was away from home when I was young. I didn't like how hard this was for my mom and for my sisters and me, too. But with the experience of my own marriage and the challenges I now see all families face, I realize that he was doing what he thought was best for the family; working to provide in very traditional terms as he was raised to believe was his Godly responsibility. Today I am blessed with very good relationships with both of my parents and I admire how they are committed to one another and to family.

WHAT WERE YOU LOOKING FOR WHEN YOU DECIDED TO MARRY YOUR PARTNER, AND WHAT DID YOU KNOW FOR SURE ABOUT YOURSELF?

I was looking for a best friend and partner in life. I knew I didn't want to be second place to a man. I wanted a partner who would see me as an equal contributor, regardless of how much money I made or what I did. When I told my dad I was engaged a few weeks before I was to graduate from college, he said to me. "But I thought there was so much you wanted to do with your life. Why are you getting married?" I explained to him that I did indeed have much I wanted to do with my life and that, with Drew, I was even more confident I could achieve my goals. I believed that then, almost 28 years ago, and I now I know I was absolutely correct! Marriage does not have to set you back. It can spring you forward with the love, support and encouragement of a true partner in life.

WHAT SIGNIFICANT MEMORIES DO YOU HAVE AS YOU WERE GETTING TO KNOW EACH OTHER? WHAT DO YOU REMEMBER MOST ABOUT THE FIRST TIME YOU MET?

I remember our strong attraction and I remember loving his sense of humor and thoughtfulness. I remember we could talk for hours and we laughed a lot. We still do! I actually don't recall the first time we met – only Drew does. I remember meeting him about a year later when he was dating a friend of mine and I thought he was so cute. Good thing he wasn't her type!!

SURELY THERE WERE CHALLENGES ALONG THE WAY IN YOUR RELATIONSHIP. HOW HAVE YOU LEARNED TO WORK EFFECTIVELY WITH THOSE CHALLENGES?

In 26 years of marriage, plus dating for four years before marrying, there have been many challenges in between the many, many good times and blessings. Drew lost his job when I was in law school. Nevertheless, he supported me fulfilling my dream to attend summer school in Europe to study comparative law. I left for Europe in the summer only a few weeks after he lost his job and just as he was starting a new job. He later moved to Arizona for a job and lived with my parents while I stayed behind in California to finish law school. Years later, Drew changed jobs following the mortgage banking crisis at a time when I was only working part time. In each of these circumstances, and when I made the decision to leave my full time job to stay at home with the boys for a while, I never felt like my career decisions were secondary to Drew's career. We faced each circumstance as a team with respect for each other's input and contributions as a whole, not based on a dollar value. Another crisis we faced together was when our first son was born. We were terrified when our son Nick was born with a heart defect and required surgery at four weeks old. All of these events and other ordinary but still stressful events such as buying and selling a house, managing a family of three boys and two careers, challenged our patience and marriage at times. We read books on marriage and family, and joined church bible study groups for couples and parents all in an effort to learn and remain committed to our marriage and family. It isn't always easy to be a spouse or parent, so we studied a lot of professionals and tried to take their advice where it fit us. There are lots of theories and experts opinions about how to have a good marriage, but each couple has to find what works for them and their circumstances and "couple personality." What worked for my parents, for instance, would not work for Drew and me, but they've been married now for more than 50 years and seem happier than ever.

Spiritual Significance

DO YOU AND YOUR PARTNER SHARE THE SAME SPIRITUAL BELIEF, AND IF NOT, HOW DO YOU FIND YOUR WAY THROUGH IT? IF YOU RAISED CHILDREN TOGETHER, HOW WERE THEY RAISED SPIRITUALLY?

Although Drew was raised Catholic, he was not concerned about remaining in the Catholic church as his family did not regularly attend church or participate in their faith. However, I was raised Lutheran and had no interest in becoming Catholic, so Drew joined me in attending a Lutheran church and our children were all baptized in the Lutheran church. We attend church regularly and are very committed to a life that honors faith and commitment to God. I truly believe it is God that helps us through the hard times in our marriage and family life. For years, I've participated in a Mom's bible study parts of which address marriage. Drew also participates in a bible study and also led a Fellowship of Christian Athletes group with the boys when they were in middle school. Losing my sister, I have learned more than ever the importance of faith at all times, so I am very grateful that Drew and I share the same spiritual beliefs.

WHAT ATTRIBUTES HAS YOUR PARTNER BROUGHT TO THIS RELATIONSHIP THAT HAVE NURTURED AND SUSTAINED IT?

Drew's sense of humor, his "can do" attitude and amazing work ethic and commitment to a partnership undoubtedly sustains me! He is incredibly supportive of me, truly acting as my biggest fan. In fact, in some ways, he is more confident in me than I am in myself!! Drew is very generous, quick to help and get things done, and very committed to his family. He prioritizes time together and doesn't let work overshadow the importance of family time, vacations and church, or his personal fitness and health. I hope our boys are learning to do the same.

LOOKING BACK AT YOUR MANY YEARS TOGETHER, WHICH ARE OF YOUR LIVES HAS BROUGHT YOU CLOSER TOGETHER?

Our children. Our children have been the most difficult thing for us to come together on, so while they are our biggest source of love, they are also the biggest source of conflict between us. We both love the boys fiercely, but we have different styles and approaches, probably stemming from our own childhoods. Facing these conflicts with honest communication, and repairing the fights and hurt that have occurred as a result, has brought us closer together. When things have been particularly difficult, I've asked myself: can I still see myself with Drew when the kids are gone? Each time the answer is absolutely YES. Nothing we have ever disagreed about has made me doubt my commitment. Asking yourself the question is not a bad thing. Sometimes you have to ask yourself if the relationship is good for everyone for the long term. But I feel fortunate to always say YES. I still look forward to the time in our lives when we once again have more time just for each other!

What advice would you have for young lovers?

Have faith. Have patience. Have humor. Be open to growth. Admit your mistakes quickly. Forgive quickly. Play together often. Don't just go through the motions or tasks of life together as partners or roommates, but stay engaged as a couple with the long term, big picture in mind! The years of young children can seem long, but they go faster than you realize and you need to keep the later innings of the game in mind, too. Be willing to lead sometimes and be willing to follow sometimes. All relationships hit valleys, but keep climbing and another mountain top moment will come!

Another thing I've realized is how important it is to "pick your battles" with your husband and let go of things that really don't matter in the big picture. For instance, I tried for a while to "teach" Drew how to load the dishwasher "the right way" and how to pick fruit "the right way" at the grocery store. Of course, the "right way" was really just "my way" and I've learned to let these things go and focus on gratitude for the fact that Drew regularly goes to the grocery store and loads the dishwasher despite my "correcting" him on how to do it. An overripe bunch of fruit isn't worth the aggravation or hurt it causes to criticize someone I love with my "teaching".

I recently decided that I see Drew and me as the pitcher and catcher in a game of baseball for our family. Both are essential, but very different key elements to a good game. The catcher and pitcher have different skill sets, but need to act in concert to win, to lead the team to victory. The pitcher has to be able to read the calls or signals of the catcher who is also motivating the whole team! The catcher misses some good pitches now and then, but also catches some wild pitches occasionally as well. In that way, Drew and I need to work in concert, reading signals, catching wild balls, and motivating our team of boys using different skills (though equally talented!).

* * *

Live brave.

PART FIVE

EMOTIONAL RESPONSIVENESS

*"Love is wanting to be with someone all the time.
It is accepting the other person with all good
qualities and bad and not wanting to change
any of them. It is wanting to give affection and
approval and comfort and everything that is
oneself, demanding nothing in return. It is...
love is very difficult, Julia. It is an ideal, rarely
achieved in reality because we are all selfish
and imperfect beings. It is a dream, a goal,
something to be aimed for."*

Mary Balogh, Courting Julia

CHAPTER SEVEN

CHALLENGES ALONG THE WAY

"Love unlocks doors and opens windows that weren't even there before."

Mignon McLaughlin, The Neurotic's Notebook

Mary Beth

With an appearance much younger than her years, Joyce is like a ray of sunshine---she approaches life with a positive attitude and is always excited for the next adventure! A successful entrepreneur, a loyal friend of many, and a woman who has tremendous empathy for those who are suffering, Joyce exudes warmth and sincerity.

As I write this introduction for my friends of 34 years, Joyce has just recently had a full knee replacement. Her husband, Norm, spent the night of her surgery with her (sleeping on a small love seat in her hospital room) and he continues to care for her during her recovery at home. Yes, girlfriends pitched in to help but the amount of physical and emotional support Norm has been providing is certainly admirable. They have dealt with several health issues over the years: cancer, stroke, and surgeries and yet the support for each other never waivers.

Joyce and Norm have been business partners for the majority of their marriage. That in itself is a true testimony to the strength of their marriage! They enjoy entertaining friends and family often and it's not unusual for them to have dinner guests five nights out of the week.

Many married couples are friends, but it is obvious with Joyce and Norm that they are "best friends", an attribute of their relationship that clearly has solidified their long-term marriage.

NORM, 73

> *"The best advice I would give young lovers is to not sweat the small stuff, pick your battles, and be somewhat flexible, not stubborn and closedminded. Listen to your spouse."*

Norm has been involved in the beauty and wellness industry with his wife, Joyce, for the past 25 years and loves every minute of it. Prior to that, he was involved in commercial real estate in Canada and the United States. Additionally, he and his wife owned three Burger King and two Sizzler franchise restaurants in California and three El Pollo Loco restaurants in Arizona, which they eventually sold back to the franchisor. Norm has a business degree from the University of California, Santa Barbara. In his free time he loves to travel, cook, and entertain friends.

Married 37 Years to Joyce

Title: Yes, Dear!

Physical Connection

WHERE WERE YOU BORN AND RAISED, AND WHAT CAN YOU TELL US ABOUT YOUR CHILDHOOD SURROUNDINGS AND CIRCUMSTANCES?

I was born in Toronto, Canada. My parents were first and second generation Italians. We lived in downtown Toronto until I was six when we moved to the suburbs. My father died at age 44 when I was fourteen years old. The next year my older brother married and moved out of the family home. My mother was a paranoid schizophrenic who spent much of her time in bed. She didn't drive, so at age 15 I did most of the shopping and much of the cooking. I grew up fast. My salvation was athletics, and I played literally all sports in high school. I married at age 18 and went to the University of California, Santa Barbara, as a foreign student. After graduation, we returned to Toronto where I obtained my real estate license and managed some commercial properties my father had built. Five years later, with four young children, I decided I didn't like the high-rise explosion taking place in Toronto and chose to raise my children in Vancouver, which I think is the most beautiful city in Canada. In 1978 my wife and I divorced, and a year later I married my current wife, Joyce.

HOW OLD WERE YOU WHEN YOU HAD YOUR FIRST CRUSH RELATION-
SHIP, AND HOW DID IT EVENTUALLY DEVELOP OR END?

I had my first serious relationship at age 17; we were married when we were both age 18 and had our first child at age 19. We had four children together. After graduation, we moved back to Toronto and then moved to Vancouver in 1972. We divorced in 1978.

In 1978 I spent a year in Houston, Texas, working on a real estate development; I met my current wife on a blind date my second day there, and we were married one year later. Shortly after marrying, a month after my development project ended, we intended to move back to Vancouver where I still had my family home and where my ex-wife and four children lived. A month before my project ended, my ex-wife called saying that she was moving out of our house, taking the two younger children with her, and that I needed to come back immediately to look after our two older children. Unable to leave, my new wife, Joyce, flew to Vancouver and moved into our home with my two oldest children, ages thirteen and sixteen. Unexpectedly, my ex had removed all the household furniture except for the children's beds and a kitchen table and chairs. Prior to this, Joyce had had only two visits with the children, so her introduction to motherhood was to move to a new city in a new country to try to hold together a very difficult situation until I could move home one month later. Fortunately, my friends rallied around Joyce and made her feel as welcome as possible under these complicated circumstances. One year later, my ex announced that she was moving to Mexico and was sending our two youngest, ten and eleven, back to live with Joyce and me.

CURRENTLY, HOW DO YOU RATE YOUR PHYSICAL AND MENTAL HEALTH, AND HOW DOES IT AFFECT YOUR RELATIONSHIP?

I am blessed with excellent health today, having endured prostate cancer twenty-one years ago and melanoma nine years ago. Mentally, I feel terrific although I'm not sure Joyce would agree with that assessment. My memory certainly isn't as good as it was twenty years ago. We go to the gym three times a week, and because we have been in the health and wellness business for over twenty-five years, we are very focused on our health, nutrition, etc. Also, Joyce suffered a stroke eight years ago. I remember the first words the neurologist told us, "Joyce, you will never be the same again!" After a period at Scottsdale Health Stroke Center, we went to see the heart group at St Joseph's Hospital who told Joyce their only solution for her afib was open heart surgery. Not liking that opinion, we then saw four different cardiologists, all of whom disagreed with that opinion, including Dr. Detrick of the Arizona Heart Institute. Our solution was to turn off our phones and focus totally on intensive rehab five days a week for almost six months. Amazingly, Joyce has enjoyed a 100% recovery from her stroke.

ARE YOU PHYSICALLY CONNECTED TO YOUR PARTNER? IF SO, HOW DO YOU KEEP THAT CONNECTION ALIVE? HOW IMPORTANT IS PHYSICAL CONNECTION TO YOUR RELATIONSHIP?

Joyce had never been married before, and she was a very attractive, fun-loving career woman when we married. Our physical relationship is still strong today, and we enjoy date nights, cooking, entertaining, taking vacations together, and simply enjoy spending time alone even if it's just reading books together. Fortunately, we enjoy each other's company. I think she is as beautiful today as when we married.

Emotional Responsiveness

WHAT DID YOUR PARENTS MODEL FOR YOU AS A CHILD ABOUT MARRIAGE? HOW DID YOU CONNECT WITH YOUR MOTHER? DESCRIBE YOUR RELATIONSHIP WITH YOUR FATHER.

My parents didn't set a very good example for a healthy marriage. Theirs was anything but healthy. My father was a workaholic, and my mother was mentally unstable, a paranoid schizophrenic. However, I loved Sunday drives with my father, often to relatives' homes, which was great fun. My mother, although somewhat unstable, loved me unconditionally, something I will always appreciate. However, there was little discipline in our home for my brother and me.

WHAT WERE YOU LOOKING FOR WHEN YOU DECIDED TO MARRY YOUR PARTNER, AND WHAT DID YOU KNOW FOR SURE ABOUT YOURSELF?

When I met Joyce, I was recently divorced with four young children, so I wasn't looking for a relationship. However, as our relationship became serious, I was looking for a responsible, well-adjusted, stable life partner that I could have a happy life with since my first marriage had been unhappy for many years.

WHAT SIGNIFICANT MEMORIES DO YOU HAVE AS YOU WERE GETTING TO KNOW EACH OTHER? WHAT DO YOU REMEMBER MOST ABOUT THE FIRST TIME YOU MET?

When Joyce and I started dating, I was impressed with her constant positive attitude, something she still has today, regardless of any challenges. As we got to know each other better and I travelled a few times to spend time with her family on their farm in Iowa, I was struck by the wholesome values they, her parents and brothers, all exhibited. There is something about people raised in the Midwest, particularly from rural areas, that develops high standards and values. They were just down-to-earth, real, hard-working people. As I contemplated marriage, these were values I wanted my four children exposed to as well. Her friends in Houston also were terrific; we had a fun courtship. Joyce loved travel and adventure and didn't seem too worried about taking on a parenting role for four children, this being her first marriage with no parenting experience. Little did she know just how challenging that role would be in the beginning because my kids were going through their own terrible time with my divorce, my being away from home for a year, my ex-wife's erratic behavior, etc.

SURELY THERE WERE CHALLENGES ALONG THE WAY IN YOUR RELATIONSHIP. HOW HAVE YOU LEARNED TO WORK EFFECTIVELY WITH THOSE CHALLENGES?

We have certainly had our share of challenges over the years. In 1982 we moved to California where we bought a Burger King restaurant in Santa Barbara, eventually expanding to eight restaurants both in California and Phoenix, Arizona. Working together in a new venture became a challenge for us both. At age fifteen our second son got involved with drugs and dealing with the challenge of rehab, etc., was a very difficult period for us. At age eighteen, our daughter who was attending Northern Arizona University had a roll-over accident while driving on I-17. Her roommate was killed instantly, and our daughter suffered very serious injuries: broken pelvis, hips, etc. We took her back to Santa Barbara where she began her very slow and painful recovery. Fortunately, today she has few residual limitations from that accident. Today, she is a highly accomplished psychiatric nurse. I think what makes it possible for us to deal with the challenges we have faced over the years is that we literally do everything together, both work and play. We truly enjoy being and doing things together.

Spiritual Surrender

DO YOU AND YOUR PARTNER SHARE THE SAME SPIRITUAL BELIEF, AND IF NOT, HOW DO YOU FIND YOUR WAY THROUGH IT? IF YOU RAISED CHILDREN TOGETHER, HOW WERE THEY RAISED SPIRITUALLY?

Joyce is a much stronger Christian than I. I was raised Catholic, and Joyce was raised Presbyterian. We attend church together but not every Sunday. Our kids did not grow up with a strong religious influence when they were young. Some attend church, and some do not. I wish they would attend more often than they do.

WHAT ATTRIBUTES HAS YOUR PARTNER BROUGHT TO THIS RELATIONSHIP THAT HAVE NURTURED AND SUSTAINED IT?

Joyce is an amazing woman who endured many extremely difficult situations early on in our marriage that few women would have. She is smart, disciplined, very hard working, and always has an amazingly positive attitude. Even when we were hurt financially in the real estate collapse in 2008/2009, she remained much more positive than I.

WHAT ADVICE WOULD YOU HAVE FOR YOUNG LOVERS?

The best advice I would give young lovers is to not sweat the small stuff, pick your battles, and be somewhat flexible, not stubborn and closed-minded. Listen to your spouse. If you are the only one talking, you will never solve any differences. Don't keep secrets from each other. We have certainly had our disagreements over the years, but we always try not to go to bed angry. For men I believe the real secret is the phrase "Yes, dear." It eliminates many disagreements!

* * *

Live brave.

JOYCE, 69

"I would say we have a healthy sex life. I learned from a Jewish friend's mother that the secret to a happy marriage is 'Never say no and always use placemats'!"

Joyce is a graduate of Iowa State University with a B.S. from the Interior Design College of home economics. After graduation, Joyce worked as a designer and sales associate for Finger Furniture Store in Houston, Texas, for ten years. While living in California, she and her husband purchased and managed Burger King and Sizzler franchise restaurants and, ultimately, three El Pollo Loco franchises in Arizona. For the past twenty-six years, Joyce has been a successful entrepreneur in the wellness and beauty industry and resides in Scottsdale, Arizona.

Married 37 years to Norm

Title: Mr. Wonderful, Blinded by a Blind Date

Physical Connection

WHERE WERE YOU BORN AND RAISED, AND WHAT CAN YOU TELL US ABOUT YOUR CHILDHOOD SURROUNDINGS AND CIRCUMSTANCES?

I grew up on a beautiful farm in Iowa. Of course, I didn't think it was beautiful at the time. I went to a one-room country school until the seventh grade. When I went to junior high in town (population of town 7,000), I was scared to death. My friend and I walked through the halls holding hands and even shared the same bathroom stall. Yes, we really did, and our classmates still remind us at our high school reunions! I really never felt accepted because I was a "farm girl." When everyone else went downtown after school, I had to get to the bus and go home. My parents weren't really strict, but driving five miles to town was not a trip you took unless there was a reason such as needing groceries or supplies. At the time I felt that living on the farm was restricting my social life, a life I wanted to have. 4-H was my big thrill, and cooking, sewing, and refinishing furniture I could do! I was a Blue Ribbon girl and even sent a blouse I made to the Iowa State Fair, "one of the places to visit before you die," according to the book with that title. My best friends were my cousin and my childhood girlfriend who lived on a farm about two miles away. I was happy to graduate and go to university and start my life there. That experience didn't start out so well with getting dropped by all but one sorority during Rush Week. I had never felt so rejected in my life, but I knew what I wanted and was accepted to the Chi Omega sorority in Spring Rush. My life was truly enriched, and when asked what influenced me growing up, I always answered, "My parents, 4-H, and my sorority."

HOW OLD WERE YOU WHEN YOU HAD YOUR FIRST CRUSH RELATIONSHIP, AND HOW DID IT EVENTUALLY DEVELOP OR END?

Oh, my first crush was with the "sons," yes, "sons" of my country schoolteacher. She sometimes "made" them come to our family parties. My girlfriend and I had a crush on both. They never paid much attention to either of us. So it really didn't develop or end because it just existed in our heads. When I was in high school, I felt pretty much invisible. Oh, sure, I had crushes, but I kept them to myself to avoid getting hurt. I did go steady my senior year, and we dated during our first year of university. He went to a different school, so it eventually ended. I actually don't remember if one of us broke it off or it just dissolved.

CURRENTLY, HOW DO YOU RATE YOUR PHYSICAL AND MENTAL HEALTH, AND HOW DOES IT AFFECT YOUR RELATIONSHIP?

My mental health seems fine. I can't believe I am the age my driver's license claims, but then I can't remember names either. As far as my physical health, I am now in perfect condition with the exception of my knees and hip. Ugh! It could be a lot worse. I am thankful for energy and overall health. We have had our health scares. Norm had both prostate cancer and melanoma, and I had a stroke eight years ago. I will talk about that challenge later. I am glad my husband and I are aging together.

We used to play golf, and my favorite golf partner was Norm. He has back issues and had to stop playing golf years ago. Golf was never the same for me. Because of some health issues, I stopped playing but do plan to get back to it this fall. We do go to the gym three times a week together. We swim, walk, and plan to start biking again when the weather gets cooler.

ARE YOU PHYSICALLY CONNECTED TO YOUR PARTNER? IF SO, HOW DO YOU KEEP THAT CONNECTION ALIVE? HOW IMPORTANT IS PHYSICAL CONNECTION TO YOUR RELATIONSHIP?

I would say we have a healthy sex life. I learned from a Jewish friend's mother that the secret to a happy marriage is "Never say no and always use placemats!"

Also, Norm and I are hand holders. We hold hands at movies, church, walking, even in bed, and when I wake up during the night, I always reach for his hand to hold.

Emotional Responsiveness

WHAT DID YOUR PARENTS MODEL FOR YOU AS A CHILD ABOUT MARRIAGE? HOW DID YOU CONNECT WITH YOUR MOTHER? DESCRIBE YOUR RELATIONSHIP WITH YOUR FATHER.

I grew up in a family where I never heard my parents argue. I always saw my dad give my mom a peck or two every day. I felt very secure and loved. To this day I don't think our kids ever heard Norm and I argue, nor can I remember us really arguing. That is not to say we always agree, but we can discuss and lovingly agree to disagree.

I loved and admired my mother so much. When I was young, I was thrilled when we wore matching pedal pushers (capris), belts, etc. I spent most of my time after school and weekends cooking, canning and preserving, and sewing with her. I was always proud of my mom and thrilled when she was the 4-H leader or camp chaperon. When I started dating, I remember asking my mom when I should be home. She would always ask, "What do you think is a reasonable time to be home?" I always chose thirty minutes earlier than my friend was to be home. She was teaching me responsibility. My mom was an example of pure grace, and my friends would all agree.

My dad was my hero. He was always happy and the funniest man I ever knew. He taught me the importance of having a sense of humor. His greatest joy was to bring a smile to someone's face. He was a hard-working farmer who was always there to help another in trouble. He lost his parents when he was five and eight from diseases of those days. He grew up in eight different homes by the time he was in eighth grade. Family members could only keep an extra mouth to feed for a short period of time in those days. Despite his childhood, he was always happy and positive. He was a great dancer, and when I stepped on top of his feet and he danced around the room holding me, I felt like Ginger Rogers.

I have two older brothers I loved and adored and still do to this day. When I was young, I just wanted them to pay attention to me. Usually, it took lots of kicking and pinching until Mom said, "Play with your little sister." When Mom and Dad brought me home from the hospital, my brothers wanted to give me to the hired man. We still laugh about that.

WHAT WERE YOU LOOKING FOR WHEN YOU DECIDED TO MARRY YOUR PARTNER, AND WHAT DID YOU KNOW FOR SURE ABOUT YOURSELF?

I met my husband on a blind date, something I had sworn I would not repeat after not having much success with blind dates. However, I was getting ready to settle down. I had had a great single life dating and hanging with my friends. I thought I was mature enough at thirty one, and I had played the single life long enough. I had a good job, owned a BMW (just me and the bank), and had no credit card debt or bank loans. In other words, no baggage.

It was interesting because most of the guys I dated had been married and were divorced with kids. So I expected to marry someone with children, but four children as Norm had? That hadn't crossed my mind. My parents had brought me up to think I could accomplish whatever I set my mind to. So when I told my mom that we were getting married, she replied (after her first gasp), "If anyone can do this, you can!" So I always believed I would be a good stepmother. Gee, I hate that Disney term! It is always associated with a wicked, ugly, mean woman. We stepmoms don't have a chance!

What significant memories do you have as you were getting to know each other? What do you remember most about the first time you met?

I remember on our first date that he was the most polite and courteous gentleman I had ever met. He wore puffs, a silk scarf tucked in his suit pocket and was very well put together. I later found out he had a clothier select his clothes. Where is that guy today? For our first date, we went to an art gallery gala. It was okay; no fireworks went off. When a friend asked if I would go out with him again, I said yes since he was recently divorced and seemed quite shy, and I didn't want to hurt his feelings. He did ask me out again, and we had a wonderful dinner at one of my favorite restaurants in Houston. The fire was starting to ignite, and when we went to lunch for our third date, I was falling in love. At lunch he dropped the bomb that he did not want to get serious. He was just out of a marriage that had started when he was eighteen, and he wanted some freedom. I remember my eyes filling with tears, and I knew I had to act FAST. So I invited him to dinner. I had to close and close fast. I served Cornish game hens, corn on the cob, and acorn squash, and no, I really don't remember what I served for dessert.

One year later we were married. I remember that when he told me he had four children I had no fear. Everyone loved me in my world, and I figured it would be the same in his world. I could see it now: his thirteen-year-old daughter and I would cook together; the boys (nine, ten, and sixteen) and I would, of course, get along. My own brothers loved me so, of course, would they! Then reality set in.

Surely there were challenges along the way in your relationship. How have you learned to work effectively with those challenges?

This is a very significant question considering I went from being single to newly married to stepmother of four children in fourteen months. Perhaps if I had become a grandmother before a stepparent, it would have been a smoother transition.

I moved to Vancouver, British Columbia, to be with our two oldest before Norm could return from Houston. He was closing a real estate project there. And, of course, he thought I could handle the situation. I arrived in a country

I was unfamiliar with to a house that had pretty much been emptied out by his ex-wife. And I was living with two kids I didn't really know very well. The only thing I knew about parenting was the way I was raised, which was NOT how they wanted their father's new wife to be. My biggest mistake was playing the role of their mother. They had a mother. Oh, how I wished there were step-parenting books available then to help me. The fact that Norm travelled a lot with projects across Canada made me feel like I was thrown into a role that I wasn't prepared for.

There was no mistaking that the two older kids hated me. In fact, I could hear them talking about how they were going to get me out of the house. Norm's daughter was threatened by another woman taking her place. Pretty normal in this case. I didn't realize it. I tried to fit in by learning to ski, a frightening experience for me at thirty two. But this was a big part of family weekends. And then Norm's two youngest boys moved in with us when their mother moved to Mexico. So at least I had Norm who loved me and his youngest son who so wanted a mom around that he and I fell in love. He used to say he was the luckiest kid because he had two moms, one who gave birth to him and one who raised him, and he loved us both.

Our first summer holiday six months after I moved to Vancouver was a disaster. About three days into the trip, I just couldn't handle it anymore. In my Christmas stocking, Norm had given me a plane ticket to Houston to visit my friends, and I planned to use that ticket to get out of the summer holiday! My plan would be to take the bus back to Vancouver and fly "home" to Houston before they returned. And that would be that and back to my old life in Houston. But when I calmly told Norm that I thought everyone would have a better time if I went back to Vancouver early and they continued their holiday, he said NO, it was a family holiday, and if I went back, we all went back. Well, that spoiled that plan. The kids came very close to getting me out of the house that summer. But Norm was determined to make this work and have his wife and children love and respect each other. I love that man to the moon and back, enough to spend upwards of twenty years on some type of family crisis directed towards me and, more recently, towards each other.

We moved to California after the oldest graduated from university. Norm's daughter was a senior in high school and stayed with a friend's family in Vancouver. We thought separation might help our relationship, but it didn't. During her first year in university, she was in a terrible car accident. Her friend who was driving was killed, and Norm's daughter landed on the highway and crushed her pelvis. Initially, she recovered at her mother's home (she had moved back to the states from Mexico by then). Later she came to live with us. She attended Santa Barbara City College for a semester. When she started, I pushed her to her classes in a wheelchair and waited outside to take her to the next class; that didn't bond us either—nothing seemed to. In hindsight, I think she felt she had to choose between her mother and me, not knowing that our heart has so much room for love. The more we love the more love we have to give. It didn't help that, for the first seventeen years of our marriage, the kids thought I had broken up the marriage. That explains a lot, and I would have felt the same as they did in that case. However, the truth is that I met Norm the week his divorce was final.

P.S. Norm and I are celebrating our 38th anniversary this weekend. We just received a card from my stepdaughter that says, "What makes a perfect pair? Partnership. Friendship. Laughter. Being in each other's corner...Sounds like some people I know." I think we finally made it!

Spiritual Significance

DO YOU AND YOUR PARTNER SHARE THE SAME SPIRITUAL BELIEF, AND IF NOT, HOW DO YOU FIND YOUR WAY THROUGH IT? IF YOU RAISED CHILDREN TOGETHER, HOW WERE THEY RAISED SPIRITUALLY?

I was raised in the Presbyterian Church. As a child, I attended church regularly and then had my mom's fabulous family roast beef dinner. (Dinner on the farm is served at noon). When I went away to university and during my single life, I broke attending church but never broke from my faith. When I became a parent, I hoped that I could introduce my family to church. I was not experienced enough and attempted this too soon. When we did attend church a few times, it was met with revolt and anger because it was my idea. Again, in hindsight, there were better ways to introduce God to our family. Norm and I attend church but not on a regular basis. We do try to live our lives as an example for our family. We are very proud of our granddaughter who loves Jesus and is a Christian example to us all.

WHAT ATTRIBUTES HAS YOUR PARTNER BROUGHT TO THIS RELATIONSHIP THAT HAVE NURTURED AND SUSTAINED IT?

Norm is the most caring, compassionate, sensitive person I know. He is strong and supportive to me in every way. He is the "wind beneath my wings." He pushes me just enough to make me stronger. In our businesses, he has always supported me and encouraged me to push myself.

LOOKING BACK AT YOUR MANY YEARS TOGETHER, WHICH AREA OF YOUR LIVES HAS BROUGHT YOU CLOSER TOGETHER?

Certainly going through and surviving together the years of raising children from a traumatic divorce. Not letting that tear us apart speaks volumes for our love and commitment to each other.

More recently when I had a stroke eight years ago, Norm was there for me each and every second. The day had started like any other day. However, after lunch I didn't feel well. Actually, I put my head down on my desk and later lay down on the sofa. I was feeling feverish, so I took my temperature, but it was normal. Norm gave me an aspirin, which, in itself, was unusual because we really didn't take aspirins. But in hindsight that could have saved my life. I had had a blood clot lodge in my brain stem. I was in the hospital for two weeks, home, and then occupational, eye, and speech therapy for weeks. Norm never once complained about the consistent care I needed and the affect it had on his life in becoming an instant caregiver. He slipped into that role like I couldn't believe. I felt so safe and protected with him by my side every minute.

WHAT ADVICE WOULD YOU HAVE FOR YOUNG LOVERS?

Take your time and wait for your Mr. or Mrs. Wonderful. You will know when it is right.

I always knew that marriage was an important commitment, which is probably why it took me so long to find the right man. I believe it is important to know their friends. They say you are the sum of the people you spend the most time with. If you don't like his friends, you might see a different person when he is not in his best behavior. Meet his family and get to know how he was brought up and how he interacts with his family. There is an old saying "Apples don't fall too far from the tree." Now this is not always true, but you will know. Listen to your gut; women have great instinct if they just pay attention to it.

Become the best you that you can be. To me this takes consistent personal development. I usually have two or three books going at the same time. One of my favorites lately is *The Power of Your Subconscious Mind* by Joseph Murphy. I will probably be buried with one in my hand! Be the person you want to attract. Enjoy the journey!

* * *

Live brave.

CHALLENGES ALONG THE WAY

"You will never know the purest love you can give a person, until the day you hurt because they hurt. You genuinely want them to succeed in life and be free from all the chains that keep them from being happy, whether you are in their life or not."

Shannon L. Alder

Mary Beth

Melissa and Keith are an outgoing, fun couple who enjoy friends and family. Confident and attractive, Melissa is engaging and warm and the self-described "life of the party". As the youngest in a family of five daughters, she received a lot of attention from four older sisters, parents, and relatives which contributes to her great self- confidence, evident in social situations and in the workplace.

Keith, with his military background, has a commanding presence and could be perceived as "macho". I, however, personally know him to have a very warm and sensitive side. He can easily shed a tear during a romantic movie and is a loyal and devoted friend to so many.

As a couple, Keith and Melissa complement each other well. Their strong personalities can sometimes clash as can be expected, but even a casual observer would note that they have a strong emotional and physical bond and love each other deeply.

I have had the opportunity to observe their marriage "up close" as Melissa is my sister. As you will read in their story, they had several challenges that most couples would not have managed to navigate and still remain a couple. I admire their faith, their bravery, and their unwavering desire to work through the challenges. What I have witnessed is a marriage and a love that has grown stronger and more dynamic over the years.

MELISSA, 51

> *"In our marriage being intimate is not only making love but also when we hold hands, cry together, laugh together, get mad at each other, cook together and dance in the rain! We keep this connection alive in our marriage by not forgetting that we are humans, humans who will make mistakes."*

Melissa and her husband Keith live in Denver, Colorado with their 16 year old daughter, Madison. She and Keith have been married for 23 years. She has two adult step-children: Breanna and Kristjan and 3 granddaughters: Kelsey, Brodie and Riley. Melissa, Keith and Madison enjoy hiking, traveling, entertaining and spending time with one another as a family. Melissa has worked in the Human Resource field for the past 23 years and finds her career extremely gratifying and enjoyable in utilizing her talents in helping others achieve goals and build relationships.

Married to Keith 23 years

Title: My Life

Physical Connection

WHERE WERE YOU BORN AND RAISED, AND WHAT CAN YOU TELL US
ABOUT YOUR CHILDHOOD SURROUNDINGS AND CIRCUMSTANCES?

I was born in a small German community in Kansas and am the youngest of
5 girls. We were raised Catholic and grew up with a strong family bond in a
traditional home setting as it was back in those days. Dad worked at the family business and Mom stayed home with her five daughters, until we had all
left home. She managed the insurance business with my father. Mom was a
big influence in my life. She always had time for her family and to this day I
surround myself with family. Living in a small town had its advantages. During the summer months, my sisters and I would play outside from morning to
dusk. We would ride our bikes all over town which included riding under the
bridges, on the dirt roads and we were always able to find some sort of adventure. Our grandma lived a stone's throw from our house and I would spend
a lot of my summer evenings with her. Grandma and I would sit outside on
her back porch swinging or rocking in her old red patio chairs and would stay
up until all the lights in town were off – just rocking and talking about life. I
remember when sleeping at Grandma's house she would always cover me with
this beautiful, thick quilt that she and grandpa received as a wedding present.
It had a wonderful smell and I knew I would be warm and safe wrapped up in
it. Now this quilt hangs in my guest bedroom.

HOW OLD WERE YOU WHEN YOU HAD YOUR FIRST CRUSH RELATION-
SHIP, AND HOW DID IT EVENTUALLY DEVELOP OR END?

I had a lot of first crushes. I look back now and feel that I was always searching
for the connection with the opposite sex. Whether it was that I felt I did not
have the strong bond with my father or not, I was always wanting that 'true
romance". I had "crushes" in high school but rarely did I ever get asked out on
a date. My first real crush was after I graduated from high school and moved to
Colorado Springs. I was 18 years old and I would go out to clubs to not only
dance but to meet guys. We met in 1983 at a night club while he was attending
the Air Force Academy. We would hang out together or with our friends on
weekends as he was only able to leave the Academy on weekends. During the
time of "hanging out" I wanted to have a commitment as boyfriend and girlfriend. However, his priority was to graduate from the Academy and go onto

flight school in Arizona. We remained friends the four years of his Academy education and for several years during his flight school in Arizona. In 1987 I left Colorado and moved to Arizona with my sister. This is where I met my soul mate and husband of 23 years, Keith.

CURRENTLY, HOW DO YOU RATE YOUR PHYSICAL AND MENTAL HEALTH, AND HOW DOES IT AFFECT YOUR RELATIONSHIP?

I am a very happy, outgoing individual. I enjoy being around others; I love to entertain and make people feel good. I am healthy, not only physically but mentally as well. My husband Keith and I try to stay active and enjoy working out together and of course hiking the beautiful Colorado Mountains. To be out in the open among God's beauty is not only calming, relaxing and breathtaking; it gives Keith and me a time to be away from the hectic hustle and bustle of everyday life. Being a ripe age of 51, I take my daily vitamins and hormones to help me keep up with life. I believe it is important to not only feel good, but to take care of oneself. If you are not feeling well, it affects not only you but the people around you. As my friends say, I am the life of the party. I love being around people and it makes me feel alive and happy.

ARE YOU PHYSICALLY CONNECTED TO YOUR PARTNER? IF SO, HOW DO YOU KEEP THAT CONNECTION ALIVE? HOW IMPORTANT IS PHYSICAL CONNECTION TO YOUR RELATIONSHIP?

Keith and I are physically connected. Keith and I do almost everything together. We love being around each other and we have many similar interests. We communicate and share stories of the day. Keith is not only my partner for life; he is my best friend. We were more sexually active early on in our marriage; however we have evolved to where we do not need to be intimate sexually as often to know that we love each other and that we are one. In our marriage being intimate is not only making love but also when we hold hands, cry together, laugh together, get mad at each other, cook together and dance in the rain! We keep this connection alive in our marriage by not forgetting that we are humans, humans who will make mistakes.

Emotional Responsiveness

WHAT DID YOUR PARENTS MODEL FOR YOU AS A CHILD ABOUT MAR-
RIAGE? HOW DID YOU CONNECT WITH YOUR MOTHER? DESCRIBE YOUR
RELATIONSHIP WITH YOUR FATHER.

Both of my parents were raised Catholic and were married in 1952. The role model my parents played in my life was an example of what I knew I didn't want in my marriage. They were not affectionate in public and my Dad had a strong and sometimes violent temper. I witnessed more fighting between the two of them than love. Even though they would fight my Dad loved his family very much and would do anything for us. Only until I was in my late thirties did I really develop a relationship with my father. My mother was a devout Catholic and she would never admit to anyone that her marriage was not perfect. Family was the most valued possession to her---we were her life. Even at rough times with Dad she would never shed a tear in front of anyone, especially in front of her daughters. It was her purpose to be a mother and to be the strongest woman she could be. My mother and I were very close and as I aged she was my friend. I always believed in her and she in me. Don't get me wrong, she and I had some rough times. Specifically the one time I remember was when I was 16 years old. As I mentioned my parents' marriage was not the best. I was the only daughter left at home and my Mom filed for divorce. Growing up in a small town, my parents were one of the very few to divorce. I was rebellious, selfish and didn't want my Mom to date anyone. She and I would fight frequently and I would go back and forth between her and Dad. It felt awkward to have friends know that my parents were divorcing.

WHAT WERE YOU LOOKING FOR WHEN YOU DECIDED TO MARRY YOUR
PARTNER, AND WHAT DID YOU KNOW FOR SURE ABOUT YOURSELF?

I was always searching for that fairy tale romance. I am a Leo so I am driven by the desire to be loved and admired. I wanted someone to make me laugh, feel good about myself and to really care about me. I was 26 when Keith and I started dating and I felt that I had grown up and had experienced life being single. I was successful in my job at that time, I had an apartment with my sister, was able to pay my bills and have money left over. I had gone out to night clubs often being single and I knew that I was ready to settle down and have a husband and a family.

WHAT SIGNIFICANT MEMORIES DO YOU HAVE AS YOU WERE GETTING TO KNOW EACH OTHER? WHAT DO YOU REMEMBER MOST ABOUT THE FIRST TIME YOU MET?

Well, the very first time I met Keith was in 1989. I was playing volleyball with a bunch of friends from work. Keith, who is the brother-in-law of my friend, was at the volleyball game. Honestly at that first meeting, I wasn't really looking at Keith as someone I would date; he was "too old" for me and he had two children!

Spin the clock ahead 2 more years and it was July of 1991 and Keith and I met again. I was still working with his brother-in-law and Keith had just gotten back from Desert Storm. His brother-in-law had a welcome home party for him and that is when we talked a bit more. He came to the office to visit his brother-n-law during which he and I would chat a bit more and flirt. He stayed in Phoenix for about a month after that as he lived in Tucson. On his last day in town, as he was leaving the office, he stopped quickly in my office and said "Hey, the next time I'm in town, can we go out?" I said sure, we exchanged numbers and it all started. Keith called me several times after he left and had to leave messages each time. I am not sure if I was playing hard to get or if I was questioning if this person could be the one. I was hesitant to call him back because he was older and had two kids. Finally at the end of August I decided to return his phone call. We chatted on the phone for hours, just getting to know each other. We called each other every night and after our first phone bill we decided we couldn't do this every day. We still called and spoke on the phone just not as much. We even said "love you" before we had our first date! Our first official date was at the end of September of 1991.

I remember that day so well. I was getting ready at my older sister's house and she loaned me a pair of her earrings and she said, "I have a good feeling about this. If this works out you can wear these earrings on your wedding day." Keith met me at work and then we followed each other to my apartment. We got a large pizza, bottle of wine and watched Dances with Wolves. It was the best date ever. We laughed, kissed and just had a great time spending it with each other.

SURELY THERE WERE CHALLENGES ALONG THE WAY IN YOUR RELATION-
SHIP. HOW HAVE YOU LEARNED TO WORK EFFECTIVELY WITH THOSE
CHALLENGES?

Challenges? Yes, we had some challenges. Keith was previously married and
had two children. To top it off he was also not a Catholic. At the time Breanna
was 12 and Krisjtan was 10. Keith was in the Air Force and stationed at Davis
Monthan in Tucson and I lived in Phoenix. We decided that I needed to meet
the kids first. So at the end of October of 1991 I met Breanna and Kristjan for
the first time. Keith drove up to Phoenix with the kids and it was a great weekend. As the kids walked into my apartment, we all were nervous and had but-
terflies. Breanna had a dance recital that morning before they left so she was in
her teal blue skirt and white blouse and she had her nails painted black from a
previous Halloween party that week. Kris was smiling from ear to ear to meet
me. I loved kids and had nephews and nieces of my own, so I knew how to be
around young ones. We enjoyed each other's company that weekend.

Keith knew that it was very important for me to be married in the Catholic
Church. We discussed the process of an annulment for him and the potential
of having a wedding in a Catholic church. Keith was very adamant in not getting an annulment after we met with a priest on what it would take. It didn't
sit well with Keith on what he needed to do or how the process would affect
his children. I knew that our marriage would not settle right with my parents
as Keith was not Catholic, was divorced and had two children not to mention
that he was 8 years older than I. We did not proceed with the annulment and
married on June 12, 1993 in Tucson at an outdoor wedding officiated by a
minister. Prior to the wedding, my parents decided that they would not attend the ceremony because it was not being held in the Catholic Church or
officiated by a Catholic priest. This was devastating to me – but I had Keith
and I just knew we were going to be starting our journey together. Two weeks
before the wedding my parents changed their minds with the knowledge that
not attending would mean that they would be setting a precedent. Any of
their grandchildren's weddings might present the same situation. They did
not want to miss out on any of those future weddings.

My step son, Kristjan (Kris), started getting into trouble at the age of 10. He
became involved with drugs, the wrong crowd, skipping school, and eventually landed in juvenile detention for his behavior. We tried tough love, in-pa-

tient and out-patient rehab, and counseling, threatened him and even thought maybe he would want to move out of state to be near other family. To no avail. Kris finally did drop out of school when he was a freshman in high school and turned to drugs and violence. During the next several years Kris would be in and out of jail. One of the hardest things we had to deal with was when he was out of jail and wouldn't come home for days. We didn't know where he was, if he was alive or dead. I would pray, Keith would be angry and Bre would cry herself to sleep. After several years of trying different things with Kris and after Keith's retirement from the Air Force, an opportunity arose for Keith and me to move to Oregon to start a business with Keith's father. We prayed about this opportunity and believed this was a door that God opened for Kris to move with us and get away from the wrong crowd and drugs. Kris was in in-patient treatment when we discussed this and he thought it was great and he was looking forward to it when he got out. Well, that didn't happen; he refused to go.

We moved to Oregon and he stayed in Tucson with the same crowd. Kris decided to continue down the same destructive path of drugs and violence. One night, Kris was driving slightly under the influence after a party and he ran a red light. If caught it would violate his parole. Thinking quickly, he drove into a residential area and ran the first stop sign he approached and pinned another car right up against a block wall. Kris fled from the scene; police arrived a few minutes later and saw that a 19 year old student was dead in the car that Kris pinned. After fleeing for several days, Kris was found and prosecuted. He agreed to 20 years of prison with no early parole.

Kris's fate has been very difficult on our marriage. Today Kris has been in prison for 10 years and during these years, we have gone to visit him and talk with him over the phone on a weekly basis. We chat about anything and everything. He likes to hear more about what we are doing, where we have traveled and even what we are eating! Kris is a very smart kid and watches the TV stations that they have available and continues to educate himself. He even received his GED in prison. He has grown into an adult and has experienced his own changes. It is a blessing to be part of his life and a beautiful experience that has majorly impacted all our lives. At first we felt it was our fault for the decisions he made. We also felt if we talked about Kris being in jail we would be judged. In getting to visit and talk with Kris regularly we now understand

HE made the choices and realize that what we have learned through these challenges is that we are not alone and that we can be a witness to others who may have gone through or are going through similar experiences.

Spiritual Significance

DO YOU AND YOUR PARTNER SHARE THE SAME SPIRITUAL BELIEF, AND IF NOT, HOW DO YOU FIND YOUR WAY THROUGH IT? IF YOU RAISED CHILDREN TOGETHER, HOW WERE THEY RAISED SPIRITUALLY?

We both believed in God and wanted the same for our children. However, as stated earlier, Keith was raised Baptist and I was raised Catholic. When Keith and I moved to Oregon our marriage began to really take shape, not only for us but also in our relationship with God. It was just the two of us and we did not have any of the stresses from back home. Keith reluctantly attended church with me at first but went regularly when we found our first GREAT church—St. Edwards Parish. The church was small and everyone was warm and welcoming and loved to see us. We had found our little loving church community in Oregon. Keith and I became so much closer and loving to each other. We were trying to live as husband and wife in the Christian way. Don't get me wrong, we were both still very stubborn and it took a while but I finally learned how to let go and let God manage my life. In Oregon we prayed more for a child – if it was God's will then let it be done. In March of 2000 we gave birth to our daughter, Madison. She was baptized in the Catholic Church in the small German town in Kansas where I was raised.

In 2001, we decided to sell our half of the business we had with Keith's Dad and move to Colorado. Our decision to move was for several reasons; we wanted to be closer to his family in Colorado, closer to my parents in Kansas and also for Keith to return to a government job which would support our family better than the family business. Living in Colorado we have once again found our "family church" and our community. We are very involved in church and know that this is where we belong. We have raised Madison in Christian schools from kindergarten to now a junior in high school. We believe that it is very important for her to know the love of God and how to serve others.

WHAT ATTRIBUTES HAS YOUR PARTNER BROUGHT TO THIS RELATIONSHIP THAT HAVE NURTURED AND SUSTAINED IT?

Keith has brought his love for others and sense of humor to this relationship. He would give his shirt off his back for anyone and I feel safe in knowing that. He has a strong relationship with his children that I admire. I believe it is very important for a father to have a significant role in his children's lives, particularly in a daughter's life to help guide her and help her understand what makes a man "tick". I also believe that our children feel safe knowing that Keith is always in their corner.

LOOKING BACK AT YOUR MANY YEARS TOGETHER, WHICH AREA OF YOUR LIVES HAS BROUGHT YOU CLOSER TOGETHER?

The areas that have brought us closer together are communication, listening and never giving up. We talk, we share our feelings, and we apologize and forgive and we listen to each other. We know we have made mistakes; we recognize those mistakes and ask for forgiveness. We have grown from those mistakes and have found comfort in each other. I think the biggest thing that I have learned is that when Keith is sharing his feelings with me, he is not asking me to fix anything; he just wants me to listen and be there for him.

WHAT ADVICE WOULD YOU HAVE FOR YOUNG LOVERS?

Be safe, be smart. When you decide to make the commitment to spend your life together realize that relationships are very difficult. We all have feelings and they are different from each other's. Make sure that you grow together and not separately. You both will change over time; your expectations will change. Talk about how you are feeling and what makes you happy and makes you feel loved. Give each other the opportunity to share and listen.

* * *

KEITH, 59

*"God has been very kind to us in that these challenges did not break us,
but only made us grow together and made us stronger."*

Keith, married to Melissa for 23 years, is the father of three children: Breanna (36), Kristjan (34), and Madison (16).

He served in the United States Air Force for twenty years (1975-1995) traveling the globe and partaking in three different "conflicts": Panama, Grenada and the Persian Gulf Operation Desert Storm. After Desert Storm, Keith was diagnosed with Post Traumatic Stress Disorder (PTSD).

After retiring from the Air Force Keith went to work with his father for a short period in an attempt to build a company in Oregon which did not materialize. Following that, he worked for the Department of the Interior (DOI) as a Security Risk Analyst from 2001 to 2016 evaluating the security systems of dams in 17 western states.

Now, fully retired, Keith has given himself the title of "Home Manager" and "Photographer" and is enjoying those roles.

Married to Melissa for 23 years

Title: Challenges

Physical Connection

WHERE WERE YOU BORN AND RAISED, AND WHAT CAN YOU TELL US ABOUT YOUR CHILDHOOD SURROUNDINGS AND CIRCUMSTANCES?

I was born in Tempe, Arizona and relocated with my parents to Lebanon, Oregon in the second grade when work in Arizona became scarce. Life was pretty simple in Oregon and we were blessed with a great home and family nearby. It was much like Mayberry in that the town was small and everybody knew everybody and everybody knew everything.

As I grew up the tension between my parents made my three sisters and me closer and stronger. My father was a demanding man, prone to angry outbursts and fits of rage. Once when I was 13, my mother threatened my father with a large kitchen knife after one of his verbal tirades and accusations. He nearly broke her arm disarming her and made sure all of us kids watched as he continued to twist her arm after she dropped the knife. He made me pick up the knife and put it away afterwards. He ruled the house with fear and loathing. In the 60's and 70's the cops were never called. It was just a part of life.

I'll never forget the look on both their faces during that night. He wanted to kill her and she was in so much pain. He was away from us for several days after the event. It was surprisingly calm during that time and my sisters and I helped Mom as much as we could in preparing meals and keeping the house clean. She never went to the hospital or to the doctor.

When he showed up again several days later, he tried to bribe us all with pocket change and told us his very lopsided side of the story. My mother never stooped to this level and only told us the truth when we were well into adulthood.

His many infidelities became known after this and we switched churches several times while growing up to avoid the glances, the stares.

I made friends easily and still do. Many of my childhood friends are still in regular contact with me and I'm always pleased to learn of their successes and help them to pray for their challenges.

How old were you when you had your first crush relationship, and how did it eventually develop or end?

I had many crushes and many girlfriends growing up. Unfortunately, my parental examples of behavior shaped my own behavior and I did not understand the meaning of a good marital relationship. My father had a long history of infidelities and flings.

The first serious crush was in high school and I married my first wife straight out of school before entering the United States Air Force. We were 18 years old at the time. The marriage lasted less than 14 years due to her infidelity and inability to cope with the rigors of my traveling schedule with the military.

We had two beautiful children, Breanna and Kristjan, and they are still the joy of my life.

My first wife was introverted, sullen, moody and very insecure. She accused me of infidelities constantly and of flirting with every woman in a skirt. The truth was that she was the one who was checking out the greener pastures while I traveled.

When my first wife's mother died, we separated. She felt abandoned and alone, and sought affection and love in the arms of another man. After the divorce, I was crushed but soon made every effort to become the best father I could be.

I met Melissa, my second wife twice. The first time was playing competitive volleyball. It was a disaster. She was younger, spoiled, and looking for a different kind of guy.

The second meeting was after the Persian Gulf. My sister threw a "Welcome Home" party for me and Melissa was there. I could not take my eyes off her and she was always right next to me asking questions about the war and asking about me. I was used to women wanting to be the center of attention. Look at me; tell me how beautiful I am. She didn't seem that way at all. Melissa is a huge extrovert . . . . like me.

It took a while for Melissa to return my calls. Like every good looking woman, I'm sure I was not the only suitor who was knocking on her door. Truth is . . . I had several strikes against me.

I was not Catholic.

I was older (8 and a half years).

I was divorced and had children.

My kids were 11 and 9 when I first met Melissa. I was surprised that it was love at first sight and the kids fell head over heels with her. She felt very much the same.

The rest seemed to fall easily into place.

CURRENTLY, HOW DO YOU RATE YOUR PHYSICAL AND MENTAL HEALTH, AND HOW DOES IT AFFECT YOUR RELATIONSHIP?

My physical health is excellent at 59 years old. I am an avid outdoorsman, love working out and strive to stay young. My personal motto is, "Never grow up, never grow old".

Melissa and I work out 2 or 3 times a week together in the mornings. She pushes me and I push her. We love our evening walks with our dog and daughter. It gives us time to catch up on the day and fill in the blanks.

I mentioned that I was in the military. I served twenty years in the military and another fifteen working for the Department of the Interior as a Security Analyst. During my military service I suffered from Post Traumatic Shock Syndrome (PTSD) while in the Persian Gulf during Operation Desert Storm.

It took many years of battling the symptoms of this diagnosis and even today I suffer reoccurring dreams that wake me in a cold sweat at night. Melissa is my rock. When I awaken from these dreams she will hold on to me and help me let it go again. It hasn't happened in years thankfully. Melissa is my rock.

ARE YOU PHYSICALLY CONNECTED TO YOUR PARTNER? IF SO, HOW DO YOU KEEP THAT CONNECTION ALIVE? HOW IMPORTANT IS PHYSICAL CONNECTION TO YOUR RELATIONSHIP?

Melissa and I are very connected physically and we work very hard to keep the magic alive in our relationship. We have regular date nights and sleep at the same times. Cuddling at night is a sure sign of our affection. Our sex life is good for our age....so I hear. We flirt and tease each other relentlessly and our children are often known to groan when we kiss. I love that.

It is extremely important to us to maintain our physical relationship. Not just sexually but in holding hands, sitting next to each other on the couch, and making eyes at each other in the kitchen.

I can honestly say that I love Melissa with all my heart.

Emotional Responsiveness

WHAT DID YOUR PARENTS MODEL FOR YOU AS A CHILD ABOUT MARRIAGE? HOW DID YOU CONNECT WITH YOUR MOTHER? DESCRIBE YOUR RELATIONSHIP WITH YOUR FATHER.

My parents were a less than a stellar example of what a loving married couple should look like. My father was often angry and violent, and my mother began to be just what he wanted her to be; subservient and sullen. They divorced after 27 years of just putting up with each other.

My mother remains a best friend to this day and we have been known to travel just for the fun of it. A recent 13-day road trip to see my children in Arizona is a coveted memory since I know it is likely that we might never have that kind of trip again. My mother's getting older and I hate seeing her health deteriorate and her mind wander. God willing, I'll have several more trips with her. We also talk on the phone at least weekly.

My father died several years ago due to the ravages of prostate cancer and we were able to mend our fences on his death bed. I often regret that I let my ego and resentment of his behavior keep me and my family away from him for so many years after a failed joint business venture between him and me. I should have approached him much earlier and looked to heal the old wounds.

I believe that he died knowing I loved him and that he was forgiven. Forgiveness was also given to me for being distant and aloof. His passing was an awful thing to observe and he admitted to me that he often regretted his behavior while we were growing up. It's a small consolation now.

WHAT WERE YOU LOOKING FOR WHEN YOU DECIDED TO MARRY YOUR PARTNER, AND WHAT DID YOU KNOW FOR SURE ABOUT YOURSELF?

Honestly, I was too immature for marriage at 18 years old. My preconceptions of marriage were vague and I had no real basis in fact. I assumed I was the boss, what I said goes, and all my physical needs would be met. Boy was that wrong.

The divorce was ugly and strained, the kids acted out and there were times my son was uncontrollable. The kids were 11 and 9 and found it easy to blame themselves for the failure of our marriage. Our son Kristjan was arrested several times on various charges and spent time in Pima County Jail in Tucson, Arizona. He currently is serving the last half of his 20 year prison sentence for Vehicular Manslaughter in Arizona.

When dating Melissa she was exposed to this behavior and even took care of my children while I was assigned to temporary duty around the world. She could have run, but she remained faithful and treated the children as her own.

WHAT SIGNIFICANT MEMORIES DO YOU HAVE AS YOU WERE GETTING TO KNOW EACH OTHER? WHAT DO YOU REMEMBER MOST ABOUT THE FIRST TIME YOU MET?

Melissa and I met playing recreational volleyball when I was separated from my first wife. I was not initially impressed. She appeared shallow, arrogant and full of herself.

The reality was that I was the one who fit the description. She was just being a single, young, beautiful woman, who was having a good time, and I was not the type of guy she was into at that time and, conversely, she was not the woman of my dreams. Yet.

It was several years before I would see her again. I met her again at a party thrown by my sister after I returned from the Persian Gulf. She was absolutely gorgeous, mature and I could not take my eyes off her. She spent a lot of time with me during the party and I was able to finally coax her phone number out of her. It took several weeks for her to return my numerous calls. When I finally felt like I should give up, she called and we began a several-month-long courtship from a distance. She lived in Phoenix and I lived in Tucson.

I knew that she was the one for me from our phone conversations, but I resisted telling her how I felt. I loved her already.

Our first date was hilarious. She invited me over and I showed up with wine and she ordered the pizza. We watched "Dances with Wolves" and drank a full bottle of wine together. It was a perfect fit.

As we continued to date I knew that she was the one. I tried hard not to tell her I loved her too soon. I loved her laugh, her weird sense of humor, her ability to see the positive in negative situations and, did I mention her laugh?

There is one thing she told me during our courtship that was a little disturbing. She told me she loved to ski because at the time I was a rabid skier and quite a racer.

As is turns out, she could barely ski. I called her out on the false advertising after a trip to Timberline in Oregon. I remember well how she went down the entire slope on her butt.

It's funny now.

Other past problems (debt, past relationships, and other somewhat typical personal issues) that came up during our courtship were sometimes tough to deal with, but we knew that together we could tackle almost anything thrown at us. Look at us now—23 years later.

SURELY THERE WERE CHALLENGES ALONG THE WAY IN YOUR RELATIONSHIP. HOW HAVE YOU LEARNED TO WORK EFFECTIVELY WITH THOSE CHALLENGES?

There were many. There were my personal insecurities from a previous wife who had strayed, a son who could not stay within the bounds of the law, and my constant deployments around the world with the Air Force.

My son was a challenge from birth. He was in need of constant support. He cried at the drop of a hat from birth and needed constant physical touch. He was arrested at 13 for possession of marijuana, and almost immediately afterwards arrested for almost torching an abandoned home in our neighborhood. He hung with a rather rough crowd. I tried very hard to bring them under my wing and include them in our family events. They rewarded me by stealing several of my guns and all the ammunition I had in the house.

We were fortunate that the guns were not used and that a quick call to the authorities ended the nightmare of what could have occurred.

He was grounded for life at that point and he was not allowed to hang with his friends.

Honestly, I was able to see myself in his rebellion and I vowed to never give up on him. I knew he was a great kid because I had seen so many glimpses of his heart along the way. He was starving for attention still.

When he got out of county jail at 18, he went to a party with friends while still on probation. A cop pulled in behind him while he was driving a friend home and he made the worst possible decision.

He ran.

Trying to evade the cops, he screamed in his car through a neighborhood and ran a light. He t-boned another car and killed the young driver instantly. His passenger had a broken leg. Seeing the carnage, he panicked and ran. He ran deep into the night and was a fugitive for almost six days.

His mother and I finally talked him into turning himself in and he was beaten brutally by the cops. A visit with him after his arrest made me churn in anger. While I understand their need to take him in, I felt that they were easily overzealous in doing so.

Then I thought about the family's loss of their own child.

My heart softened and I was able to move forward. Thank God.

Melissa weathered every event. She even held me when I could no longer be the tough guy and sobbed on her shoulders.

She actually was the glue that held us all together.

Our faith was a huge part of us, even though I was not a Catholic. We worshipped together at our local parish and it soon was very apparent I felt the desire to convert to be able to be fully engaged in the faith.

Melissa's mother, Twila, was very helpful during the process of conversion. She was an amazing woman. She answered every question I had about the faith, and when she couldn't, she would reach out to her church family and immediately respond with a suitable answer to my query.

After making the decision to join the church, I began the arduous journey of getting my first marriage annulled. It took nearly five years of near mental torture and many thoughts of just giving up, but we finally prevailed. I became a Catholic in 2009 and was married in the Catholic Church with Melissa amid throngs of friends and family.

Now, our faith is the glue. We are deeply involved in our local parish and we look forward to events with our parish family.

I am also involved in the Knights of Columbus.

Spiritual Significance

DO YOU AND YOUR PARTNER SHARE THE SAME SPIRITUAL BELIEF, AND IF NOT, HOW DO YOU FIND YOUR WAY THROUGH IT? IF YOU RAISED CHILDREN TOGETHER, HOW WERE THEY RAISED SPIRITUALLY?

As stated before, Melissa and I were raised in different faiths. I was raised Baptist and she was raised Catholic.

One of the many promises I made to her mother was that our children would be raised Catholic. At the time it was a huge concession for me to agree to such a thing.

A pivotal point in our lives was when I retired from the Air Force and we moved to Oregon to begin a joint business venture with my father in Oregon.

During the stresses of building a business, our relationship began to really take shape. Not only for us personally but for our faith in God. When the business relationship began to sour, our faith only grew. We knew God was in charge and all we had to do was remain faithful to Him and to each other.

I reluctantly began attending Catholic Services at St. Edwards Parish in Keizer, Oregon. The parish was small but welcoming of two new young people. I felt at home there.

Melissa and I had been praying for a child since our marriage and it seemed that nothing was working. We had tests run, and spent time in research for things that would help. It was only when we gave up and gave it to God, that we were finally blessed with a positive pregnancy test. Madison was born in 2000 and she was baptized in Melissa's home church in Victoria, Kansas.

From the beginning of Madison's education, we were blessed to be able to enroll her in Christian schools. We feel fortunate to have gained many long-lasting relationships with the families that we have met because of the schools Madison has attended.

Colorado has become home for us. Our church family is here and I have two sisters who live near us.

WHAT ATTRIBUTES HAS YOUR PARTNER BROUGHT TO THIS RELATIONSHIP THAT HAVE NURTURED AND SUSTAINED IT?

Melissa has the ability to forgive. Not that I was a terrible husband, but I was prideful and arrogant. Honestly, I still struggle with these issues, but now I am so much more aware of both of these problems.

She also has the heart of her mother. She's stubborn to a fault, but it has worked to her advantage in dealing with her clients and her know-it-all husband.

Melissa has the ability to love fully. She adopted my children as her own and stayed with it even when she could have said, "enough is enough". She is still lovingly called "Mom" by both of our adult children.

LOOKING BACK AT YOUR MANY YEARS TOGETHER, WHICH AREA OF YOUR LIVES HAS BROUGHT YOU CLOSER TOGETHER?

All the struggles and trials we faced together are certainly key factors. The expression, "What doesn't kill you makes you stronger" applies fully.

Evidence of what doesn't kill you makes you stronger include; a son in prison;

a failed business venture; the birth of our miracle daughter; a move to Colorado and finding new opportunities for both of us; an annulment; recently full retirement for me; and now new employment for Melissa.

God has been very kind to us in that these challenges did not break us, but only made us grow together and made us stronger.

WHAT ADVICE WOULD YOU HAVE FOR YOUNG LOVERS?

It's easy to say you're done....that maybe it's not worth the fight or the battles.

Don't even think about it.

It's more of a victory to stay in the battle and work together to get through the challenges.

Give your love freely, don't use sex or silence as weapons to hurt the other because in the end it only hurts you both. Do silly things together. Make sure you know what each other likes to do and spend time doing those things; sports, hiking, operas, even chick-flicks. Be open.

Hold hands. Whisper sweet nothings. Remind her how beautiful she is. Buy a better wine than you think you can afford at dinner. And buy dessert. Relish it together.

Life is too short to forget why you fell in love in the first place.

Oh, and kiss each other goodnight.

And guys . . . . Make your wife coffee in the morning. They love that.

Postscript:

Kristjan is on the downside of a 20-year hard sentence (a fixed sentence without a chance for parole). We visit him several times a year in Buckeye, Arizona and we are fortunate to have several of Melissa's sisters who live in the Phoenix area. This makes trips less of a financial hardship and well, honestly it's always great to spend quality time with them too.

Physically Kristjan is in excellent health and he works hard to stay fit. Several of his fellow inmates do literally nothing while there to improve themselves. Kristjan takes every class he is afforded the opportunity to attend; he has a regular "steward" position which allows him some extra spending money on phone services and even some additional food items he is not exposed to normally.

Mentally, he is recovering from having to "renounce" any past affiliation with a known white supremacy gang in prison. Over time and discussions with family, he came to realize that his thought process was wrong and that all lives indeed do matter. Currently, he is in a protected yard and is housed with many others who have "renounced" membership with gangs while in prison.

Another Significant Emotional Event (SEE) for me was when Kristjan and I had a heart-to-heart conversation several years ago during which he apologized for any pain he had caused us as a family. There were many tears and hugs, and I also confessed that I felt I had failed him in ways as a father. He calmly assured me that any actions he had taken were of his own volition. His confession was huge for me since all I had seen in the past was an arrogant narcissist; with his hand always out for more. I have already described previously that he is a mini-me. I recognize my own past behavioral issues in his past behavior patterns, too.

So, the past behind us, we now share visits filled with laughter, making plans for the future, and even reminiscing about the past.

Kristjan is very appreciative of all we do for him now. We are able to send money regularly and provide him with special foods that are available online. We also speak to him weekly as he is allowed phone privileges.

Life is good. I cannot wait to spend time showing him around the world when he gets out.

God has been very good to us.

* * *

Live brave.

7

PART SIX

SPIRITUAL SIGNIFICANCE

"Just don't give up trying to do what you really want to do. Where there is love and inspiration, I don't think you can go wrong."

Ella Fitzgerald

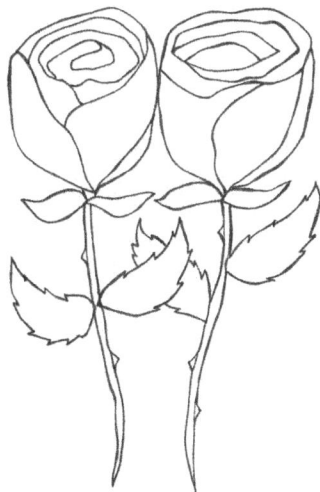

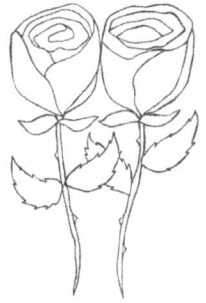

CHAPTER EIGHT

CLOSER TOGETHER

*"Words Matter...What we say—and how we say
it—can have a powerful effect on bringing us
closer to or farther from another person"*

Dean Ornish, M.D. Love and Survival

Hilda

There are no accidents. We meet those who we are meant to know and if by chance they stay for a while, then there is a good reason.

We met when Sue and John's niece came to work with us at the salon. When her time ended with us, Sue remained a client and John a salon friend. As with others who bring out the joy of service in us, Sue is a favorite and you will soon see why. I do think that someday we will be reading a book written by this couple. They have much to share. It's my pleasure to introduce this couple to you...their love story.

JOHN, 54

"We live in a "me now" and disposable society. In order to create a successful long-term relationship, it can no longer be all about "me"; it has to be about "us" and being of service to the other person."

John has double majors in accounting and German language studies. He currently works as a business analyst for a local home builder. Previously, John spent several years with a Kansas-based consulting company and, prior to that, worked as an accountant with a well-known, privately held Minnesota corporation. He is a proud father of three children and is a world class "pool man" at home.

Married 31 Years to Sue

Title: Through the Years

Physical Connection

WHERE WERE YOU BORN AND RAISED, AND WHAT CAN YOU TELL US ABOUT YOUR CHILDHOOD SURROUNDINGS AND CIRCUMSTANCES?

I was born and raised in Fridley, Minnesota, a quiet suburban city north of Minneapolis. I was the first of three sons born to my parents, both of whom were on their second marriage. My mother also had a son from her first marriage whom she brought into the union. He is four years older than I. My father had adopted his first wife's two children; however, she took them back to California with her when she left him. There was no conversation about their prior relationships growing up; we kids just knew they had existed.

My parents had a tumultuous and tense relationship. They were typically bickering back and forth with each other over things that would often boil over to a verbal blow-up between them. It was never physical, but we kids would usually clear the room when this happened. It was a strained relationship.

My father worked in banking until he was elected as the county treasurer. He was involved in a community service organization and in the church. We had a three season lake cabin where we spent weekends and summers. He had two brothers, one of whom owned a fishing resort in northern Minnesota. During high school, I worked up there for three summers, which were very formative summers for me. It was a very unique and important experience that very much shaped who I am today.

My mother was a stay-at-home mom. She had operated her own beauty salon before marrying my father, so she took pleasure in styling and perming the neighbor ladies' hair. I'd say she battled us to cut our hair as kids. It was a constant chore to keep us boys sitting still. She was also a singer and took voice lessons from an opera instructor. She sang in church and community choirs.

Music was a big part of her life and my father's life as well. I took piano lessons from kindergarten through high school and played trombone in the band starting in the fifth grade. I also was involved in the scouting program until high school when our troop disbanded. I went on to study accounting and German language at St. Cloud State University.

How old were you when you had your first crush relationship, and how did it eventually develop or end?

My first "crush" relationship that I recall was when I was in the first grade. I was to play Flower the Skunk in our performance of "Bambi." My costume was incomplete until my teacher, Mrs. Anderson, found a black and white striped sock to pin on to me as a tail. I remember that she drove me home after school one day after a late rehearsal and on the way she told me how she had found the sock in her husband's sock drawer. I recall how crushed I was to find out, "You mean—you're married??" I knew then it was never meant to be.

I had many friends who were girls over the years, but it wasn't until the ninth grade when a girl showed real interest in me—and I reciprocated. It started with notes passed surreptitiously in the hallways, sometimes couriered by other mutual friends. And then it continued with rumors among other classmates. Eventually, it evolved into a dating relationship where we would go out with other couples to movies, dinners, and other activities. It was an awkward time for me. I was growing and maturing, and at the same time, I feared and shied away from intimacy. Our relationship was very platonic. We held hands, but rarely hugged and never kissed. Affection was something rarely shared between us in our family and extended family, so it was difficult and uncomfortable for me to express to anybody outside the family. At this same time, my oldest brother had a girlfriend who got pregnant by him, which was very scandalous for the family, and I vowed to myself—and to the parents of the girl I was dating—that this would not happen to me! The relationship lasted through the school year. Over the summer, I went to work at my uncle's fishing resort in northern Minnesota, so we were separated. While we wrote back and forth a little along with one brief visit, it didn't take much to grow apart. We met again at the end of the summer, but before the start of the tenth grade, the relationship ended. She was looking for more than I could give.

I dated other girls, but the fear of intimacy and other judgments I placed on them prevented them from developing into anything serious. It wasn't until I met Sue and knew that I wanted to turn this into something more that I knew I would have to let that fear go, open up, and be vulnerable. I know it was excruciating for her, but she was patient, understanding, and above all, diligent and allowed me the time to work through it.

CURRENTLY, HOW DO YOU RATE YOUR PHYSICAL AND MENTAL HEALTH, AND HOW DOES IT AFFECT YOUR RELATIONSHIP?

Of course, over time our bodies change. Over the past years, I allowed myself to become overly obese. A few years ago the company I work for created a wellness program that did quite a bit to open my eyes to ways in which I could improve my physical well-being. In the last six years, my father died of a stroke and was himself very large and not very healthy. I was also treated for a varicose vein, which was also a bit of a wake-up call. So there have been a number of signs encouraging me to mind my health.

Sue and I have tried to stay active over the years with walking, health club memberships, and other forms of exercise at home for us and our children. We encouraged our children to find activities that interested them but never forced them into things. They tried every sport, and we supported them.

Today I am steadily but gradually losing weight through more conscious and conscientious choices and participating with Sue on different forms of diets and diet programs. Going to a gluten-free, reduced sugar, and dairy diet has had the most significant impact. To date I have lost 25-30 pounds from my highest weight in 2009, and my blood pressure and other biometric health indicators have improved to more healthy levels.

I think working together to be healthier has been something we have in common and has brought us closer together as a couple.

My mental health is starting to be a concern, although it is something I do not want to over-dramatize or dwell on. Dementia and Alzheimer's is something that affected many of the women on my mother's side of the family, including my mom. She died in 2014 at the age of 78 from the effects of dementia/Alzheimer's. She showed signs of it 10-15 years before that. After my father passed in 2010, she lost her footing and failed rather quickly. In their final years together, I always said that between them they were one whole person. My mother was a workhorse who was physically strong, but failing mentally; whereas, my father was mentally sound, but failing physically. It was their stubbornness that kept them both going.

While I see myself becoming more and more forgetful, I do not worry myself over it. And to be honest, it isn't something that Sue and I discuss too seriously. It's just a part of aging, and I compensate for it by using lists and other written reminders. I believe that we are aware of "signs" that will identify when it becomes an issue and then we will need to investigate further. While forgetfulness can be frustrating at times, I believe it is another phase that will bring us together as we go on.

ARE YOU PHYSICALLY CONNECTED TO YOUR PARTNER? IF SO, HOW DO YOU KEEP THAT CONNECTION ALIVE? HOW IMPORTANT IS PHYSICAL CONNECTION TO YOUR RELATIONSHIP?

I have very much enjoyed our physical relationship over the years. We have never been afraid to display our love and affection towards each other in front of our children, family, friends, and general public. Affection was something that my family did not share as I was growing up. I had never noticed this until I met Sue and her family. It wasn't until I was in college and after I was married that I routinely recall hugging my parents when we saw each other.

While the fire and frequency of our physical relationship has diminished a bit, the passion is still there between us. We have accepted that our bodies are changing, but the physical love between us still exists.

I think a physical bond is extremely important to the health of our relationship. It helps to keep us connected emotionally, as well. The two go hand in hand.

Sue and I spend a lot of time together, commuting to our workplaces together, at home together, and with friends. We do not fear silence between us and do not require non-stop conversation to feel connected. All it takes is a handhold and squeeze, a gentle rub of the arm, a hug and a kiss, a peck here and there. On weekends when we are busy with chores and activities, one of us will make it a point to stop and hug the other with a verbal, "I love you."

Emotional Responsiveness

WHAT DID YOUR PARENTS MODEL FOR YOU AS A CHILD ABOUT MAR-RIAGE? HOW DID YOU CONNECT WITH YOUR MOTHER? DESCRIBE YOUR RELATIONSHIP WITH YOUR FATHER.

Wow. My parents were the example of a couple who stayed together for the sake of the children, but then got to a point where they depended on each other to the point where they could not separate. It was such an odd love-hate relationship I could hardly understand it. My mom frequently said, "If I had it all to do over again, I wouldn't."

On one hand, she couldn't stand that man, and on the other, he was the best thing that happened to her. They modeled how I didn't want my marriage to be but also how to stick through thick and thin. While many families disintegrate, they stayed together after my youngest brother committed suicide. If they could survive that, there must have been some stronger bond between them than appeared or than they demonstrated.

I believe that in my mother's eyes I could do no wrong. But then I think I did everything possible to stay on her good side to avoid the wrath that she was capable of. I was always quiet, usually obedient and helpful when I could be. And other times, I just stayed clear and out of the way. As I grew up and left home and started my own family, she eventually came to rely on me as an outlet. She called me just to talk about her feelings, frustrations, and problems. I couldn't solve any of her issues, but at least she had somebody that she could talk to in confidence. She did see counselors here and there, but she usually complained about them, too. Furthermore, as Christian Scientists, it wasn't part of their religious beliefs to seek out medical or therapeutic help other than their own church practitioners, so there was a bit of guilt for doing that. After my father passed, I became her rock in the storm. Even though I lived states away, telephone conversations helped ease her mind to work through the life changes she faced.

My father always seemed distant to me growing up. He was supportive of what we did but not too overly involved. He was usually a man of mystery who didn't talk much about his past or youth. Occasionally, he would open up to us and tell us stories. He was always a fun guy to be around when our friends were with us at the lake cabin, driving in the car, or at other outings with them. He and I became much closer after I was out of college and had my own family. I think that this was when he could relate to me better. My father essentially grew up without a father, so I tend to think it was a role he struggled with. He was a very independent person, and I think that was how he wanted us to be. On the other hand, he was quietly responsible, which may be a trait that he passed on to me and my younger brother. As he aged, he eventually opened up to us more about his childhood, youth, and life experiences. One thing that brought us closer together in his older years was our interest in genealogy. Together, we traced back our shared family history. It was fascinating to him, gave us common ground, and forced him to think back on his life.

WHAT WERE YOU LOOKING FOR WHEN YOU DECIDED TO MARRY YOUR PARTNER, AND WHAT DID YOU KNOW FOR SURE ABOUT YOURSELF?

I believe that while dating I was always looking for the life partner. I believe that I looked not only at the girl but her whole family and situation.

I know I shied away from one girl because her father was divorced and had a girlfriend over at the house while we were there together. It was a situation that quite frankly freaked me out and one that I just wanted to get away from. Looking back now, I see that I was a horrible guy to date. I'm quite certain that I left a lot of girls confused and wondering what they had done or what had gone wrong because I simply stopped talking to them when I ended a relationship. That was it. Just over. I had no idea what I was doing, and I never talked to my parents (or anybody else) about my relationships, and they never spoke about them with me—or even asked me about my dates that I can recall. And likely if they did, I found a way to avoid that conversation. Communication, being open and honest, sharing my thoughts and feelings, was very foreign to me, and I was allowed to live that way for a very long time.

All I did know is that I would eventually find the right girl for me. When I started dating Sue, it took a while for me to meet her family. On our first date, I didn't even approach the house. She came out to the car, and off we went.

Again, I had no idea what I was doing.

During our time together, I realized she was what I was looking for. As I got to know her family, they got to know and accept me, too.

We dated five years before we married. I feel like we grew up together and just became a single unit. We evolved and survived so many things together that I simply couldn't see ourselves as anything but "together." It only made sense that we would get married. (I recall singing the Beach Boy's song, "Wouldn't it be nice," back in college.)

It was during our junior year in college that we formalized our relationship by getting engaged. We had originally planned a fall wedding but moved it up to an earlier June date based on my job at the time.

So, I don't know that I knew anything for sure about myself at that age and after high school except that I was going to attend St. Cloud State University, I was going to study in Germany, I was going to study accounting, and Sue and I would go to school together—and I couldn't wait to see what would happen next.

WHAT SIGNIFICANT MEMORIES DO YOU HAVE AS YOU WERE GETTING TO KNOW EACH OTHER? WHAT DO YOU REMEMBER MOST ABOUT THE FIRST TIME YOU MET?

I remember that Sue and I first met in band when I was in the ninth grade and she was in eighth. I played trombone, and she played saxophone. We played a song in band that included a Dixieland quartet. We had a blast playing in that combo, but I was also dating somebody else at that time (see "crush"). That was our first meeting, but it wasn't until my junior year that we really "met" each other. Again, it was a band activity where we went on a trip to play at various college campuses in Minnesota. It was on the bus where we talked and chatted and goofed around, but I was also a bit distracted because I had a crush on an older band member at the time. I wasn't ready to connect on a deeper level yet...By my senior year when I decided to ask Sue out on a date, I had dated and been friends with a number of girls. I sheepishly asked her out to a movie to which she said yes (and likely thought, "FINALLY!"). That first date was funny looking back on it now. We went to see the original Fantasia. I was so nervous, I watched the movie intently and barely acknowledged Sue when she spoke to me at one point during the show. After the show, we went to a taco place where I think we had a great conversation. We hit it off quickly. We spent hours talking and getting to know each other. Sue was always accustomed to speaking openly while I was very reserved and quiet. I was slow (and sometimes excruciatingly so) to share some thoughts and feelings. But we didn't just talk, we talked about deep topics and had long conversations about life, dreams, hopes, aspirations, the number of children we wanted, how we would raise and discipline them, beliefs and faith and everything else imaginable. She introduced me to Catholicism, and I found with her a family that supported and loved each other.

SURELY THERE WERE CHALLENGES ALONG THE WAY IN YOUR RELATIONSHIP. HOW HAVE YOU LEARNED TO WORK EFFECTIVELY WITH THOSE CHALLENGES?

Every relationship is faced with challenges, internal and external, and ours has been no different.

When faced with external challenges, I think the lesson I've learned is that we faced them together as a unified front. We may not have always agreed with each other, but once a decision was made, we moved forward together in that direction. We don't remember spending time bickering about things back and forth. We managed to work through them together.

Even at the outset when we became engaged, the response from our parents was less than enthusiastic, somewhat condescending and "challenging." You are so young. Yes, looking back now, we were very young, but that's not the way we saw it. We had already been together over five years, and there was nothing that we couldn't handle together. Bring it on. When our oldest son recently became engaged and, subsequently, married, my initial reaction was not unlike that of my parents. I was immediately brought back to our engagement experience, and I mentioned this to Sue. It wasn't my place to judge their decision and their future; it was my job to be as supportive and enthusiastic as I could possibly be. The next time I saw him I congratulated them both and told him how proud I was of him and the family he was building.

When it comes to internal disagreements, hurts, and challenges between us, I'll admit that I have a hard time recalling them. Very early on, I heard something that struck a chord with me and became a sort of mantra. It was a simple question. I think it had to do with "being right." The question was, "Is this more important to me than this relationship?" This question has become the basis for almost every situation I have found myself in—whether it is at home, at work, or in the general public. I believe that this is the foundation for avoiding most challenges that couples face. It's the desire to "be right," "be on top," and "come out ahead" that can be the root of most issues. Perhaps this is also why I have been told by more than one person that I tend to "stuff" my feelings. I found that typically it's my own misinterpretation of a situation and then acting on it that has been the cause of issues. So, I will tend to wait and see before jumping headfirst into a situation and saying something that I will later regret.

After ten years without one, I finally decided to purchase a piano. I have been told over the years that I needed to actively bring music back into my life, not just to listen to, but to create. The first few days I began to play I realized that this was not going to be as easy as riding a bike. It was going to take a lot of time and practice to get back to where I wanted to be. Of course, one of the reasons that I hadn't already had a piano was that life was already full. How would I be able to carve out time for this? As weeks went by and I didn't have time to play, I became more and more frustrated. Here I had the piano, but no time for it. It finally got to the point where I was angry about it, so I announced to Sue that I was going to sell it, that I didn't want it around if I wasn't going to be able to play it. Sue was upset by this because, in the meantime, our son had come to enjoy playing on it, and she liked having it in the house to play for herself and to listen to me play. My selfish desire for perfection (all or nothing) shouldn't get in the way of the enjoyment that it brought to the family. Maybe I should change my perspective and simply enjoy what I am able to do now and stop striving to be what I thought I once was.

The bottom line here is to forgive and forget. Learn the lesson and move on. Don't hold a grudge, don't keep score, and don't dredge up the old stuff. See it for what it is and get over it. Is it more important than this relationship?

Sue and I operate under different styles. I am a very planned, thought-out, and really quite controlling person (ISTJ Myers-Briggs personality type), whereas Sue is very spontaneous and "go with the moment" (ISFP Myers-Briggs personality type). When I figured this out, it was a huge eye-opener. I learned to just go with her flow, instead of trying to fight it and impose my more stringent processes on her. When I let go and just go, I have found it to be a fun ride.

Spiritual Significance

DO YOU AND YOUR PARTNER SHARE THE SAME SPIRITUAL BELIEF, AND IF NOT, HOW DO YOU FIND YOUR WAY THROUGH IT? IF YOU RAISED CHILDREN TOGETHER, HOW WERE THEY RAISED SPIRITUALLY?

Our common faith and beliefs are the glue that holds us together. I was brought up by my father and mother in the Christian Science Church. I did have a belief in God and Jesus, but it was something distant, something to achieve through study and practice. When I met Sue, she introduced me to the Catholic Church. I went to church with her and her family, and I was introduced to a relationship with God and Jesus that was much, much, closer than anything I had ever imagined. I came to love the Catholic Church and studied at college. I took a course offered by the university parish priest that eventually prepared me to convert and to be baptized into the church. Throughout this conversion, Sue was there. This became the foundation for our marriage and life together.

When we had our children, they were raised in the church together with us. Sue and I both taught the catechism at church, so our children didn't just learn about church from others as we were right there with them. Certainly, there were years where we were not weekly attendees, but our faith was always there, and we often spoke with our children about our faith and beliefs.

As the kids grew up, each was confirmed into the Catholic Church; however, after that, we let them choose the way they wanted to live their spiritual life. This is not something that can be imposed on a person without their own will. While they do not practice any particular religion today, I believe that their actions and lifestyles confirm that they are grounded in a spiritual way.

In fact, today, our own spiritual practice has changed as we have moved away from the practices of the Catholic Church toward a more direct spiritual connection to God, Jesus, and the universe in general. While this is a new path for both of us, it is also a path that we are walking together.

WHAT ATTRIBUTES HAS YOUR PARTNER BROUGHT TO THIS RELATIONSHIP THAT HAVE NURTURED AND SUSTAINED IT?

Oh, where to begin with this. First there is love. Sue is love, and love is the basis for everything. As I mentioned before, she is also very patient with me, and I know that's important. But it is also very important with children. It's not always easy, but it is always there.

Sue is an eternal optimist and has the kind of faith and trust that I lack even today. If I have faith in anything, it is in her and in her faith and trust. On the other hand, we both believe that everything happens for a reason. There is a lesson in everything. Sue has been very flexible and supportive of my career choices and experiences. As a result, we have moved around the country a lot. Everything happens for a reason and things that worked out were meant to be and things that didn't work or happen simply weren't meant to be. It has brought us to where we are today.

Sue herself is a nurturing person. We have raised three children and, at the same time, have been a part of raising three nephews and two nieces. Our door is open to anybody, including family and friends in need.

Sue is a generous person and by showing me the value of being generous has made me a much more generous person than I would have ever been. We have always given of ourselves, our time, money, and talents where we can. There is really no better feeling than doing something good for somebody else.

LOOKING BACK AT YOUR MANY YEARS TOGETHER, WHICH AREA OF YOUR LIVES HAS BROUGHT YOU CLOSER TOGETHER?

As you can tell from reading this story, there isn't one aspect of our life together that brought us closer together. It's the everyday things—living, laughing, loving, working, doing, and relaxing. Having children, creating a home (or, in our case, thirteen homes), solving problems, experiencing every aspect of life together—all have brought us closer together. Every birth, death, and marriage we experience has been something we have shared together that works to bind us closer. Even the challenges and arguments and differences we have bring us together as we work together to resolve them and work through them. Underneath it all is the commitment that we made to each other on our wedding day, and the knowledge that while I may not like you right now in this moment, I will still always love you. Our life has not been me versus you; it has been me and you. It has not been something we are testing to see if it will work; it's something that we committed to make work together. And as we move forward into new chapters of our life, there are many new things waiting for us to discover together.

WHAT ADVICE WOULD YOU HAVE FOR YOUNG LOVERS?

This is advice that we got from a family friend that I share with every newly-wed couple in the wedding card we give them:

"Remember—true love is not made in heaven; rather it is sent to us in a kit which we must assemble together." I let them know that what I have learned is that some days the pieces seem to fall into place easily; other days you will really have to work together to figure out how they fit. I end by wishing them a lifetime of joy and happiness as they assemble the kit of their love together.

We live in a "me now" and disposable society. In order to create a successful long-term relationship, it can no longer be all about "me"; it has to be about "us" and being of service to the other person. And when children come into the relationship, the role of self diminishes further. This is not to say that everything and everybody else comes first as it is still very important to be yourself and have your own identity and interests. This just has to be weighed and balanced equally. Being selfish, self-centered, and self-serving will be the downfall of a successful relationship. When one person feels like the only one carrying the ball, that's when the relationship will become a burden.

Do not rush into marriage—it is the most important decision you will make. Do not go into a marriage with the thought, "if it doesn't work out..." or it will be doomed. Truly know your partner; talk about the important topics and not just the superficial. Take the time it takes. And lastly, laugh! Life is way too serious already. Find a way to make your relationship fun. I've always said, "If it isn't fun, I don't want to do it. And if it isn't fun, I'm going to figure out a way to make it fun!"

* * *

Live brave.

SUE, 53

"Learn to love yourself. Spend as much time getting to know yourself and loving yourself as you do someone else. But – do it first! It really is true that to love someone else, you must first love yourself. To care for someone else, you must first care for yourself."

Sue is a law office manager in a small Phoenix law firm. She lives in Mesa with her husband of thirty-one years, as well as two of her three children, two nieces, her niece's two cats, her son's cat, her niece's dog, and, finally, her and her husband's two tortoises.

Married 31 years to John

Title: Weekend Romance

Physical Connection

WHERE WERE YOU BORN AND RAISED, AND WHAT CAN YOU TELL US ABOUT YOUR CHILDHOOD SURROUNDINGS AND CIRCUMSTANCES?

I was born in Billings, Montana, on November 13, 1962, fifth in line in a family of twelve children. According to my mother, I had colic as an infant, so I was a bit of a handful in the beginning. With four children already in tow, I'm sure that created some hardship, and I do believe it led to a lag in addressing my infantile needs. Our home was a small, three bedroom on a quiet Billings, Montana, street with a large, empty plot of land behind us. I say empty, but I know there were horses in it occasionally, but I don't remember if it was a ranch, farm, or what. I don't know if we were *allowed* to play in that area, but I do recall being in it more than once. I've never felt I can remember much from this time of my life, as we lived there until I was six. We were close to extended family, as my grandpa and grandma lived nearby, as well as two sets of aunts and uncles. Other extended family lived in cities within driving distance, so we saw them every once in a while.

When I was five years old, the majority of my friends started first grade, but I had just missed the cutoff. A neighbor boy brought me to school with him on a day you could bring a friend. There were LOTS of kids around when we first got to the school yard, and we became separated. I frantically searched for him, but never did find him, so I ended up walking back home. I was **so** disappointed!

I remember feeling the need for attention and connection and sought that away from the home. This was not just in my early childhood, but throughout my growing up years. To this day I could list at least five mothers who nurtured me to adulthood. I still feel very close to all of them, even though several are now gone.

I felt very close to my grandfather on my father's side, who I felt was an amazing man. He built his own home, and I can almost remember the smell of it if I think deeply about it. The things I remember about him and the house were that every time we visited, he would set out two packets of Fig Newtons (loved them at the time!). He and Grandma owned a huge, round dining room table where we enjoyed many wonderful meals. The attic wasn't scary but was built to house extra beds and that is where we children often slept when visiting. I don't recall if there was a ledge that went around the room, but I do remember many items up there—old cigar boxes, worn out hats, etc. And the icing on the cake—a border of nudie (or maybe just topless—I don't recall exactly) women around the room. I always felt safe at that home and hold fond memories of it today. It is now a parking lot for the city hospital, as it was torn down many years ago. What a lost piece of history that was.

A bigger loss was moving from this beloved birthplace and leaving behind family and friends to move to Minnesota. It wasn't long after we moved that my grandfather passed away, which absolutely devastated me. I remember his funeral vividly because my aunt, his daughter, was crying throughout, and I got to a point where I just couldn't take anymore. I knew I was going to break down crying also, so I ran out of the funeral home into the parking garage where I sat and bawled my eyes out.

This may sound strange, but I always felt like Heidi (from the movie) after we moved to Minnesota—I *really* missed the mountains and the wide open sky! We traveled back to Montana every summer until I was twelve. After that, trips were generally for funerals, weddings, etc. Even at twelve, because we stopped taking that annual trip, it took me a long time to get over my homesickness for the mountains.

How old were you when you had your first crush relationship, and how did it eventually develop or end?

As I recall, I was four or five when I had my first crush. It was on an older boy (I believe he was seven), and it made my first cousin really mad because he wanted to marry me. I think I even knew then that it wasn't right to marry a cousin. Gary, the boy on whom I had a crush, lived on the same street as my grandfather, so I only got to play with him when we were visiting Gramps. We would actually kiss (he knew about those things), so I truly felt I loved him. Even though we eventually moved from Montana, I believe his family moved out before we did. I remember a deep loss at that and how lonely I felt when we visited my grandparents, since he was no longer there. That made my cousin happy, but I remember feeling very sad and depressed for quite some time. Other details surrounding our relationship are just not there anymore. I think the years between this loss and then the loss of my grandfather caused a block in my memory because of the deep pain I felt throughout those early years.

CURRENTLY, HOW DO YOU RATE YOUR PHYSICAL AND MENTAL HEALTH, AND HOW DOES IT AFFECT YOUR RELATIONSHIP?

My current physical and mental health is excellent, and I continue to work on that every day. I would certainly not say I started that way, which reflects my husband's patient, accepting nature in working through life together. I'm sure there are some who would say I was straight up crazy in my younger years, and I don't know that I could argue with that. I attribute it to being an "open" personality type, which took a toll on me while I was in my teens through about thirty. Let me explain. I was expected to help with household chores, as well as help with the younger children. Not that there's necessarily anything wrong with that, but one does mature a bit faster in many ways, while remaining stunted in others (think inner child). I mean, here I am meeting the needs of my younger siblings, but who is meeting mine? Yes—my older siblings whose needs, I'm sure, went unattended at times. And that progression continued down the line of children until the last few. But even they weren't necessarily "doted" upon, not in their formative years anyway. By the time they were the remaining children in the household, patterns were in place and weren't going to change unless through the help of a good therapist, concentrated self-reflection, and/or self-help. I worked on myself through reading and self-help study, self-hypnotism, and meditation. Being an "open" person, this type of work flooded my inner being with a deeper awareness—some of which I have to say was supernatural—thus, the *crazy*. When John and I made our first move to Schenectady, New York, I felt we lived in a haunted apartment. I would awaken some nights in a panic feeling that aliens wanted to take me. (I said crazy, right?) Well, I never was taken, but a psychic did confirm our place was haunted—at least she saw a spirit in the home. I felt vindicated on that one! But you can see that I was perhaps a little "odd" in my younger years.

We all feel our family situation is <u>normal</u>, right? I know I did. I could never understand the fuss about other parents not wanting my friends (their children) to spend the night because it was adding another body to the mix, or why they felt so sorry for us over all the hollering my father and mother did throughout the day. I figured ALL families were like that. Then, I moved out and went to college. My first weekend back home I almost had a panic attack! I saw it, and I got it—there was *a lot* of chaos in our home! With this memory in mind, I think of what it must have been like for my poor husband, boyfriend at the time, to come into that mix. Yikes! Picture this—the first time John stepped into our front door, he immediately had a seven year old grab his leg, sit on his foot, and hold on while he tried to walk around with at least three other curious young ones at his side to see "the new guy." As he entered our family room, my mom, dad, and a few other siblings are milling about. Now the questions start flying—and I mean a <u>barrage</u> of questions from everyone in the room—except my dad, who was formidably quiet at such times, putting up a seemingly impenetrable wall of protection. He didn't smile, he didn't speak unless spoken to, and then he responded with a one or two word answer. It might have gone like this: John, "How are you?" My dad, "Good." (Awkward silence.) John, "A little crazy in here, huh?" My dad, "Yep." How embarrassing! I always tried to get John out of the house as fast as possible. Don't misunderstand me because I loved my dad and wanted him to approve of my boyfriend and vice versa, but I knew a relationship with my dad was a process that could never be rushed. Happily, they both did warm up to each other over time. In the beginning, I don't know that either of my parents thought I had made the best choice in a partner, but does any parent initially? In the end, however, we all got along swimmingly. So early in the relationship and probably throughout the birth and first five years of our children's lives, I was a bit unstable as I worked to educate myself in the areas I felt I had missed out on as a child to not only heal my inner child but to work to do better for my own children. The funny thing about that is that I understand my parents probably did the same. We all do the best we can at the time.

ARE YOU PHYSICALLY CONNECTED TO YOUR PARTNER? IF SO, HOW DO YOU KEEP THAT CONNECTION ALIVE? HOW IMPORTANT IS PHYSICAL CONNECTION TO YOUR RELATIONSHIP?

Much of the physical connection between John and me occurred early on. Like most young lovers, we kissed <u>a lot</u> and explored our bodies. Three to five hour make-out sessions, interspersed with pretty deep conversations throughout, were the norm for us when we started dating. Because those dating years lasted five years prior to marriage, I felt I knew every piece of John straight to his soul. Today, just a hug or interlocking of fingers as we drive rekindles that connection in a subtle, yet reassuring way. We often hug and kiss at home, hold hands when out together, and share strokes and caresses while commuting to work. The physical connection of sex is not the important aspect in our relationship at this point (not that it doesn't happen); however, the snuggles, caresses, hugs, and kisses definitely are! After thirty-one years of marriage, our connection is as much psychic as physical. We are more attuned to the physical *energy* between us. We truly are more "one" than "two."

Emotional Responsiveness

WHAT DID YOUR PARENTS MODEL FOR YOU AS A CHILD ABOUT MARRIAGE? HOW DID YOU CONNECT WITH YOUR MOTHER? DESCRIBE YOUR RELATIONSHIP WITH YOUR FATHER.

I grew up Catholic, and my parents modeled a deeply committed, faithful, and loving relationship to us kids. My parents rarely fought or rose their voices to each other (to us kids was a different story!) although they did have disagreements. I saw that two people could be at odds, discuss it, and come to a mutual agreement without a huge conflict. That doesn't mean I didn't notice one or the other of my parents wasn't a little ticked off with the outcome, but it was dealt with in a civil manner. I also saw my dad "flirt" with my mother, as well as kiss and hug in front of us. PDA (Public Displays of Affection) were almost always pointed out and made fun of by everyone, yet they were a nice reminder of the love between our parents.

As far as connection to my mother, I love her dearly, and as kids we knew she was the one we could work on if we really wanted something. I think she wanted to be loved as much as we did, but having grown up in a home where they never said "I love you," she didn't really know how to express her love.

Because of that, she would find other ways to make us happy to receive the thanks (from us) and the good feelings that follow—often that was breaking down and saying yes to something we had been told we couldn't do. Like all of us, my mother had her faults and we saw those--especially as we got older, but I'm not perfect either. I know we all do our best when it comes to raising our children, and my mother was no different.

I was somewhat fearful of my father but loved him dearly and sought his praise and approval. I was an early riser as a child and would often sit in the bathroom with him as he shaved. I'm not sure why that enthralled me, but it did, and I loved being close to him. My father was an authoritarian who ruled the house. We often got the "Wait 'til your father gets home" line from my mother (cop out if you ask me). Yet dad had a true love of children, and we would do anything to make him smile. He was a tough one to crack, but when we did—even if we only got a snicker—our chests swelled with pride. I remember wishing I were a boy when I was young because my dad did more with the boys. He enjoyed male sports over female sports and attended my brothers' sports games more often than he attended the girls' games. I was in choir—NOT his thing, but also band, and he did love big band music. I played the tenor sax and when I made the Dixieland and Jazz Bands, he would often attend those concerts. I had a special connection with my dad and actually feel I came into this family as somewhat of a "buffer" for him. When, at age 67, I hugged him goodbye to winter in Arizona, I knew in my heart it would be the last time I would see him. It took everything I had not to break down sobbing right then and there, but I didn't. It was like he went through me as we embraced that day because I felt a wave of emotion run through me. It's a feeling I'll never forget. He died of a massive heart attack on Christmas Eve that winter in Arizona.

WHAT WERE YOU LOOKING FOR WHEN YOU DECIDED TO MARRY YOUR PARTNER, AND WHAT DID YOU KNOW FOR SURE ABOUT YOURSELF?

When I was of dating age in high school, I knew <u>exactly</u> what I wanted in a husband—a good father who was good with kids and could express his love for them, a soul mate who would remain "connected" with me always, a happy person who enjoyed humor, a responsible person who could provide for his family. I knew for sure I could be a loving spouse and a wonderful mother to our children. John and I dated for three months when I knew I would marry him. I knew I could provide for his physical and emotional needs and raise his children in a loving, caring atmosphere. I believe I stated earlier that John and I spent hours making out, but also talking hours on end. And we talked about *everything!* A typical talk could include religion, children, abortion, politics, family life, our fears, and even our deepest secrets. There was nothing he didn't know about me, and I felt the same about him. We knew how many kids we wanted, the type of house we would have, the philosophy around which we would raise our children, the church we would attend, the pets we would have, and on and on. And quite honestly, if we were to look at that list today, we were pretty spot on, except for the house thing. We actually wanted to live in one of those octagon type homes!

WHAT SIGNIFICANT MEMORIES DO YOU HAVE AS YOU WERE GETTING TO KNOW EACH OTHER? WHAT DO YOU REMEMBER MOST ABOUT THE FIRST TIME YOU MET?

I'm not sure what you would call significant. I do remember that at the time John and I were just getting to know each other, things were going very well with another young man and me. To this day I know that either would have worked just fine (for me), but I had come to a crossroads where I had to choose. Olivia Newton John's "Torn Between Two Lovers" was truly what I felt like at the time. The reason I chose John is that I am a "fixer," and John not only needed some fixing but saving from a family that I saw as nearly opposite to that of my own (and when we're still with our family – we often think it's the best family there is, don't we?). I think that's funny as I reflect on it now because I hadn't yet come to see the fault of my own family—nor my own faults. It's amazing how we always see the needs in others, yet neglect our own. Anyway—I don't believe I knew all of this at the time I made my choice, but in looking back and knowing who I was at that time, I can see that it was. The other boy was wonderful, and I loved him with all my heart too. Unfortunately, a choice had to be made as it's socially unacceptable to go through life with two husbands.

The first time John and I met was at a grade school music event, but I didn't think much of it. I saw him and thought he was "cute." It wasn't until eighth grade Dixieland band that the love bug bit me. John played trombone, and I was there on my tenor sax. He was cute, funny, and had a beautiful smile with a thick head of curly hair. I pursued him that year, but being the "big freshman," he was too busy going after a different girl to even notice. It wasn't until my junior year that he finally asked me out. Prior to that, we would walk from our band class to each other's lockers and enjoyed each other's company. We were at one of our lockers the day he asked me out. I laugh now because he made it sound like a group of us were going to a movie. When he showed up at my house to pick me up, it was just him and he didn't come to the door. (Not a good first impression on the parents). I ran out to the car, opened the door, and asked him where everyone else was. He couldn't understand why I thought there was anyone else and said it was just him. I certainly didn't mind, but I always remember that. We went to the movie *Fantasia* where he never once took his eyes off the screen to look over at me. I was laughing at that inside but thought his awkwardness was cute. We then went out for tacos and had a fun time eating and chatting. After that, he dropped me at home, said goodnight, and that was it. I think it was two or three weeks of dating before I pecked him goodnight on the lips. I remember feeling ecstatic when that finally happened!!

SURELY THERE WERE CHALLENGES ALONG THE WAY IN YOUR RELATIONSHIP. HOW HAVE YOU LEARNED TO WORK EFFECTIVELY WITH THOSE CHALLENGES?

There are always challenges, no matter *what* your relationship. A big one was our weekend romance status during our early years together. John worked days and I worked nights, so we only had weekends to spend time together. That was really difficult, but you do what you have to do. We did that for four years after my youngest was born. It was really difficult, but I believe it gave John the opportunity to bond to our children in a way he wouldn't have if that had not been our lifestyle. After a handful of years of normalcy (meaning we spent evenings AND weekends together), we moved to Kansas, and for the first several years there, John traveled eighty percent of the time. The weekend romance was once again the norm. Then came 9/11, and his travel came to a screeching halt. It started up again prior to our move to Phoenix but was never quite as hectic and often as it had been in the beginning.

One of the biggest challenges for me came about five years into our marriage. I was extremely upset over a decision John made that went against one of our pre-marriage agreed upon items, which was the number of children we would have. We had agreed on five, and I had just given birth to our third child when about two weeks later, John came to me and said he just couldn't do it anymore. He was stressed out and just didn't have it in him to have more than three children. I have to tell you I was quite taken aback by that and extremely upset. That was one of our agreed upon items! In my mind, he was now basically killing off two of my children. Those of you who have had miscarriages or have lost a child in pregnancy will understand what I mean. And not to make light of that—I know that experience would be an even more horrible situation to endure, but you have to understand that in my mind I had already created and fantasized our life with five children. As I did during pregnancy, when John and I determined the number of children we would have, I fantasized about how our children would look, what they would grow up to do, and whether they would be male or female—all the dreams, hopes, and wishes built on those five children were already ingrained within my soul. And now John was taking two of them from me. It really, really hurt!

It was probably about six months after his decision when I found myself absolutely hating him. And I know hate is a strong word, but that's truly how I felt, and it was deep and extreme. My mantra for a long time became "if you can't say something nice...." So I didn't talk much. After the first couple of weeks, rather than dissipate, the feelings seemed to intensify. I had to have a little talk with myself. I knew nothing had changed with John, so I had to start looking at myself. I discovered there was a lot of negative self-talk going on in my head, so I sought help. I found a tape (I don't think they had CDs yet) that was a couple's talk on relationship. I listened to that hour-long tape at least once a day during the work week over the next several months (I had the luxury since John worked days, and I worked nights). By about month three, I could finally talk civilly to John again, but it took a full six months to let those negative feelings go and get back on track. Divorce occurred to me many times during that trying period of my life, but we had entered into marriage for better or worse, and we took that seriously. I cannot express how grateful I am today at having not only that experience, but also having been able to work through it. I knew (and now know) that if I could work through that, I could work through anything! I still hold that sorrow in my heart—I can't help that. But I have come to understand that people's situations can change, and you either make the decision to change with them or move on.

Today, as challenges come up, we discuss them, find solutions, and set a path to resolution. We have been through a lot: ten moves from one home to another; three children, all born in different states; the addition of nieces and nephews into our home at different points in time; several pet transitions; the loss of my father; the loss of both of John's parents; the difficulties of correctly diagnosing both health and mental issues in some of our children; working through transgender issues with one of our children; multiple financial issues throughout a thirty plus year marriage; job changes, and as in any relationship, the list goes on and on. When needed, we'll call a family meeting so discussion is open to all. Rarely does it take a full meeting of the minds, but I believe everyone would agree it's the best way to resolve problems.

Spiritual Significance

DO YOU AND YOUR PARTNER SHARE THE SAME SPIRITUAL BELIEF, AND IF NOT, HOW DO YOU FIND YOUR WAY THROUGH IT? IF YOU RAISED CHILDREN TOGETHER, HOW WERE THEY RAISED SPIRITUALLY?

Spiritual belief has always been a significant part of my and John's relationship. He was raised as a Christian Scientist, and I a Catholic. Funny as it may seem, we still held many of the same beliefs. John also felt a "stigma" around his faith, and growing up in Minnesota, the majority of folks were either Catholic or Lutheran, so he always had it in his mind that he would become one or the other at some point. My guess is that it was going to depend upon who he ended up marrying, and in this case, John converted to Catholicism. My faith meant a lot to me at that point in time, and I was very proud of him. Many of you who are Catholic are familiar with the pre-marriage "test," which is basically a compatibility test to give the couple an idea of how their beliefs and aspirations compare. A high score means you're very much in sync, and the probability of a successful marriage is good. A low score means there is work to do in getting to know each other better and in getting on the same "wavelength," as I like to call it. John and I received one of the highest scores our college priest had ever seen. We basically only differed on one question and when the priest reviewed that with us, we really were saying the same thing, but it had just been interpreted differently by one of us. But then—we could have told them that!

We raised our children within the Catholic faith also, but in time, the kids, as I had, saw the hypocrisy in both the church and those who worshipped there. Knowing this, as the kids got older, I began to direct them more to nurturing their spirituality in whatever way felt most genuine to them, whether that be appreciating nature and the beauty in the world or finding an alternative church group in which they were interested. The Godself within each of us does need nurturing, and that was my soapbox with my kids. Once they were older, I didn't make a big deal about them not wanting to attend church services, especially since I was on that same path of revelation regarding the "purity" of formalized religion. I know our local church leaders would like us to believe every word of the Bible is completely true, but come on—how many times have we played the game where one person starts a sentence, whispers it to the next person, and by the time it has gone around the room, it's something completely different? *That's* how I feel about formal religion. The truths are there, sort of, but nothing in the Bible today is as it was said 2000 plus years ago. And just the translations of the Bible itself—how many times has that happened? There are certain words that don't even translate, so don't think for a second that every word in the Bible came directly from God or even from a pure heart. In ancient times, the kings ruled the people and did whatever was necessary to maintain power and control over them. With the powerful and mighty running the early churches of the world, I can't accept that their influences, greed, and desires didn't affect the way religion formed, was taught, and even written down.

The biggest hit in the spiritual area for John and me came when our youngest declared herself transgender (wasn't a big surprise), as it made us really have to think about what we were promoting in the religion we were supporting. Not so much that we made a complete change right away, but it definitely changed the way in which we celebrated our faith. Rather than attending church services, we chose to spend our time at a holy hour in the wee hours of the morning. This was a once a week practice that John and I both did for about ten years. It came to an end when we felt we had to finally make a stance on where our church stood on gay and transgender issues versus our own beliefs and feelings on the matter.

This, obviously, was a thoughtful process and one that spanned our daughter's lifetime into her twenties. I stated that our child's transgender status wasn't a surprise. And it wasn't, *totally*, as we always knew there was something different about her. This could be a book in itself, but she was, of course, born as a he, yet even from infancy she was totally different from her two older brothers. As infants, my first two boys would scream when another woman picked them up to hold them. My youngest would scream when I took her out of the arms of another woman holding her! (I definitely picked up on that and thought it different.) As she grew, she always sought out families with girls and had a ball playing with them. As she continued to grow, her best friends were always girls or, if a boy, it was a boy that was "different," much like her.

My husband did have a difficult time during this journey. I allowed our child to play with dolls and such, as that was her preference. (And understand that I now refer to her in the female gender with which she associates.) All the "boy" toys were around, but she rarely played with them. Our older boys had no desire to play with the doll toys preferred by her, reinforcing the fact that there was a difference between these boys. I gently nudged my husband during this lifelong process to open his understanding and perspective. It was difficult in the early years because there was only so far I could push, which meant our daughter was often left hurt and feeling unsupported. One case in point came at Christmas when she was five. She desperately wanted one of those life-size (for a five year old—36") dolls that came with dresses for the owner to not only dress her doll but also wear herself. And when I say desperate, she even said to me that she would "hide it in her closet" if anyone came over. That statement made me so sad. If only she knew what she was saying! I could tell how much she wanted this. She was almost in tears the day she pleaded with me to get it for her. I relayed her desire to my husband and worked on him several weeks to push for it, but this was one he just couldn't do. Not at that time, anyway. And all of that is nothing but society. It's a "but what will people think" type of mindset. To that I say—who cares! Does the way a person chooses to identify himself affect anyone but that single person? Let me answer that for you—no. And would a God whose Golden Rule is to love thy neighbor as thyself follow that up with...but not these neighbors? Again—no. Our job is to love all. That's it. Love them. God will be the judge—that's not our job.

So the journey with our child has not been without its bumps and bruises—for both us and her. John, over time, was able to open his heart and accept his God-given child as she was given. That's a testament to the security he has in his own sense of self and the understanding God led him to in dealing with this situation. As parents, all we ever want is the best for our children.

We want them to be happy, to find love, to fulfill their potential, and to be self-sufficient. We are both now on an even richer spiritual journey that we're taking together. I personally feel I'm in a great space right now when it comes to spirituality and its place in my life. I am richly blessed—not only with the love of my spouse, but God's great love as well.

WHAT ATTRIBUTES HAS YOUR PARTNER BROUGHT TO THIS RELATIONSHIP THAT HAVE NURTURED AND SUSTAINED IT?

Wow. Well, I have to say that without John, our family would not be the family it is today. He brings a lightness to us all when needed. If I start getting too upset at one of the kids and head down a dark path, he'll step in and speak up and remind me to slow down, breathe, and take a break. Sometimes that pisses me off at the time, but I know he's right, and I appreciate that he does it. He is also funny and loves to interject humor into any situation. It's a joy to watch him do this with our kids (now full grown, of course) because they all have the ability to build on it and move it to belly-laughing splendor.

John has been open and accepting to the children we've had come into our home. When our children were young, my sister worked differing shifts with a local police department. Her son was often with us, and many nights she just slept at our place, as we lived closer to her work than she. We also took in two of our nephews at a time when they were causing problems in their adoptive home. John never asked for that, but he was always open and willing to let me do what I felt was my purpose in this life—to help others, especially children and young adults. We currently have two nieces who live with us and that again is testament to his patience and his willingness to allow me to walk my life's path. I know my husband would love to have it be "just the two of us," but I also know he has come to the understanding that that will most likely never happen. Perhaps it will happen for a few years of our life, but with my large family, I can totally imagine that, at some point even after the kids are on their own, it will then be my siblings' turn for assistance. We even joke with a couple of our good friends that their room in our home is "reserved" for their time of need. Being able to share our good fortune makes me happy. I don't know that it necessarily makes John happy, but his desire to bring joy to my life is fulfilled when he allows me to do this. This is such a special quality of his. He truly fulfills me.

John is also extremely detailed and disciplined, unlike me. He has had to get used to living on the fly and going with the flow, as that's more me. That probably makes sense having come from a family of twelve, but I'm sure it drives him nuts sometimes. I don't know how to put his nurturing attributes into words. He truly is my soulmate. I wouldn't be the same person I am without him. I would be—I would exist—but I would be different. He brings a peace to me, and I truly love being with him.

LOOKING BACK AT YOUR MANY YEARS TOGETHER, WHICH AREA OF YOUR LIVES HAS BROUGHT YOU CLOSER TOGETHER?

We started close together and have worked to stay there. I believe growing together throughout time is what **keeps** you close together. Finding an activity to do together, especially if it's something where you discover more about the inner workings of each other, is a great way to stay connected. I guess if I had to give a specific area that has strengthened our closeness, I would have to say the birth of our children and our ever-expanding world of spirituality. It's so much easier when you work to walk the same path. You might not be on the same level of the path as your partner, but as long as you're striving to reach a similar goal, it will do you both good. Let's look at that a second on the spirituality front. If John and I both were on a path of enlightenment, although he chooses to follow a different faith, full enlightenment is still the end goal. Even though he's on a different level of the path than I might be on, we would both be able to discuss what we're going through and look for the similarities, as well as the differences between our two choices. In effect, we are both now learning two different faiths, yet working to obtain a similar goal, which keeps us on a similar path and provides a stimulus to learn more about each other. The opposite of that would be one partner with a desire to reach enlightenment with the other having no spiritual drive at all, leading to an incongruent path. So find something, whatever it is, to work on together.

WHAT ADVICE WOULD YOU HAVE FOR YOUNG LOVERS?

Start talking to each other again!! The introduction of the cell phone and computer has so ruined it for so many people. Text and email are __not__ the way to communicate. There is *so* much more to communication. It includes body language and voice inflection, tone of voice, and speed of dialogue. Learn to read those body cues again! Yes, it's uncomfortable at first, but like anything, practice makes it second nature.

Take relationship seriously. I never heard a more discouraging phrase when it first appeared than "starter marriage." What?! It's not a game! Wait patiently for that someone special to enter your life and then **really** get to know him/ her before moving forward. Spend time finding out everything you can about each other, enough to be serious if you choose to vow a wedded life to each other. Know that it comes with bumps and bruises, and you'll have to pick yourself up time and again, get back on the horse, and do it all over. Love to love, and love to be loved. It's a two-way street, so walk down it with someone who has your back as much as you have his or hers.

Learn to love *yourself*. Spend as much time getting to know yourself and loving yourself as you do someone else. But—do it *first*! It really is true that to love someone else, you must first love yourself. To care for someone else, you must first care for yourself. Learn to be at peace with who you are inside and out. Put in some time to discover how you ended up the way you are today. Do an exercise like this one where you delve into your early childhood and how you felt about your relationship with your parents, siblings, etc. Explore how spirituality plays into your life and how all of it put together has helped shape who you are today. Surrender to it and be comfortable with it, knowing that you are a beautiful soul given to this world to do tremendous things because we are all and have been beautiful souls. Within this discovery of self—meditate. Take time from your busy, hectic schedules to connect with your inner soul.

Remember to **breathe**! Breathing deeply is important to live a long life, reduce stress, and release toxins. It can even make general aches and pains feel better. Google it—do it!

* * *

Live brave.

CLOSER TOGETHER

*"When you graduate from "Being In Love" to
"Loving Someone" you understand Love is not
about owning, Love is about wanting the best for
them, It's about seeing or helping them achieve
great heights, with or without you. Love is not
what you say, it's what you do."*

Wordions

Hilda

I am convinced that we should all put in writing our life stories and carry them around with us to introduce ourselves. Although I have known Victoria and Donald for many years, I didn't truly know their essence and struggles and gains, both individually and as a couple. I met with Victoria for a 'get reacquainted' meeting and then had the honor of presenting for her networking group of successful women. It has been inspiring to observe what she is accomplishing in both her business and personal life. I am currently receiving Donald's *Being 80 and Thriving* monthly newsletter and again excited and not afraid to someday arrive to 80 and continue to thrive. Allow me to introduce my friends.

Victoria, 69

"I have grown in confidence and self-belief that would not have been possible outside a loving relationship."

Married 27 years to Donald

Victoria began her career at Stanford University as a software engineer designing and developing one of the first word processing software systems, a field dominated by men. Her system was utilized for 25 years in universities and research centers around the world and caused the typewriter to become a thing of the past.

The next 20 years of Victoria's career were spent in Silicon Valley, rising quickly through management ranks and ultimately becoming vice president of engineering, marketing, business development, and sales.

A marriage and move to Arizona led Victoria to entrepreneurship as a franchise owner and trainer to over 2000 small business owners in how to build power networks and procure business through network referral marketing techniques. After five years, Victoria launched a coaching and consulting practice in which she found great joy in basing her business success on mutually beneficial relationships.

Following that experience, Victoria became more aware of the differences between men and women business owners at all levels. Women's inequality was well known in the circles of power in corporate America but not talked about as much in small business. With a belief that women must change their relationship with money to have the success they deserve, Victoria's mission became helping women to see their value, to charge appropriately, to build their confidence and to ask for help. In her current career as a financial advisor to women, Victoria is fulfilling her mission by helping them become comfortable with their finances and financially secure.

Title: Finding the "We in Me"

Physical Connection

WHERE WERE YOU BORN AND RAISED, AND WHAT CAN YOU TELL US ABOUT YOUR CHILDHOOD SURROUNDINGS AND CIRCUMSTANCES?

I was born in San Francisco, the second in a family of three girls and one boy. We were raised overseas living in Asia and the Middle East with some stateside years in Alaska. My father was with Pan American airlines, so we could travel anywhere and were able to return home to visit relatives in San Francisco on a regular basis. There were many large family reunions at the home of my grandparents, and they seemed to balance our somewhat unusual world with a sense of normalcy.

My father was a typical corporate executive with long hours away from home. Work was a very high priority. The pressure of work would often follow him home. I felt a lot of stress and tension in our home, mixed with times when my dad would play with us kids with complete abandon.

My mother was a responsible woman, always doing the right thing for her family and friends. She didn't spend much time taking care of herself. The most she would do was get up a few hours earlier than the family to write letters and have her quiet time.

My parents raised us as Catholics amidst the variety of religions we encountered living in foreign lands. There could be a lot of guilt in our house; it was a powerful presence that was emphasized by the teachings of our church.

We had a very strong sense of family and values that I appreciate to this day. While we were raised with servants in exotic places for much of our childhood, we somehow valued a strong work ethic and doing for others who had less.

It was a good family by outside appearances but we lacked any sense of carefree joy within our walls. Strange lands, an unusually large number of medical problems among the kids, and a single income left its mark, causing a great deal of stress and worry at times for my parents.

We had everything we needed and more than many and from parents who loved us. We didn't express much affection in our home, but I never left the house or went to bed without saying goodnight to my parents with a light kiss on the cheek.

How old were you when you had your first crush relationship, and how did it eventually develop or end?

I was very shy and didn't have much interest in boys. I had friends who were boys through high school but no boyfriends.

I finally had a crush in my senior year, and it was a big one. Pete was very tall and good looking. Tall was important since I stood 5' 10" in high school. Pete was fairly popular and already out of high school; he made it very clear he wasn't interested in me even as a friend. I felt so rejected and hurt that I decided not to let my heart be broken again. Going back to my comfort zone, I went to my senior prom with a boy who was just a friend.

I did date in college but not very much. In a women's college, we met boys in artificial situations like mixers at men's colleges and frat parties at universities, which were not the most comfortable settings for me. I finally met the man I thought I would marry in my junior year, and we were informally engaged as I entered graduate school. He went on to his first job, and the real world showed his values were quite different from mine. Judging potential friends by what they could do for his career, he left my friends out of the picture. Friendships were very important to me, and I was not ready to abandon them. He abruptly broke up with me, leaving me puzzled and disturbed that I knew someone so little and yet was planning to marry him. Once again I was disillusioned about love and threw myself into my studies and then my career.

I never dated casually like most of my friends. I had several long-term committed relationships with men who were connected to my field of high tech in Silicon Valley. They could understand and even share a commitment to career and long hours at work. I was engaged one more time over the years only to break the engagement, knowing deep down it wouldn't work.

I was passionate about my career and loved the excitement of high tech challenges and professional achievements. It did get in the way of most of my relationships as I continued to be promoted beyond my boyfriends in both title and income. By my 40th birthday, I was grateful for my wonderful friends and my rewarding career and decided that was enough. I concluded that as women we can't have it all, but I did love the part of life that was mine.

CURRENTLY, HOW DO YOU RATE YOUR PHYSICAL AND MENTAL HEALTH, AND HOW DOES IT AFFECT YOUR RELATIONSHIP?

My physical and mental health are both excellent at this stage and age in life. My husband taught me to make health a priority. We share a healthy diet and exercise routine that serves us well as we continue to age with excellent health. It is very important in our relationship as a value and as a state of mind. Being healthy starts with an attitude that inspires the discipline to do what it takes to be healthy.

My emotional health has been problematic for much of my life. My addiction to work, achievement, and perfectionism wreaked havoc on my inner joy, self-acceptance, and relationships. I have found the deepest emotional healing through the loving trust-based connection I have with my husband. He continually sees me as wonderful, strong, and remarkable. Daily expressions of his delight in me for almost 29 years have healed the deepest wounds from childhood and given me the space to discover I am a remarkable person with many gifts to contribute to the world. I have grown in confidence and self-belief that would not have been possible outside a loving relationship.

Both physical and mental health are important to enjoying our relationship and life together, as well as being a gift of the relationship.

ARE YOU PHYSICALLY CONNECTED TO YOUR PARTNER? IF SO, HOW DO YOU KEEP THAT CONNECTION ALIVE? HOW IMPORTANT IS PHYSICAL CONNECTION TO YOUR RELATIONSHIP?

Yes, we are physically connected and make that part of our relationship a priority. At the lightest level, we never walk anywhere that we don't automatically hold hands. We sit side by side on the couch to watch a movie. I feel the loving energy anytime he touches me with even the lightest touch.

Our deeper physical connection is a place of deep emotional connection for me while Donald feels more from a physical perspective. While I think this may be common for men and women, I know Donald appreciates the deep emotional connection of love and trust that I enjoy.

I have never experienced this level of intimacy before and never was able to trust enough to enjoy it or feel truly connected. I can feel totally vulnerable and trust when Donald fills my entire being...both body and soul.

Emotional Responsiveness

WHAT DID YOUR PARENTS MODEL FOR YOU AS A CHILD ABOUT MARRIAGE? HOW DID YOU CONNECT WITH YOUR MOTHER? DESCRIBE YOUR RELATIONSHIP WITH YOUR FATHER.

Marriage was "until death do us part" for my parents. They didn't display much affection at home; my mother seemed to be embarrassed by it. Their issues and discussions were hidden from us children. Mother made it clear they lived at a different level from the children, and we were not allowed any insight into that world.

They didn't discuss money or sex and thought it should never be discussed outside the bedroom. I often felt the tension but never knew what was causing it. I lived a tentative life, not wanting to set off an explosion of emotion, which would happen when things got too tense. The cause was always some incidental trigger that had very little if anything to do with the real reason.

It felt as if the children were the cause of most of the upset and unhappiness with my parents. Feeling very guilty for their unhappiness, I tried very hard to be a good girl and not cause them grief. I learned to read the emotions and feelings of others at an early age. I was the peacemaker of the family and, in many ways, the caretaker of my mother's upset feelings.

My older sister didn't experience the emotional tension in the same way. Today she remembers the temper flare-ups and anger from my father but not the deep emotional things that set it off. My other sister and brother were ten years younger and seemed to be raised in a different family. My older sister and I were buffers for them in many ways, and we clung to each other for support and understanding.

As a young adult I wondered why they stayed together, in spite of the apparent unhappiness much of the time. I don't know if it was being Catholic, for the sake of the children, or just not knowing how to dissolve the marriage and find a new life. It was a different time, and divorce was not the solution it has become today. I think this view of marriage kept me from risking a mistake. While I never experienced the pain of divorce in my childhood, I knew I would rather live single than risk the emotional destruction that seemed to accompany divorce.

WHAT WERE YOU LOOKING FOR WHEN YOU DECIDED TO MARRY YOUR PARTNER, AND WHAT DID YOU KNOW FOR SURE ABOUT YOURSELF?

I was not looking for anything or anyone when I decided to marry Donald. I met him at 41 and had decided my life was too happy to compromise with a marriage that was less than ideal. I enjoyed an independent life, close friendships, and an exciting career.

I had left corporate earlier that year thinking it wasn't as satisfying as it had once been, and I needed to rethink my life direction. That didn't include marriage as an option. When I met Donald, I knew I was happy on my own, and I had decided to give up looking or risking another painful and disappointing relationship.

I decided to marry him because it seemed like the natural thing to do. We had been dating only a few months, yet we knew and trusted each other at a deep level. I revealed to him all the flaws that I hid from the outside world, and he loved me for my true self. I had never been able to be so authentic with anyone in my life, and I knew I wanted that for the rest of my life, no matter what the risk of heartache might be in the future.

I was not even conscious of my deepest need until Donald filled it. I wanted more than anything in the world to feel like I belonged. To find the "we in me" that I had never known before. That feeling, that bliss I felt when I married him, continues to this day with an exclusiveness that can be frightening at times. There is no one who knows me better than Donald. There could be no one who loves me more completely and unconditionally.

WHAT SIGNIFICANT MEMORIES DO YOU HAVE AS YOU WERE GETTING TO KNOW EACH OTHER? WHAT DO YOU REMEMBER MOST ABOUT THE FIRST TIME YOU MET?

I will never forget the first time I saw Donald. I was at a stop sign on one of those famous hills in San Francisco. With my car poised at the top of the hill, I saw him outlined against the blue sky walking across the street. He had such an eager bounce in his step; I could only think this man must be wearing comfortable shoes. I was very surprised to see him sitting in the seminar room when I arrived for the session.

A mutual friend asked us to sit in on a dry run for a two-day workshop called Life Planning. She wanted our feedback to help them prepare to roll this seminar out across the country.

In this workshop we evaluated our life and looked at how to live at the highest level in relationship, financial, learning, career, health, family, and other important areas. Unlike Donald, I had never done any personal development work. Having just left corporate some six months earlier to find more meaning in life, I was ready for the questions and the opportunity to design my life. I was not, however, ready to meet anyone and, in fact, had decided a relationship was not in the cards for me.

Looking back on the workshop, Donald and I were clear on our life values and how we wanted to live. We were able to share that as we started our relationship after the workshop. The workshop designer went on to develop the curriculum that became the well-known Coach University that launched the life coaching industry. We went on to develop a partnership for life that gets better with each year.

We chatted at breaks and lunch during the weekend workshop. We made a lunch date the next week to discuss collaborating on a consulting project. I didn't think anything other than a professional opportunity. In fact, I thought he was married.

We were both very surprised to learn by accident that neither one of us was in a committed relationship. Suddenly, our business lunch turned into a personal conversation that ended by making a date for the following weekend.

After our first date, we both said goodbye to the people we were dating and have been together every day since. It felt so comfortable to be in the same space with him. I had never even lived with anyone before. Feeling safe and easy sharing my space was a new feeling for me.

He was different from any man I had ever dated. My life had been so corporate, so career minded and serious. This man stretched my comfort zone and led me into many new adventures that were fun and, at the same time, a bit scary. I knew deep in my heart, however, that it was safe to love him and that he would never knowingly hurt me.

People we met at events thought we had been together our entire lives. Seven weeks after we met, he asked me to marry him. While we waited a few months to tell the world, we felt like a couple, and I finally knew the feeling of belonging in the world.

It happened so easily and effortlessly. I could hardly believe it and waited every day to wake up from a dream. It was wonderful, and I never had to wake up!

SURELY THERE WERE CHALLENGES ALONG THE WAY IN YOUR RELATIONSHIP. HOW HAVE YOU LEARNED TO WORK EFFECTIVELY WITH THOSE CHALLENGES?

I was plagued by severe depression during my 20s and 30s. Being a workaholic allowed me to succeed professionally while staying crippled emotionally. A month before we were married, I checked into a women's hospital in the worst emotional state I had ever experienced. My long-time therapist explained that turning on the faucet of my feelings allowed all the feelings to come out after years of suppressing them. I was not ready to handle all the memories of child-hood wounds. I knew I could not start our married life this way.

Donald came to the hospital every evening for weeks on his way home from work. It was a very intense time. Women around me literally turned schizo-phrenic as they tried to hide from their deepest fears and darkness. Donald never worried. He saw the light side of me and encouraged me to explore my own shadows and trust in his love for me no matter what. The power of love is beyond description and can dissolve any challenge. It brought us closer than ever, and the trust we knew deepened even further. We haven't had many chal-lenges after that, at least not that severe. I continued to heal.

I was surprised how quickly I trusted Donald. We were dating less than two months, and I agreed to marry him. I was afraid my family and friends would think it was a mid-life crisis so we hid our engagement from them for two months.

I knew in my heart we belonged together when I realized I was easily sharing my space with him. I showed him my true self, no masks, no hiding. I had never lived with anyone before, but I felt safe and comfortable having Donald move in very quickly. I trusted my love for him was real because I felt like we really belonged together. It was not fireworks and chemistry so much as a feel-ing of deep trust, safety, and feeling cherished that helped me recognize it was a forever love.

After we were married, we grew in love and friendship. We are fortunate to have good health, thanks to Donald's priority of healthy living. Our physical needs have always been met, and we have always enjoyed a strong circle of friends and support.

We have had many stressful life changes that allowed us to learn and grow. We took on those challenges together, and he supported every major change that I felt compelled to make. I appreciate his trust and support for me through every major change. The reward has been a better life at every turn.

I asked him to move to the desert from the Bay Area after spending a weekend in Scottsdale and falling in love with the desert. We left friends and family behind without question. This is truly home for us and the best move we ever made.

I changed careers, leaving the security of a paycheck to become an entrepreneur. I continue to make career changes even into retirement with his full support. Each time I start over and find a deeper way to make a difference for people. I am driven by passion that fuels my energy. It is rewarding even if tiring along the way. Donald is a calm, low stress person. It is like riding on the top of a moving train to live with me sometimes. He always handles it and keeps me grounded. We have succeeded with every leap forward, and the adventure continues.

The way we work through challenges big or small is to sink into the security and comfort of our love and friendship. There have been challenges, but I never had to face them alone and that has made all the difference.

Spiritual Significance

DO YOU AND YOUR PARTNER SHARE THE SAME SPIRITUAL BELIEF, AND IF NOT, HOW DO YOU FIND YOUR WAY THROUGH IT? IF YOU RAISED CHILDREN TOGETHER, HOW WERE THEY RAISED SPIRITUALLY?

We came from two very different sets of beliefs. I considered myself very ecumenical having lived among so many different religions. Donald was not religious...he was truly spiritual. He seemed to feel a deep connection to the creative power of the universe while I only had well-defined concepts from my Catholic upbringing. He was free to explore without fear of punishment.

When we were first together, we had a lot of experiences that were typically "California" but not typically me. We went to a metaphysical church on our first date! After dating for two weeks, we decided to go away for New Year's with a group of people from the church who promoted the idea of starting the New Year planting trees in an area of California that had been burned out by forest fires. I loved the idea of "planting our hopes and dreams" for the year ahead with every sapling we put into the ground. I never imagined until we arrived that this group were "tree worshipers"!

The food was supplied by Pagan Plates, a group of women who were truly earth mamas who had somehow held onto their hippie image into the late 1980's. I was ready to leave the minute we arrived. Donald assured me we could leave at any time. With that reassurance, we literally took it one moment at a time.

We met some delightful, kind people and had a weekend to remember forever. I will never forget the New Year's Eve celebration, a ritual performed by the caterers, the four earth mamas, who danced inside a circle with hair flying amidst the children who beamed with their little faces painted fanciful colors. The women called in the New Year by addressing the four directions and chanted to the spirits of good much like a Native American ceremony. I was fascinated and terrified all at once. All I could think was how horrified my Catholic mother would be if she could see me now. At 41, I was highly sophisticated in the business world and very protected in life and love. I kept repeating to myself "breathe" and "he will never hurt you; this man loves you." I would use those mantras on other occasions throughout our courtship as he introduced me to his world of adventure and discovery.

I think that would have frightened me away actually if we didn't express and share the same values. We had met in a workshop called Life Planning where one of the exercises was to rank a list of values and discover your top three. At the end of the day, we had the same values of spiritual growth, relationship, and learning. That foundation made it safe to explore other ways of thinking and believing that helped me take more responsibility for my life.

Donald has discovered many teachers over the years who contribute to our spiritual growth. I had trouble being open to a new perspective. I shift my paradigms slowly while Donald seems to recognize a new truth and eagerly embraces it to learn more. To this day I feel increasingly empowered to create my life in partnership with my spiritual self. My human failings of the past have become teaching tools versus cause for punishment and condemnation.

I enjoy discussing spiritual beliefs and learning from the different perspective of others. Early in our relationship, we explored many new ideas. I honestly wondered if he was leading me astray with his spiritual freedom and if I would suffer eternal damnation for my foolishness. I have come to realize I am truly in partnership with my creator, and I am allowed to explore my spirituality and grow.

I now embrace a truly light and loving creator of all that is versus a power that demands obedience and adherence to a set of rules. Guilt was slowly replaced by hope. I had to trust him and his inherent goodness to move into that way of thinking. It has been freeing and contributed immensely to my highest value of spiritual growth.

**WHAT ATTRIBUTES HAS YOUR PARTNER BROUGHT TO THIS RELATION-
SHIP THAT HAVE NURTURED AND SUSTAINED IT?**

Donald has always believed a perfect relationship was possible. He searched for half his life until he found me. He truly believed he had reached success when he found the perfect relationship for me.

I never believed in perfect relationships. I think that doubt caused me to test our relationship in many unconscious ways in the early years. Steadfast in his belief, he never took the bait and was not threatened by my tests. He saw them as ways to grow and deepen our trust with each test he passed.

His perspective keeps him focused on what is good in our life and how grateful he is for our partnership. He overlooks my flaws and growing pains as I work my way through them. He sees all as a process of growth and, as he says, it is getting better all the time. He easily brings me back to the feeling of being adored.

I think it is natural to blame discomfort and negative emotions on your trusted partner. It is often safer to find excuses outside ourselves than it is to face what needs to change within us.

We have the same quirks and differences that naturally exist in any relationship between two people. We can't possibly hear every word as it is intended or understand the motivation and intention behind every action.

I have always noticed I can stop short of blaming when I remember and trust that he would never knowingly hurt me. Little things that I observe causing upset between spouses are short-circuited somehow before I snap at him. I am able to catch my knee-jerk reaction and choose my response. My relationship with Donald is the only area of my life that I notice a consistent ability to stop a reaction. The emotional reactions that get the better of me with other people don't have the same power with Donald. We aren't perfect, but we are aware and can talk about things that come up between us.

There was a brief period of our life when we were under a great deal of stress! I would find myself snapping and reacting before I could stop it. He never hung on to any of it, and we ultimately came back together. As soon as the stressful situations (yes, there were four going on at one time) were resolved, we returned to our state of intentional awareness and gentleness with each other.

I learned from that experience not to allow anything to stress me so much that I forget what we have and risk any bruises or damage, no matter how temporary. Our relationship is truly a gift and the most precious thing in life. We both agreed the stress had caused risk to our relationship, but we came through the year with a sense of renewed partnership and happiness.

Is it possible for a couple with a great relationship to go to the next level after 25+ years? Absolutely, and the excitement and gift of rediscovery makes the journey worthwhile.

Donald sustains our relationship with his regard for me. He expresses his love and deep appreciation for me daily. Feeling precious is a great reminder that he would never knowingly hurt me and that will sustain us forever!

LOOKING BACK AT YOUR MANY YEARS TOGETHER, WHICH AREA OF YOUR LIVES HAS BROUGHT YOU CLOSER TOGETHER?

Emotional growth and new adventures! Evolving as a person brings challenges and pain that can only be shared with a trusted partner. It is hard to see the one you love in pain. It is worth it to see them discover who they are. Donald does that with ease and grace.

He believes I am a remarkable woman. He never worries that I will hit the wall. It is empowering to experience that trust in me. At the same time, it can be challenging when he just won't go into the rabbit hole with me. Sometimes, sympathy and company feels better than belief.

His consistency over the years and his certainty that all is truly well with me and us bring us closer together. I sometimes see myself flying into the chasm of worry and fear only to feel the welcome tug of a safety line when I want to come back into the comfort of gratitude and trust in life.

His practicality and belief that our life together gets better all the time is at once a source of frustration and humor. I often joke that he doesn't need to worry because I do enough for both of us. Even a few friends who know us well can see him as a "bubble man" living in the belief that bad things have never happened to him and never will.

On the light side, we love new adventures. He typically thinks them up, and I go along with some trepidation, mixed with excitement.

We have had many adventures over the years that involved new places, new people, and new homes. We still make note of firsts and appreciate that we have so many even though we started our marriage half way through life. While our adventures have shifted from physical to more mental and learning, they are fun to share and to allow us to satisfy the love of learning and growth we both share.

WHAT ADVICE WOULD YOU HAVE FOR YOUNG LOVERS?

Be completely authentic in your relationship. Allow your beloved to see all the areas you hide from the world and you will find a deep trust that can last a lifetime.

When someone truly knows you and loves you for who you are, it becomes unconditional and a source of belonging that is rare. A feeling of being loved and accepted by another person can help transcend any challenges and misunderstandings.

Share your values early in your relationship. Understand and honor each other's values, and you will maintain trust. Small misunderstandings can be resolved. Your values are truly who you are and cannot withstand betrayal.

If you build a relationship of trust and authenticity, you will have what I know as the greatest gift in life.

* * *

Live brave.

Donald, 81

"Looking at my failed relationships, I realized that I had never allowed myself to be vulnerable, to completely trust my mate with my heart, and I realized that I had to do that in order to receive it."

Donald's professional career was nearly all about telephones! He began his career as a technician for the Bell System, held management positions at several aerospace companies, and served as consultant/project manager on large telecomm installations. His last eight years of employment were with DHL as a telecomm engineer. At age 62 he was laid off and never worked for another corporation.

Donald has been assisting his wife, Victoria, with her businesses since he left corporate in 1997. He has found that it requires less and less of his time and that the secret to aging gracefully is to be engaged with projects that matter to him and, hopefully, others.

Several years ago he decided to learn the most beneficial habits to keeping healthy and vibrant as he neared his 80th birthday, and it's working! He decided to share this information with a blog called "being 80 ...and thriving" (www.being80.com) and sending a monthly health bulletin to his subscribers from whom he receives a gratifying response.

Married 27 years to Victoria

Title: Blissful Partners

Physical Connection

Where were you born and raised, and what can you tell us about your childhood surroundings and circumstances?

I was born in 1935 at the site of a huge construction project, the building of the Grand Coulee Dam on the Columbia River in Washington State. When I was about two, my mom divorced my dad and moved, along with four kids, to a small town in the San Juan Islands in northwestern Washington where she had a sister. My mom had no income, but she managed to get us a house on five acres with a barn and a stream running through. We had no running water, but that house was my favorite.

When I was about five, my mom married Frank Trafton, who was a least twenty years her senior. She married him for the financial support; there was no love. Frank adopted me and my little brother and gave us his name. He was well-meaning but never showed any affection. (My mom didn't either.) As it turned out, Frank wasn't a very good provider, but my mom stayed with him until my brother and I were out of high school.

HOW OLD WERE YOU WHEN YOU HAD YOUR FIRST CRUSH RELATIONSHIP, AND HOW DID IT EVENTUALLY DEVELOP OR END?

In high school I longed to be with girls, but I lacked the confidence to even talk to them, let alone ask any girl out on a date, so I missed all the proms and parties. At the very end of my senior year, I finally worked up the courage to ask a girl on a date. She let me know that she knew it was my first date. You can't get by with anything in a small town.

The following summer I operated a machine that loaded pea vines on trucks in the pea fields to transport the pea vines to nearby canneries. Two of the truck drivers were teenage girls, both really cute, and they flirted with me constantly. They didn't know about my limited girl experience, and with much more confidence, I dated both before we all went off to different colleges. That was my springboard to the dating game, and I got pretty good at it. No sex yet.

I was 19 and in my second year at the University of Washington, Seattle, when I met and fell in love with Jeannie. She was cute and smart and loved sex. We were in love and planned to get married, but I had to drop out of college (poor grades, no funding). After two years of floundering and finally taking a low-paying job with the telephone company, she gave up on me. I really couldn't blame her. She and her family were right; I didn't have a very bright future.

CURRENTLY, HOW DO YOU RATE YOUR PHYSICAL AND MENTAL HEALTH, AND HOW DOES IT AFFECT YOUR RELATIONSHIP?

I'm very pleased with my physical and mental health. Over the years I've made it my top priority, and now it's paying big dividends. I've attracted the all-time best love of my life. In my wildest dreams, I couldn't imagine that life could be this good.

ARE YOU PHYSICALLY CONNECTED TO YOUR PARTNER? IF SO, HOW DO YOU KEEP THAT CONNECTION ALIVE? HOW IMPORTANT IS PHYSICAL

CONNECTION TO YOUR RELATIONSHIP?

Our physical connection is a very high priority for us both. We make it special every time. I feel that it's the ultimate way to nurture. We do every physical activity together that we possibly can, including walking, exercise, yoga, movies, eating; we relish the opportunity to be together.

Emotional Responsiveness

WHAT DID YOUR PARENTS MODEL FOR YOU AS A CHILD ABOUT MARRIAGE? HOW DID YOU CONNECT WITH YOUR MOTHER? DESCRIBE YOUR RELATIONSHIP WITH YOUR FATHER.

My mother divorced my father when I was about three years old. It was a bitter divorce, and my father was not allowed to visit. When I finally met him (I was 15), I immediately liked him, and although he lived 400 miles away, I made it a priority to get to know him as best I could. When I was 18 through my early 20s, I'd drive the 400 miles to spend weekends with Don (yes, I am Don, Jr.) and his new wife and kids. I did that trip about six times. He was a truck driver, so I'd ride with him on some long road trips. Unfortunately, we couldn't really talk much in the truck cab though.

My mother was not physically affectionate. I don't remember her and my stepfather ever embracing or kissing. My stepfather tried to be a good provider, but I never felt close to him.

WHAT WERE YOU LOOKING FOR WHEN YOU DECIDED TO MARRY YOUR PARTNER, AND WHAT DID YOU KNOW FOR SURE ABOUT YOURSELF?

This is my third marriage. I had to get this one right. First and foremost, I was looking for real intimacy. Looking at my failed relationships, I realized that I had never allowed myself to be vulnerable, to completely trust my mate with my heart, and I realized that I had to do that in order to receive it. One way that I am vulnerable and completely trust my wife with my heart is when I make financial decisions without her agreement that could make us liable for thousands of dollars. She is very angry, of course, but she's never made me feel that she would withdraw her love. Now we have an agreement about spending: if the pending expenditure is over $200, we must consult the other before either of us can proceed.

WHAT SIGNIFICANT MEMORIES DO YOU HAVE AS YOU WERE GETTING TO KNOW EACH OTHER? WHAT DO YOU REMEMBER MOST ABOUT THE FIRST TIME YOU MET?

The first time we met I was very impressed, but I thought she was already in a committed relationship. Later, when we met for a business lunch, I learned that she was dating but open to exploring a relationship with me. Our backgrounds and experiences were not very similar, but she trusted me right from the start, demonstrating the willingness and courage to explore my unfamiliar world. I kept thinking, "This is the most courageous woman I have ever known."

When we met, I had been doing years of self-development classes (like EST) and had developed a rather "free spirit" lifestyle. She was a practicing Catholic. I had been raised as a Christian Scientist. On our very first date I took her to a very unorthodox church where they practiced "messages from the spirits" and did tarot card readings. I was so impressed with her openness and acceptance of ME and my very different lifestyle.

There was a poster at the church announcing a three-day tree planting event at a "rustic" hot springs resort in northern California, and she agreed to go with me. It turned out to be more rustic than either of us expected. Our sleeping accommodations were in sleeping bags with more than 100 tree worshipers on the floor of an auditorium. The resort turned out to be "clothing optional." Thankfully, it was quite cold (January 1st), so there weren't many people running around naked.

SURELY THERE WERE CHALLENGES ALONG THE WAY IN YOUR RELATIONSHIP. HOW HAVE YOU LEARNED TO WORK EFFECTIVELY WITH THOSE CHALLENGES?

There were a few big challenges in the beginning. She admitted to being seriously flawed and unfixable, and I kept assuring her that she was fine just the way she was, and I wasn't going to leave her ...ever. I've watched her blossom into the most incredible woman I've ever known. Our years and experiences together have brought us closer and closer. Today our relationship is the best it has ever been.

I can't recall a single time that we've been so angry at each other that we've had a shouting match or needed a "cooling off" period. Typically, our disagreements involve her being fearful of something that I am not. I have learned to acknowledge the reality of her fear even when there is no real basis and to agree with her that we don't make an important decision unless she is sufficiently comfortable. Yes, we talk and share our feelings, and yes, we take turns listening to each other ...all the time.

Spiritual Significance

DO YOU AND YOUR PARTNER SHARE THE SAME SPIRITUAL BELIEF, AND IF NOT, HOW DO YOU FIND YOUR WAY THROUGH IT? IF YOU RAISED CHILDREN TOGETHER, HOW WERE THEY RAISED SPIRITUALLY?

The spiritual belief we share is that the universe and everything in it, including us, evolves from one source, and that source is what we call God or Love. There is no beginning or end for us, just the continual evolving. We exist simultaneously in physical and nonphysical form, which means that while our physical self will end, our nonphysical self continues forever, and we can return to the physical world whenever we choose. (This removes all fear of dying). Our purpose here is to expand our experience of joy ...that's it. We have felt at home attending both Unity and Science of Mind churches, and currently attend the Scottsdale Center for Spiritual Living, mainly for the fellowship. We practice a guided meditation as part of our morning program ...each and every morning.

WHAT ATTRIBUTES HAS YOUR PARTNER BROUGHT TO THIS RELATIONSHIP THAT HAVE NURTURED AND SUSTAINED IT?

The list is long. She is smart, attentive, caring, giving, perceptive, trusting (that's a huge one). She also cares a lot about how she looks and feels, which is very important to me. Undoubtedly, her presence in my life has helped me become a whole, more loving human being. I am more than grateful to have her as an essential part of my life.

LOOKING BACK AT YOUR MANY YEARS TOGETHER, WHICH AREA OF YOUR LIVES HAS BROUGHT YOU CLOSER TOGETHER?

Honestly, I relish the time I get to spend with Victoria, no matter what we're doing. I can't remember any time that I wanted to be by myself. But if I had to choose one area that is absolutely my favorite, it has to be those "most intimate" connection times. Amazingly, these "play times" are getting better and better.

WHAT ADVICE WOULD YOU HAVE FOR YOUNG LOVERS?

Try to keep your attention and focus on those qualities you most admire about your partner, especially when he or she does something that angers you. I know our first impulse is to let that person know that you feel threatened. But can you see how destructive that is? Remember, trust is fragile. Everything you think and everything you say about your mate either brings you closer together or pulls you apart.

This is the moment, the opportunity, to bring your partner close, to bond, to make your union tighter. Remind them about the qualities you admire most in them. Give some examples of where they have shined. Point out that although this is a slip, it's not a fall. You've got their back on every action they take. Let them know that they will have your unwavering trust, and together, you two will resolve whatever comes your way for the greater good.

* * *

Live brave.

CLOSER TOGETHER

"I love that you get cold when it's 71 degrees out. I love that it takes you an hour and a half to order a sandwich. I love that you get a little crinkle above your nose when you're looking at me like I'm nuts. I love that after I spend the day with you, I can still smell your perfume on my clothes. And I love that you are the last person I want to talk to before I go to sleep at night. And it's not because I'm lonely, and it's not because it's New Year's Eve. I came here tonight because when you realize you want to spend the rest of your life with somebody, you want the rest of your life to start as soon as possible."

Nora Ephron, When Harry Met Sally

Hilda

These days EVERYONE is busy! Everyone has piles of stuff to get through and even the ones who are semi-retired, like Ron, have much going on to fill their plates with delicious things to savor. Both Ron and Lory are involved and engaged in their professional, personal and creative lives. As you will read, their interests are varied and adventurous and they have kept their lives this way from the beginning. But, just as all of the others who have so graciously taken the time to contribute to *Living Brave In Love*, neither hesitated to say yes to us. We are grateful for their open and generous hearts in sharing their lives. I am truly honored to introduce this amazing couple to you.

Ron, 69

"I fell in love when I least expected it and at a time when I had my guard down. I found my best friend and soul mate."

Ron attended Harvard College, Dartmouth, and Harvard Medical Schools and completed pediatric residency at Tufts and the University of Colorado. He spent three years in the Indian Health Service in San Carlos, Arizona, and became Assistant Professor of Family Medicine and Pediatrics at the University of Arizona College of Medicine in Tucson, where he published scientific papers and won awards for teaching and community service. He moved to Phoenix to become Director of Outpatient Pediatrics at St. Joseph's Hospital and, at age 40, started his private practice of pediatrics in north Scottsdale. Over the years, the practice has grown to fifteen doctors; he has been voted "Top Doc" and "Best Doctors in America" and continues to teach medical students. He has been involved in medical leadership as Chair of Pediatrics and President of the Medical Staff at Scottsdale Healthcare and as President of the Arizona Chapter of the American Academy of Pediatrics.

He is now semi-retired, works part time, and spends summers on the coast of Maine with his wife, Lory, and family. He has recently taken up silversmithing and enjoys sailing; he and his wife share an active sports life playing mixed doubles tennis, golf, and skiing.

Married 47 years to Lory

Title: Friends and Companions for a Lifetime

Physical Connection

WHERE WERE YOU BORN AND RAISED, AND WHAT CAN YOU TELL US ABOUT YOUR CHILDHOOD SURROUNDINGS AND CIRCUMSTANCES?

I was born in Boston as the only child of older parents. My father was 47, my mother 45. They emigrated from Austria in 1939 to escape the Nazi persecution of Jews. We lived in a lower-middle-class area of Boston in a three room apartment. I shared the bedroom with my mother; my father slept on a couch in the living room, which doubled as his office. My mother was a milliner, making hats in the city; my father was a wholesaler of phonograph records, a small business he conducted from our apartment. I walked to school but had to watch out for gangs after dark. When I was ten, we moved to Brookline, a middle-class and largely Jewish neighborhood a few miles away, with excellent schools. We rented a five room apartment in a house, and I now had my own bedroom.

When I was eleven, my mother had several lung operations for cancer. We went to see her homeland--Austria for the summer, and a year later she died. I spent adolescence trying to patch the large hole left by my mother's absence, helping with household chores, doing well at school, and struggling against my father's strong views about what I should do. I was accepted to Harvard on a full scholarship, and my fortunes changed.

HOW OLD WERE YOU WHEN YOU HAD YOUR FIRST CRUSH RELATION-SHIP, AND HOW DID IT EVENTUALLY DEVELOP OR END?

My first crush was as a junior in high school with a girl named Barbara. She was very sweet and cute, and came from a good family. We went out together to movies, bowling, and "necking." While it lasted over a year, it was obvious to us at senior prom that going off to college meant it was time to move on. We parted as friends.

CURRENTLY, HOW DO YOU RATE YOUR PHYSICAL AND MENTAL HEALTH, AND HOW DOES IT AFFECT YOUR RELATIONSHIP?

My physical health has been largely very good with a few chronic back pain issues that have not limited physical activity. I have struggled at times with anxiety and depression. Clearly, I am the one in the relationship who has been "high maintenance," and my wife has been a steady source of comfort and counsel over the years. At times I have resorted to professional counseling.

While I dated a lot in college, Lory was the first woman that I was attracted to physically and as a friend at the same time. Prior to meeting Lory, I found I was either physically attracted or had friendships but never both together, and it didn't take very long to appreciate how special this relationship was.

ARE YOU PHYSICALLY CONNECTED TO YOUR PARTNER? IF SO, HOW DO YOU KEEP THAT CONNECTION ALIVE? HOW IMPORTANT IS PHYSICAL CONNECTION TO YOUR RELATIONSHIP?

I think the physical connection is very important. I think Lory also valued the importance of nurturing the physical attractiveness part of our relationship.

At times her weight made her feel less attractive; we'd talk about it, and she worked hard to get it back into control and she did. I saw that as a gift to us and to me. There were times when we drifted apart emotionally and physically but have always been open with each other and found our way back. We both share the commitment to our romance; we have always made time for dates together and romantic getaways, even during our childrearing years.

Emotional Responsiveness

WHAT DID YOUR PARENTS MODEL FOR YOU AS A CHILD ABOUT MARRIAGE? HOW DID YOU CONNECT WITH YOUR MOTHER? DESCRIBE YOUR RELATIONSHIP WITH YOUR FATHER.

My parent's relationship was not something that I wanted to emulate. Nor do I have an adult's understanding of it since my mother died when I was twelve. I remember my mother's warmth and her being social. My father was a loner, worried a lot about everything, and had very strong views which he foisted on me. He did model enjoying life when on vacation and out from the burdens of daily life and work. He encouraged me in sports like skiing and tennis. I started working at fifteen so I could buy things that I wanted. There were many conflicts between us as I began to assert my independence.

WHAT WERE YOU LOOKING FOR WHEN YOU DECIDED TO MARRY YOUR PARTNER, AND WHAT DID YOU KNOW FOR SURE ABOUT YOURSELF?

I fell in love when I least expected it and at a time when I had my guard down. I found my best friend and soul mate. I felt better in her presence, and the more time we spent together the better I liked it. I was twenty two and a first year medical student when we met. At three months we became exclusive, at six months we became engaged, and we married about a year after we met. We shared views about family. She was willing to be adaptable to my career, and I was committed to making sure that the choices I made about where to go were acceptable to her.

WHAT SIGNIFICANT MEMORIES DO YOU HAVE AS YOU WERE GETTING TO KNOW EACH OTHER? WHAT DO YOU REMEMBER MOST ABOUT THE FIRST TIME YOU MET?

Lory called me a week before I was heading from Cambridge, Massachusetts, to Hanover, New Hampshire, to start medical school. I was not looking for love but was open to meeting this charming and forward woman who called to invite me to play bridge. She was trying to arrange a date for her roommate and had learned from a mutual friend that I played bridge. Lory had just come off a summer relationship in Italy and also was off guard. I brought the fourth, a high school friend who was heading off to law school. They cheated, we won, and we laughed a lot. The next night she called again; this time her friend made a pass at me, which I rejected. The mood in the room became seriously deflated, so Lory and I went for a walk. We walked all over Boston and wandered into an old movie theater where they were playing the trailer for what would become the movie *Woodstock*. It was the summer of 1969 and a magical time. Lory visited me at Dartmouth every other weekend. We went hiking, horseback riding, skiing, and hanging out with my friends and fellow students. She fit into my life. She passed all the "physical tests" of endurance. We shared a love of theater. After our marriage on a very rainy day, we spent our first year as caretakers of a gorgeous farm house in Vermont overlooking the Connecticut River. Lory taught English and drama at a local high school. We drove to California for the summer where I had a summer job near the beach, and then back to Boston where we lived in a studio apartment in a high rise building near the medical school. Lory took a job as an administrative assistant at Massachusetts General Hospital. After three years in Boston and because of my low draft number in the Vietnam War era, (they were drafting doctors then and I was very opposed to the war), I joined the Indian Health Service and was sent to San Carlos, Arizona, about a two hour drive from Phoenix, and our next adventure was to begin.

It was a rural community; we lived on the hospital compound and we shared a special experience and made lifelong friends. We worked on trying to become pregnant but struggled. Lory had an infertility evaluation and had several procedures, which, at that time, were ineffective. We spent three years in San Carlos, where we explored the Southwest, learned a lot about Native American culture, and collected baskets, and Lory began painting. She played basketball and volleyball in local leagues and taught weight reduction classes for the Apaches. Then we moved to Denver for me to finish residency training. We bought our first house—I made the furniture out of pine; she made cushions and decorated the house. She found work at the University Poison Control Center as an administrative assistant.

While we would have liked to stay in Denver, there were no openings at the university, and since I wanted a teaching job at that point in my career, we decided to accept an academic position at the University of Arizona College of Medicine in Tucson. She found work with the Az Poison Control Center as the communications officer. We decided to apply to become adoptive parents, went to classes for six months, and one day received a call that our baby was ready to be brought home from the hospital at two days of age. We loved being parents, and our son was an easy baby. Our family and circle of friends accepted him with open arms. He was an easy baby and youngster until about fourth grade. We found a grandmother who had an in-home day care and became friends with several other families who brought their kids there. We entered the world of parents and parenting, happy to be there after so many years of trying and watching friends become parents.

Meantime I proceeded with my career at the university. But I was not happy in my role there. Being on a tenure track, I was expected to teach, provide service to patients and the community, and publish in peer-reviewed journals. It was very difficult for me to feel like I was measuring up in all of these areas, and I found the "politics" of the university challenging. As I was obsessively preparing my case for tenure in my sixth year, Lory told me that she was late in her cycle and feeling tired and nauseated. We laughed it off since we had had many false alarms over the years, but I brought a sample of her urine into work in a clean pickle jar and tested for pregnancy, and it was POSITIVE. On the same day, I received notice that I did not attain tenure. I was ecstatic and disappointed at the same time. I called her, and she was in shock on both accounts.

We retested her urine in a proper container and again it tested positive. Eleven years after beginning our efforts, six years after fertility surgery, and four years after adopting our son, our daughter was born. Shortly after learning about her pregnancy, I received a job offer in Phoenix for twice as much money and doing the kind of work creating programs that I had dreamed of. So our disappointment about leaving Tucson was replaced with the excitement of a pregnancy and a new opportunity. The pregnancy was challenging but had a very happy outcome, and we were blessed with a beautiful and healthy daughter.

After staying home for six months, Lory, in her usually adaptive way, found an opportunity in professional training with Motorola University and embarked on a new career as a training consultant. We found child care first in centers and then with a series of German au pairs, each of whom lived with us for a year and generally worked out very well.

After three years in my teaching role at St. Joseph's Hospital, and with growing disenchantment with my boss who did not follow through with what he had promised, I decided to open my own Pediatric office in Scottsdale. I have never looked back. The practice grew rapidly, and my reputation spread which attracted great clients and great associates. With success came satisfaction. For the last several years, I have been in the process of retiring slowly. In the meantime, Lory's career also flourished as mine was winding down; she has written two books with her partner and has had national and international clients. We have had a bit of a role reversal with hers being the dominant career the past few years.

SURELY THERE WERE CHALLENGES ALONG THE WAY IN YOUR RELATIONSHIP. HOW HAVE YOU LEARNED TO WORK EFFECTIVELY WITH THOSE CHALLENGES?

For many years, we had a motto, "Don't go to bed angry"… meaning fight it out and make up before bed. That worked for many years. Later we weren't so adherent to this rule, but I think we have always believed deep down in the relationship—the marriage—and our ability to work things out with each other. I think a big part is allowing each other to pursue our passions and our friendships.

While we share more than most couples in terms of shared activities, there are still some that she likes that I don't, and I encourage her to pursue those; likewise, she has allowed me to go on golf trips, ski trips, sailing trips, etc. to keep my male friendships alive and satisfy my need for adventure.

Like most couples, money, sex, and kids probably are the basis for most of our fights. But we've managed to talk things out time after time. I recall that our early years of parenting were largely conflict free. When our son was in about fourth grade, he began to display problem behaviors. He had a hard time sitting still, studying, doing his work independently, and turning it in. He was caught shoplifting. We began to fear the worst, (were we raising a criminal?) and our home became a site of conflict. Everything seemed to focus on our son, staying on top of his schoolwork and behavior, and the next few years were challenging. I tended to be firm and consequence driven. Lory saw me as harsh and jumped in to rescue, which made me feel undermined. So what started with our son became a fight between Lory and me. Finally, we sought counsel from some wise therapists, tried medications for ADHD, and in high school, we found a wonderful school for our son which really saved him. During this time, we later learned our daughter felt overshadowed by all the attention (mostly negative) directed toward our son. She had to teach me an important lesson about the nature of parental love as unconditional. I had been raised with love being unstated and based on conditions of performance. I had a very hard time expressing love if I was upset or disappointed by my children. Lory was raised with a very different model. She believed in herself while I was raised to doubt myself. I had to work hard to adopt her model, and I had to learn it from my children as they became young adults and I grew to admire them for who they were and no longer feeling "responsible" for raising them .

Fortunately for our kids, they did feel loved and both emerged from this very difficult time. After a short stint in college, our son enlisted in the Army, and one of our proudest moments as a family was attending his graduation from boot camp in Missouri. He was sent to Iraq after 9/11, served a tour there, and returned with minor injuries and PTSD that he has largely gotten over, but it cost him a marriage. Our daughter completed college and embarked on a career in marketing. She has done very well, lives in New York, and is currently in a serious relationship. I feel we have grown a lot as they reached adulthood and that our relationship with both our kids and with each other as parents is better than ever. We are patiently waiting being grandparents if and when. It is out of our hands. Meantime we enjoy watching our great niece and nephew grow and the grandkids of friends and family.

Spiritual Significance

DO YOU AND YOUR PARTNER SHARE THE SAME SPIRITUAL BELIEF, AND IF NOT, HOW DO YOU FIND YOUR WAY THROUGH IT? IF YOU RAISED CHILDREN TOGETHER, HOW WERE THEY RAISED SPIRITUALLY?

Both Lory and I were raised as Jews. We went to religious school, had a bar/bat mitzvah, and wanted a Jewish wedding. We were not particularly observant and began the search for a religious community when we became parents. In Phoenix, we first joined a synagogue and have been very actively engaged. Lory served as president and participated in the selective Wexner fellowship program for young Jewish leaders; I have sung in the choir, participated in advanced Jewish studies, chaired capital campaigns and served on the board. I am clearly the more "spiritual" and more "observant," but she is highly participatory in the social and activist components.

Although we raised our children to be Jews, and both had religious school, Bar/Bat Mitzvah, and other experiences like camps and BirthRight Israel, neither of our children currently practices Judaism or any other spiritual tradition. My daughter reminds me that it wasn't until we had children that we became observant of Jewish customs, rituals, and synagogue membership. She identifies herself strongly as Jewish. My son says he is Jewish but rarely participates in Jewish holidays or rituals. I am hopeful that at some point in their lives they will come to it as we did. And if we are blessed to have grandchildren, I hope they will be raised with a strong foundation in Judaism. I have a strong connection to the Jewish people, especially since my grandmother was murdered in the Holocaust. I have a strong desire to see the Jewish people survive and thrive from one generation to the next.

WHAT ATTRIBUTES HAS YOUR PARTNER BROUGHT TO THIS RELATIONSHIP THAT HAVE NURTURED AND SUSTAINED IT?

Lory's commitment to our relationship, her good energy and enthusiasm, her desire to be together, and her shared sense of how we want to live our lives together has sustained and nurtured us. Lory is an identical twin. Her sister married a friend of mine on our seventeenth wedding anniversary, and for nearly twenty years, the four of us got along famously. We bought a house together on the Maine coast to spend summers together as we approached retirement with the idea that they would come to Arizona for the winters. Unfortunately, that marriage fell apart, but we have continued as a threesome. We travel together and somehow manage to enjoy our life together while giving space and respect for each individual.

LOOKING BACK AT YOUR MANY YEARS TOGETHER, WHICH AREA OF YOUR LIVES HAS BROUGHT YOU CLOSER TOGETHER?

We share a love for most things and especially for each other and the partnership we have. We've been there for each other in good times and through bad.

WHAT ADVICE WOULD YOU HAVE FOR YOUNG LOVERS?

Trust your love and treat it with respect—your love will get you through the tough times, but you need to nurture it.

Make time for romance, especially in busy times—if only a date night or dinner together or a special trip or visit when you can.

Embrace conflict, learn how to fight fair, and not hold grudges and make up.

Allow each other the freedom to grow as a friend and in key relationships.

Allow each to go off on their own at times to pursue their individual dreams or friendships.

Avoid telling the other what to do but express what you think and what you wish for.

Keep the vision of a healthy marriage and your love alive in the present.

As parents, recognize you each bring strengths and challenges based on experience, but if you engage, communicate, and ask for help when you need it, with the strength of your love, you can get through most anything.

* * *

Live brave.

LORY, 69

"One of the ways we deal with our challenges is walking and talking. Ron loves to walk and usually likes to talk out an issue, often a work issue or a leadership issue."

Lory is senior associate with Leadership Development Services and the associate director of Center for Mentoring Excellence. She has over twenty-five years of experience in consulting, training, and coaching clients from a diverse array of organizations, including the health-care, manufacturing, government, and non-profit sectors. She is the coauthor of *The Mentor's Guide: Making Mentoring Work for You and Starting Strong, A Mentoring Fable—Strategies for Success in the First 90 Days.*

Married 47 years to Ron

Title: 47 Years and Still Going Strong

Physical Connection

WHERE WERE YOU BORN AND RAISED, AND WHAT CAN YOU TELL US ABOUT YOUR CHILDHOOD SURROUNDINGS AND CIRCUMSTANCES?

I was born in Boston, Massachusetts, in 1947, as was my twin sister Lyn. We have a sister 18 months older, as well. It was basically our mom, three girls, and a female dog in a household with my father, who was outnumbered. My dad was the founder and CEO of a successful advertising company, but when he came home, the business persona was off, and it was all about family. My mom was the disciplinarian and probably didn't love having to stay home with children. Dad was the "funny man" who came home and played games with us. My dad adored my mother, who was very smart, well informed, and well read. My mom was a Southerner living in the East. Her first cousin was Woody Guthrie, so her roots were in civil rights and fighting for liberal causes. Living with her Jewish in-laws, she raised us Jewish, although she remained an atheist all her life. Growing up, dinner was family time and family conversation. We talked about what we learned at school and often had to bring a new word to the table to define and use in a sentence. My mom was big on table manners and told us she wanted us to be able to eat at the table with the Queen of England. I spent summers at camp, which I loved, and we went away in the winter skiing. Some summers we would go out West to ranches or to visit my mother's parents. Whenever our family drove somewhere of any distance, we sang our way to and from our destinations. We always ended our trips with "East, West, Home's Best." Being a twin is probably the single most defining thing about me although we fought every day until we were fifteen and didn't really become as close as we are now until the age of about twenty six. But it is amazingly special to have someone in your life who is so much like you and thinks just like you. Growing up, however, we didn't like to be compared, and we fought to be individuals. In fact, my mom never called us "the twins" and never dressed us alike. We didn't share a room. I think our older sister played us against each other for a number of years, as siblings will do. Growing up, we lived pretty well, upper-middle class, but my mom grew up poor and always kept us thinking there wasn't a lot of money. I didn't actually realize how privileged we were until I went away to college and compared notes with classmates.

HOW OLD WERE YOU WHEN YOU HAD YOUR FIRST CRUSH RELATION-SHIP, AND HOW DID IT EVENTUALLY DEVELOP OR END?

In sixth grade I had my first boyfriend, Jay. I was a late developer (I didn't wear a bra until 9th grade) so there wasn't anything physical. I don't even think we kissed. We just sort of called ourselves boyfriend and girlfriend. I believe that each year of school I had a new boyfriend, but when summer came, the relationship was over, and I took a break.

CURRENTLY, HOW DO YOU RATE YOUR PHYSICAL AND MENTAL HEALTH, AND HOW DOES IT AFFECT YOUR RELATIONSHIP?

I think of myself in good physical health. I am active in sports (golf, tennis, skiing, kayaking, biking, walking, etc), but I am definitely not as fit as I was a few years ago when I was running—and a lot thinner too. I am working very hard now, and although there is some stress to the work and travel, I am thankful the work is challenging and invigorating. I have been partnering with a colleague in town for the past sixteen years who asked me to join her in delivering mentoring training, coaching, and consulting. She had already written two popular books on mentoring, and together we have written two more; in addition, she got me writing journal articles, which have been widely published. Our most recent book, *Starting Strong*, was a divergence from our usual more academically-oriented approach and is written as a fable. We work with diverse clients all the way from the Navy, to the folks who make Gortex, Dallas Community College District, and UN Women. In fact, we just returned from Cairo where we rolled out UN Women's first leadership mentoring program, which we will be taking to all the continents...very exciting.

I have always had a strong mental fortitude which has held me in good stead most of my life and certainly helped with this most recent demanding work load and travel. The upswing in my work has had an interesting twist on our relationship. Ron is working less but is not yet retired. However, he takes off four months in the summer when we live in Maine with my sister in a house we co-own. Ron keeps himself busy in the garden, tinkering, and playing tennis, golf, sailing, kayaking, and silversmithing. I found myself completely swamped with work this summer and having to travel to clients. So I wasn't available to either Ron or my sister, so I know they were a bit impatient with me, and I a bit jealous of them. I hope not to have work continue at this pace although Ron appreciates the revenue. This summer I was glad he decided to act as my "bodyguard" and accompany me to Egypt for my work.

ARE YOU PHYSICALLY CONNECTED TO YOUR PARTNER? IF SO, HOW DO YOU KEEP THAT CONNECTION ALIVE? HOW IMPORTANT IS PHYSICAL CONNECTION TO YOUR RELATIONSHIP?

First and foremost, we like to kiss and hug each other. We hold hands. We cuddle. We have sex several times a week. Our physical relationship falls into two categories. For Ron, our sexual relationship is really important as is our ability to do physical things together. Ron and I do many sports together—tennis, golf, biking, skiing—and travel is really important to him too. Our physical connection beyond sex is important to Ron and also to me. He wants an active partner both sexually and as a life partner. I wouldn't expect sex to stop for some time.

Emotional Responsiveness

WHAT DID YOUR PARENTS MODEL FOR YOU AS A CHILD ABOUT MARRIAGE? HOW DID YOU CONNECT WITH YOUR MOTHER? DESCRIBE YOUR RELATIONSHIP WITH YOUR FATHER.

My parents really defined for me the marriage partner I wanted. My parents were physically demonstrative with each other, always kissing and hugging. So

I expected that in my marriage. My father truly adored my mother until the day he died, and he told her and me that all the time. I felt loved by my mom, but when I look back, I think she was overloaded with the responsibility of three girls all so close in age. And as a twin, I had to always share special times, namely birthdays. But I do remember when I was eleven, my parents took me to my first opera, *La Boheme*, by myself. I remember feeling very grown up and special. My dad was the affectionate, fun one. I could curl up in his lap, always get a joke, or kid around with my dad. He used to say that one of us (the twins) was adopted. That was his humor.

WHAT WERE YOU LOOKING FOR WHEN YOU DECIDED TO MARRY YOUR PARTNER, AND WHAT DID YOU KNOW FOR SURE ABOUT YOURSELF?

I knew I wanted to marry someone smart with potential. I had dated so many men that when I met Ron, I was pretty sure he was the one. I remember saying to my mom shortly after I met Ron that I would marry him because I would never be bored. And I never have been. Ron and I were engaged after about two months—we were both pretty sure. By the way, Ron went to the same elementary school, high school, and college (Harvard) as my Dad. I am so close to my family that I knew whoever my partner was, it had to be someone who would appreciate my family and want to be a part of it. Ron was definitely into that.

WHAT SIGNIFICANT MEMORIES DO YOU HAVE AS YOU WERE GETTING TO KNOW EACH OTHER? WHAT DO YOU REMEMBER MOST ABOUT THE FIRST TIME YOU MET?

The first time we met was over the phone when I got his number from someone because I was looking for guys who could play bridge as I was trying to fix up my roommate. We schemed together to find two bridge players as the ruse. But Ron was just about to start med school, and the guy he brought with him was about to start Columbia law. Neither was interested in getting started in a relationship, nor was I interested in meeting anyone. Ron came over to our apartment wearing bell bottoms (this was 1969); he was cute so my roommate liked him and made a bold pass at him. He ended up rejecting her, and she left. Ron and I ended up alone, and my lack of interest was appealing to him from the start. Our first conversations that evening kick-started our relationship. I remember that two days later, he brought over raw oysters, and we went into my room, sat on the floor, and hammered them open. Who does that but a romantic adventurer? Pretty soon, it was clear that Ron and I were connecting, and the rest is history.

SURELY THERE WERE CHALLENGES ALONG THE WAY IN YOUR RELATIONSHIP. HOW HAVE YOU LEARNED TO WORK EFFECTIVELY WITH THOSE CHALLENGES?

Two strong personalities are going to clash, and we clash around power. Neither of us likes to feel bossed around, and we both can get into that mode. When it goes over the top, one of us pushes back. On a rare occasion, we clashed over child rearing philosophies. I am of the motto "firm, not harsh"— Ron tends to be tougher than I like to be. I tended to be softer and more generous than he. We both could easily criticize the other's style. One of the ways we deal with our challenges is walking and talking. Ron loves to walk and usually likes to talk out an issue, often a work issue or a leadership issue. So early in our relationship our fights were over the kids with Ron thinking that I was spoiling them. Later, as Ron wanted to cut back on work (aka cut back on income), his favorite word was "downsizing." I, on the other hand, had (and have) no interest in moving out of our house. This was the source of a lot of spats for several years. For the moment, we have laid that one to rest.

Spiritual Significance

DO YOU AND YOUR PARTNER SHARE THE SAME SPIRITUAL BELIEF, AND IF NOT, HOW DO YOU FIND YOUR WAY THROUGH IT? IF YOU RAISED CHILDREN TOGETHER, HOW WERE THEY RAISED SPIRITUALLY?

We very much come together in our love of Judaism and our pleasure of celebrating Shabbat together with friends. Ron is more spiritual than I am, and he studies Torah and reads more in depth in the area. I admire his commitment to his own education and evolution in this area. Earlier in our life together I was part of a Jewish leadership program and was also president of our temple so my involvement was often more on the political side and his on the spiritual side, but we both appreciate this part of our life. I don't think we exactly share the same belief in an afterlife, but that doesn't get in our way.

Ron was an only child, so he has tried to reenact with our family the way he idealized life could have been in his own childhood. I think he believes from his "old world" father that a parent's role is to teach their child—and for the child to learn from the parent. For the children's birthdays, in addition to whatever fun thing I bought them, Ron would buy them a book. He also loved teaching the kids tennis, skiing (his mother taught him to ski), or whatever. But what kid wants to learn from their parents? Our kids certainly didn't like it. But we took them skiing; we hit balls with them at the tennis court; we took vacations in Maine and at the beach. We also left them home periodically and travelled as adults, which we all appreciated, I'm sure. Our Sunday was family time and that usually meant a hike or tennis or bike riding or roller-blading—something outdoors and physical. Ron definitely drove that.

WHAT ATTRIBUTES HAS YOUR PARTNER BROUGHT TO THIS RELATIONSHIP THAT HAVE NURTURED AND SUSTAINED IT?

Loyalty and love of family, love of travel, financial acumen and caution, romance, adventurous spirit, interest and energy for sports and being active and fit, commitment to Judaism, and especially the ability to fix things. I love that about him. I especially love how Ron has embraced my family as his. We spend considerable time living as a threesome with my twin sister (without the three way), and he has come to love and appreciate her the way I do. We intend for the three of us to grow old together.

LOOKING BACK AT YOUR MANY YEARS TOGETHER, WHICH AREA OF YOUR LIVES HAS BROUGHT YOU CLOSER TOGETHER?

All the ones I listed above. They all make a difference and enrich our life together. We would be missing something if one of them wasn't present.

WHAT ADVICE WOULD YOU HAVE FOR YOUNG LOVERS?

- Be your own person first, love yourself first, and then be partners and love him/her. Each of you should make the other better because you are together and your strengths and weaknesses should complement each other.
- You need to have the other fill some of the gaps you lack—and appreciate them for having those strengths rather than let them annoy you.
- Find activities you truly like doing together—whether it be sports or cards or movies or whatever—although having something physical

that you enjoy doing is important. If your partner plays golf, I would suggest you learn that game because it just takes too much damn time if you don't.

- Men need to be appreciated, so show appreciation and learn to say thank you.
- Ask for what you need. Don't expect your partner to be a mind reader. If it is important to you, then say so, and coach your partner to deliver what you need in a way that is sufficient for you; maybe not great, but it will do. Hopefully, you will marry someone who is coachable and is willing to work to be the partner you need. Hopefully, you are doing the same thing.
- Don't ever take each other for granted, or stop celebrating, appreciating, kissing, hugging, loving, and saying I love you. It never gets old.

PART SEVEN

SUSTANING MEANINGFUL LOVE

*"Love doesn't sit there, like a stone, it has to
be made, like bread; remade all the time,
made new."*

Ursula K. Le Guin

CHAPTER NINE

WORDS OF WISDOM FOR SUSTAINING MEANINGFUL LOVE

"I have just three things to teach: simplicity, patience, compassion. These are your greatest treasures. Simple in actions and in thoughts, you return to the Source of Being."

Lao-Tzu

Hilda

I appreciate the above quote by Lao-Tzu and as I have matured and grown wiser, have tried to keep my life simple, practice patience, and show compassion. But as author Mark Nepo wrote in his book, *The Book of Awakening*, about this very same quote: *"...let me confess that while stumbling about my own path, I have found that I must continually learn and relearn these things—not just once, but again and again, in deeper and deeper ways. They appear now like a spiral staircase and with each stepping, I find myself deep in the life of my soul".* I as well have stumbled along the way and know that I'm not alone in my process of returning to the *Source of Being,* or at the very least, arriving to a sense of being at peace with the choices that I have made along the way. But the light on my own spiral staircase is absolutely beginning to shine a way for me to see and step by step, day by day I am making the changes necessary to love more and fear less.

As Mary Beth and I listened and read the stories and added them to the pages of this book, we felt a sense of related connection with each and every one of our contributors. Of course both of us have loved, lost and loved once again. We have also married with every intention of being married for a lifetime to our spouses, and we have missed that mark. And along the way we have once again reached a deeper sense of love for ourselves and for others. Through the stories we have relearned that thoughts and actions do manifest the future and that each one of us is responsible for where we will someday cross the finish line.

Not too long ago I wrote an article for a newsletter titled, *"It's Not That Complicated!"* The point I presented in the article was that keeping our lives simple, being patient and showing compassion toward ourselves and others would indeed lead us to uncomplicated lives. But the truth is, life has now become very complicated and it is even more so as we add the complexities of our connections to the entire world at our finger tips. The Internet and many other fresh modes of uniting us are coming our way daily. They have entwined our lives and have added to a complex way of living. Without having to be at home for the morning or evening news, we now carry our constant information channels with us by phone. We are updated from births to deaths and from religion to politics in an instant of any global event. We are stretched out and moving quickly to stay afloat. And for many, friendships are relegated to the tracking devices on the Internet.

With that said; the simplicity of the human desire to love and be loved, the patience that it takes to sustain love, and the commitment to compassionate love for those around us, are definitely possible for all of us to attain. As all of the authors that we quoted within the pages of this book wrote and sincerely believe, love is necessary for genuine happiness and for our human survival. And quite possibly, for reaching the greatest treasures of them all; simplicity, patience and compassion.

As with our previous book on living brave lives, we have identified seven areas of life expression that we know sustain meaningful loving relationships. Whether our love is toward a partner in a committed relationship, with our children and family members, friends or co-workers, it is imperative that we learn to sustain connections that fill our hearts with love...our lives depend on it.

We are fortunate to have a group of wise contributors who have consented to share their views and words of wisdom that have supported them along their way on matters of love. Once again, we suggest that you not rush through reading these in one sitting but savor each one separately and enjoy the offerings. After all....love takes time to appreciate.

Words of Wisdom for Sustaining Meaningful Love

Attention

Trust

Playfulness

Shared Interest

Authenticity

Vulnerability

Respect

ATTENTION

D. J. Vanas

I met the love of my life by paying attention. I'm still with the love of my life almost twenty years later – through joy and pain, challenges, losses and adventures – for the same reason.

I met Arienne while out with friends at a dance club. The music was good but my friends and I were bored and ready to leave but before we did, I told them, "I'm going to walk around one more time." And as such things go, that "one more time" changed my entire life. Across the dance floor I saw Arienne and her beautiful smile illuminated bright purple under the black lights. I moved towards her as if pulled by a magnet. I was paying attention with every fiber of my being, so much so that I couldn't pay attention to anything else. The music faded away and the people around me became a blur until I could only see her.

Attention in love, in the beginning, is exciting and easy. But when the chaos of the world crashes in – friends, family, careers, bills, travel, stress and every other thing this world shoves at us – attention must be given with intention or else it doesn't happen at all. We must put first things first, like the relationship we have with those we love. We tend to neglect the things we don't value and if we lose sight of what is vital, the ones we love feel it and the love bond you've created can wither.

Our time is the most precious resource we possess. It's non-renewable and what we do with it defines every aspect of our life, including love. It's the best thing we can give the ones we love and there is no substitute for it. In my mind, attention is the time we willingly give to the ones we love to share the same space, the same breath and solely focus on them. To simply share thoughts and listen to each other, without the assault of TV, cell phones or myriad other distractions, is not always easy but necessary to continue feeding the fires of love.

One of my favorite movies is *Avatar*. The aliens in the movie have a greeting that translates into, "I *see* you" and a linguist is explaining this to the main character, both of whom are human. The linguist is adamant in making the point that the greeting isn't just the physical act of recognizing there is a person in front of you, it means I see you, recognizing the person in all its being-- eyes, spirit, life force. I feel that is what real attention represents and the only way to achieve it is to intentionally carve the time away from all the other things in the world and get back to the human-to-human connection that love requires and craves.

Even today, when I give Arienne my attention, the music fades and the people around me become a blur until I can only see her.

D.J. Vanas is an internationally-acclaimed motivational storyteller whose expertise is in leadership and personal development. D.J. is an enrolled member of the Odawa Tribe, a former military officer, and author of "The Tiny Warrior:" A Path to Personal Discovery & Achievement (printed in six countries). His latest book; "Spirit on the Run." is his first novel. D.J. demonstrates to people and organizations how to use traditional warrior spirit principles to thrive in tough, changing environments, to lead with courage, and to serve others well regardless of circumstances. He has delivered over 7,000 programs with 500 tribal nations, Intel Corporation, NASA, Subaru, Boston Children's Hospital, P&G, and has been twice invited to speak at The White House.

Live brave.

TRUST

Shayla Roberts

For me, learning to trust love was a long, complicated process. Trusting the men I hoped would love me was the hardest part. My father came into my life when I was two years old, having been off to the war. For me, it was love at first sight, and unqualified trust until he called me into his office five years later to tell me that he loved me and would always take care of me. And then. . . . .he quickly exited my life forever, leaving me, my mother, and two brothers on the edge of destitution.

Mom, God bless her, mustered all of her feminine wiles, to provide us with a stepfather. He was a solid, sensible man whom I learned to trust deeply until he physically battered my mother into the hospital. No wonder, that on the eve of my wedding, she sat me down for this motherly advice, "Never trust a man. They are all scum-dogs."

And so, I began my first marriage with the goal of proving my mother wrong. Surely my husband was a good guy, a faithful man who would cherish me forever until after 17 years of marriage he slept with my best friend. It wasn't long after, that I learned my 'faithful' man had been sleeping with other women for years, and liked to brag about it to his guy friends.

So I went on a 20 year sabbatical from trusting men and love. I took my love nature into my own hands and acted out in every way imaginable, wallowing as a victim of men's deceit. Heartlessly experimenting with every kind of love, I found it all wanting until I reconnected with a friend from high school at a 40th class reunion.

I don't know why I decided to trust him. Maybe it was because he was a big, unpretentious man like my sweet grandpa. Maybe it was because I sensed that he, too, had been victimized by love, and by life, and we might be able to heal together. Maybe it was because, we both sensed that our outrage at life would mirror the other's outrage, and finally find expression. Maybe, because somewhere deep inside me, I knew he had come to co-create a life with me, and to unconditionally support me in forwarding my life's work.

Whatever my reasons then, I found in my second marriage, that I was finally growing up, becoming someone who could express outrageous anger, and still not judge myself too harshly; someone who could tolerate my mate's righteous raging at the way life had treated him, and not judge him too harshly. It turned out that I had attracted a man who trusted himself enough to learn, in his sixties, that his suffering was impacted by undiagnosed autism. It turned out that I too, had been misunderstood, and mistreated for being deeply introverted, and quite abnormal.

It turned out, that we could grow together, learn together, work side by side, hug each other, be kind to each other, cook for each other, respect our differences, and relish our shared interests. It turned out that we had each trusted ourselves enough to choose against all odds, our perfect complement in a life companion.

So what I've learned from my complicated process is that, as we learn to love and accept ourselves, our sense of our unique value grows. With a true sense of our value, we make choices that are self-nurturing. As they are nurtured by our choices, our hearts begin to open. Open-heartedly, we step away from needy, I-centered love, and relax into generous, trust-centered love.

Shayla Roberts is a highly creative, serial entrepreneur in the fields of personal growth and professional development. Over the past thirty-eight years, she has helped clients build conscious business successes, and make self-honoring life transitions, by providing products and services including one-on-one entrepreneurial coaching, intensive personal development retreats, phone and on-line courses, best- selling books, and inspirational audio and video products.

Shayla launched Yansa Music in 1982, an independent record company and in 1989 she launched her entrepreneurial coaching practice. She is currently in prelaunch mode with her latest cutting-edge offering, Sparkle School, a revolution-

ary, online personal development curriculum and wise-women community, that enhances a woman's natural capacity for achieving success in all areas of life.

Shayla is coauthor of the 2006 Amazon.com best-selling business book, "Bold Moves - Jump To Outstanding Self-Managed Action" and ghost wrote "The Corporate Shaman," published in seven languages. Shayla brings essential creativity to all of her endeavors. She was awarded 'best of' status as a musician and composer, by the Governor of Arizona, and Billboard Magazine, and her fine art has been exhibited in galleries and museums, nationally.

Live brave.

PLAYFULNESS

Lonnie Whittington

So, what's so humorous about making your partner spew toothpaste at bedtime? What's so special about laughing until your stomachs are sore? What's the big idea of finishing each other's reference to a television comedy episode, sparking more laughter?

It's about fun, it's about playfulness and it's about experiencing a deeper relationship with each other. Being playful with your partner is good on many levels. Humor helps you connect with your partner and makes them feel loved and comfortable. Humor and laughter are now proven to have health benefits. Laughter decreases stress hormones and increases immune cells. Laughter is the best medicine. Besides, it feels good to be happy.

I really enjoy making Michele, my wife of more than twenty-five years, laugh. It's not that I try hard to think of things to do or to go out of my way to find funny things to say, our playfulness is always spontaneous. For us, playfulness seems to be automatic because we are at ease with each other and we want to please each other. To behave otherwise in a lifetime relationship seems tragic.

Before we were married Michele created a list of the desirable characteristics that she wished to have in a future mate; a sense of humor was close to the top of her list. Humor has always been a big part of my life. I met most of my friends in primary school while spending time in the corner with them as punishment after I acted out in class. But, that's another story.

As with most boys growing up in the 50's and 60's I watched many Three Stooges shorts after school. Their antics are rife with physical abuse and women don't particularly care for their brand of humor, but it's classically funny in a crude way. I have a collection of Stooges CDs and watch them when I need a jolt of humor, particularly before going to the dentist. While sitting in the dentist chair having my teeth cleaned I will often chuckle to myself or even laugh out loud, replaying a Stooges episode in my head. This used to puzzle my hygienist (imagine sitting in a dentist chair and laughing without the aid of chemicals!) until I told her the secret of my mirth. Now, she and the dentist will sometimes recommend to their patients a dose of Stooges as a "pre-treatment" to their appointment. Humor can help take the pain away for yourself, or when you and your partner are experiencing an event in your lives that could use a little diversion.

Playfulness is defined as being light hearted and full of fun. There can be many different levels of what can be considered playful. To some couples, it could mean dousing each other with a hose or chasing each other around with a soapy sponge while washing the car. I know Michele would never think that chasing or tickling her was funny and being aware of her aversion, I don't taunt her like that. I like to do things that are unexpected and harmless.

An example of harmless, playful fun is when I found a plastic replica of a red pepper and placed it in the vegetable bin in the refrigerator for Michele to find. The idea of fake vegetables is not real funny by itself but the big difference in this piece was that it had a face molded into it with wide eyes, a big nose and a toothy grin. It has been there for more than 15 years and is still smiling at us as a playful reminder to have fun – even with vegetables!

"Do not underestimate the power of humor in your union. Take your relationship seriously; but don't take yourselves too seriously. Be able to laugh together, remember that laughter is always good medicine."

Michele and I are both ministers. And, as such, we have the pleasure of marrying couples. The passage above is usually included in the wedding ceremonies that we perform. That wisdom was in our vows when we were married in 1991 and we enjoy practicing it every day.

Much of our playfulness has shown up in word play or a spontaneous outburst that seemed hilarious at the time. There have been many nights that we have laughed ourselves to sleep while bantering back and forth after the lights are out. Playfulness; it's good for the relationship and good for the soul.

Lonnie Whittington has been a minister of Religious Science since 2010 and serves as staff minister at Creative Living Fellowship in Phoenix, Arizona. His wife, Michele, is the senior minister and it is Lonnie's passion to support her in her ministry.

In his day job, Lonnie is an independent graphic design consultant to high-tech business-to business clients and also serves consumer clients.

He is the author of "From the Heart, Experiences, Lessons and Stories to Help Make Your Life Easier."

He also says this about himself: "I have absolutely no musical talent!"

Live brave.

PLAYFULNESS

Michele Whittington

It was 1989, and I was finally getting my act together in the one area that really mattered, which sadly had been the one area I hadn't been able to get right to save my life. Two failed marriages and too many relationships to count suggested that I didn't have a clue how to create a sacred and holy partnership. But, that is what I wanted more than anything!

So, a year or so earlier, I had embarked on an emotional and spiritual journey that was preparing me to actually be the person who could have the kind of relationship I wanted.

Spirituality played a key role in my journey, so not long after I met a smart, sexy, seemingly delightful man that had potential to be "the one," I invited him to attend church with me. For him to be "the one," he would need to share the spiritual journey with me, so I figured I better find out early on if he would. Much to my surprised delight, he said yes, so the next Sunday we were front and center at a service.

And then, the strangest thing happened.

He sat through the entire service giggling. Yes, giggling! I had never heard such a thing. The minister didn't say anything particularly funny, so I was quite perplexed. When service was over, I asked him what he thought about the service, and, in particular, what he thought was so funny. He did not answer the latter portion of my question, because he was too excited to answer the first. He said he sat throughout the entire service in amazement that there was a spiritual belief system -- a religion -- that espoused everything he had always believed. He said he was in awe at it and questioned why he had never heard of it before. He said he couldn't wait to go back next week to learn more. Hearing all of this was such a great relief to me that I forgot about being perturbed over the giggling.

As our relationship progressed and I got to know him at a deeper level, I learned something about him that I now find to be one of the most (of many!) endearing qualities he has. When his heart is opened and he is moved, he giggles. And I've learned something else about him. He giggles a lot – not only when his heart is opened and he is moved, but on a frequent basis, because he can find humor in pretty much anything! And he takes great enjoyment out of making me giggle as well!

This smart, sexy and absolutely delightful man turned out to be "the one," and Lonnie and I have been married for over 25 years. One of the reasons our life works so well together is that from the get-go, playful humor has been a key element.

After my abysmal record of relationships before Lonnie and after I became the person who could have the kind of relationship I wanted, I decided to be very clear about the partner I desired. In fact, I wrote a long laundry list of qualities and attributes. Because I enjoy laughter and playfulness, one of those qualities was humor, but a very specific kind of humor.

My second husband actually had a keen sense of humor. He had a quick wit and regularly had a humorous observation to make. However, his wit had one little problem. It almost always had a harsh edge to it and it was often at the cost of someone else – and that someone else was usually me!

So, when I made my laundry list of the ideal mate in 1989, kind-hearted humor was at the top of the list. And that is the kind of humor Lonnie has. It is never at the cost of another, but it is always funny.

I feel so blessed to be able to laugh through life with him. Although we don't necessarily appreciate the same kind of comedy (I just don't get Monty Python or The Three Stooges!), that doesn't matter. We share a playful heart and delight in creating space in our lives for laughter and joy. Having this as a staple in our relationship has sustained us through loss, health issues and career challenges. We know we always have one another, and one of us will find the joy in any situation.

Our wedding ceremony included the profound reminder that "laughter is always good medicine." For more than 25 years we have put that to the test . . . and the jury is in. Laughter is definitely good (actually great) medicine for a sustained happy relationship!

Rev. Dr. Michele Whittington *is an Emerson Theological Institute graduate and the Senior Minister at Creative Living Fellowship, a Religious Science church and teaching center in Phoenix, Arizona, for over 20 years and is the founder of New Thought Seed Thoughts, a support service for New Thought ministers. She graduated from Arizona State University, summa cum laude, with a Bachelor of Arts degree in Organizational Communication. Having come from a varied business background before entering the ministry, she combines her spiritual depth with her knowledge of business and organizational structure in her ministerial work. She and her husband Lonnie of over 25 incredible years are certified Real Love coaches and have a vibrant couples coaching practice. Dr. Michele believes her life's purpose is to travel an ever-ascending spiritual journey and to serve others with love, light, compassion and laughter as they travel theirs, helping them to reveal their inherent, but often unrealized, Divine nature.*

Live brave.

SHARED INTEREST

Sabra House

Unattended, even the most loving relationship can grow stale. Repetition brings on boredom. Doing the same things, traveling to the same vacation spots, eating at the same restaurants all dull the shared experience because there is nothing new.

What keeps a relationship vital and alive? When a couple investigates new and different projects, activities, skills, interests – and can share the exciting energy that comes from experiencing something new.

I'm big on planning vacations which take us to new countries and new experiences. But I have to give credit to my partner and wife, Lou, for finding us new projects and new interests that become part of our life together. A year ago we received a rock covered bird house as a gift from my daughter. Lou loved the item so much that she researched how it was made and actually began to buy the supplies for making one. I, who love jig saw puzzles, found it fascinating too. For over a year now we have decorated bird houses with rocks, gems, crystals and charms. Then we had to find a place to sell them, and that led to craft fairs, where people oo'd and aa'd over our birdhouses and even bought a few!

Our latest newly added interest is pickleball. Lou and our friend, Cindy, tried it a couple of times and then roped me into playing with them. Tennis lessons, from when I was 12, kicked back in and now I'm an enthusiastic participant. While we share aches and pains from the unaccustomed activity, we laugh at ourselves and then head back out to play either on the courts or on the street in front of our house, whichever is easiest.

During our most recent trip to Florida, Lou found a kite that had become entangled and abandoned. She restored the kite to working order and flew it happily on the beach. We bought another kite and felt like children – happy and free and having a blast. My sister says that Lou has brought out the child in me, and she has!

Then there is the volunteering that we do, also initiated by Lou. Our two cairn terriers are pet therapy dogs and we take them to a memory care center to bring a sparkle of recognition back into the resident's eyes. We volunteer weekly at a cancer center doing Reiki on cancer patients and survivors. We also provide support and comfort for end of life situations. These experiences always give us a renewed appreciation for our lives, our health and our togetherness.

Lou and I have been together for 16 years and in that time we've added many new activities to our life. First it was kayaking and then that turned into kayak-camping where we pack our sleeping bags, camp stove, and groceries into our kayaks and paddle across the lake to some remote and idyllic spot where we enjoy nature at its best.

We've tried classes in painting with acrylics, glass blowing, and music lessons. We've gone on hikes to find petroglyphs. In Sedona we sought out the Palatki Indian ruins and their rock art alcoves. We traveled to Canyon de Chelly to view the rock art there with a guide. We searched out cave paintings in Uluru, Australia. And always, we look for rocks, crystals and charms to put on our rock covered birdhouses.

It's the diversity and the new additions to our lives that have sustained and enriched our relationship. While I think shared interests are important to a relationship, I think newly discovered interests are even more important in keeping the relationship vital and alive and loving.

The key to happiness is: Someone to love, something to do, and something to look forward to.

Sabra House, LCSW is a Licensed Certified Social Worker in the State of Arizona. She has been a psychotherapist for over thirty-five years. She first practiced in Flint, Michigan and then moved to Scottsdale, Arizona in 1990 where she opened her private practice, The Lighthouse Center. Sabra is also the author of a personal development book entitled, "Who's Walking Around in Your Head With Muddy Boots?"

Live brave.

AUTHENTICITY

Michelle Medrano

"When you are authentic, you create a certain energy....people want to be around you because you are unique." Andie McDowell

"To be yourself in a world that is constantly trying to make you something else is the greatest accomplishment." Ralph Waldo Emerson

Imagine that as a child you had a favorite Halloween mask. You wore it one Halloween and people around you raved about it! They thought it was an unusual and beautiful mask. Because you got such raves about it, you decided to wear it as often as possible. Wearing the mask helped you to feel attractive and confident. It became a habit.

During personal private times, or at night, the mask had to come off of course. It is uncomfortable to sleep in a Halloween mask. Plus, if left on too long, it irritates and damages the skin. However, from that time on, no one saw your true face.

Upon growing up, you decided that you wanted to have a romantic relationship. You made sure your mask was nice, clean, and fresh and you headed into the world to find a beloved. Eventually, you found one to fall in love with and this beloved one loved you and loved your mask!! In fact, the mask is part of what your beloved loved most about you. "It is so unique that you wear such a cool mask," your beloved tells you.

Now you have a dilemma. Because the most intimate relationships involve nakedness. Not just physical body to body nakedness; at some moment you will have to likely be seen by your beloved without the mask. In the beginning, you did everything you could think of to keep that mask on all the time with this person. Eventually, it became challenging. Your real skin broke out into a rash, and you knew that sooner or later, you were going to have to show this special person your real face.

Yet, it is such a risk. What if they don't like or love you without the mask? What if they leave you because you show them your true face? What if...........

While we really don't wear Halloween masks in life, we have all grown up and come to believe that our authentic self, or certain parts of it are unacceptable, or unlovable. When someone loves us for our "masked" self, we cannot feel truly seen, or loved. Yet being loved just as we are is something we crave deeply.

As a child, I became an expert mask wearer. I was even good at changing my mask and figuring out just what was the best mask to wear so that someone would love/like me! But it was hollow and irritating to my authentic self. As I felt the emptiness of being loved for my shallow self, my true self became harder to find and exist. Yet, I knew that what I craved most was to be with those who loved me for who I really was, but it would require me to show this part of me to others.

In the safety of some family relationships, and in my spiritual community, I finally began to take the risk of "simply" being who I really am and being loved, occasionally rejected, but still, TRULY loved.

From that risk, I was able eventually to attract into my life a man who loves the authentic me. It is not always easy. The authentic me has her weakness, ugliness and challenges. Yet, she also has amazing beauty and grace and to find someone to partner with who is willing to be with me as I risk this way, and to risk the same himself, is thrilling!!

So how do we learn to take down the mask and live authentically in our relationships?

First, we may have to literally forgive anyone who ever made it clear that our authentic self was not welcome in our past. Living authentically can be very intimidating to some people. Generally our society seems to appreciate the easy way of relating; just do what is "normal" and what you are asked. Just be in alignment with what our family, religion, culture thinks is normal and right. Yet, almost all of us have some uniqueness that disqualifies us from that demand. So, when we have felt wronged, or judged, or rejected in the past from that, it is important to learn to forgive. Otherwise our wound from the past inserts itself on our present and we cannot be or feel loved for who we really are.

Secondly, take a risk!! Many times people appreciate when someone is willing to show up authentically. We can be guilty of talking ourselves out of our authentic voice because we THINK we know how someone else will respond. Yet often, we are simply wrong and staying in a comfort zone for our own comfort. Take occasional risks to speak authentically and see how it lands. It may be surprisingly refreshing.

And lastly, keep in mind that being ourselves is what we are to do and be. We can find those who love and appreciate our authentic self the more WE appreciate our authentic self. We teach people how to treat us. Upon experiencing such radical self- acceptance, we discover that the acceptance of others is no longer so important to us because we have the best prize of all....ourselves.

The reality is that not everyone in our life will come to love and appreciate our truest self. But when we take a risk, and find those who can love and appreciate us in this way, it is totally, completely 100% worth the wait!!

Rev. Dr. Michelle Medrano found Religious Science at age 15. Upon walking into the Mile Hi Church of Religious Science in Denver, Colorado, she knew she was "home." As a teenager, Michelle started volunteering at that church and eventually joined its administrative staff where she worked for six years. She continued her studies, became a practitioner, and in 1991, after receiving her degree from Ernest Holmes College, became a minister.

Michelle became an assistant minister at the Huntington Beach Church of Religious Science where she served four years in various capacities. Michelle then joined New Vision Center for Spiritual Living in Scottsdale, Arizona as its senior minister in 1995. Her vigorous involvement in her local community is matched by her work on the international committees of her denomination. She has served in many capacities of leadership in the New Thought Movement.

In 2013 Dr. Michelle was invited to return to Mile Hi Church as an Associate Minister. In the congregation she serves and in the many churches and organizations she visits each year, Michelle is known as an inspiring teacher and leader who deeply touches her audiences with her humor and profound insights.

Live brave.

VULNERABILITY

Doug and Becky

Vulnerability is easy in the first blush of love.....prior to the onset of those emotional papercuts destined to occur in any long-standing relationship. Between the two of us we have over 65 years working as therapists with couples and individuals. One would think vulnerability would come easy to such trained professionals. And it is true that we intellectually know how to fight fair, use "I" statements and express vulnerable feelings. But we, too, have personally experienced from each other those emotional papercuts that occur over time, and like everyone else, we can automatically move into self-protection when we sense emotional danger. For unlike our *canine* companions who love unconditionally because of their extraordinary ability to "be in the moment," we humans have a tendency to store up every slight that occurs especially in our relationships that matter the most. And therefore, ironically, it is our *most important* relationships that ultimately invite the greatest defenses.

So what are our chosen defenses? At times of emotional distress, Doug is likely to seek refuge in an emotional cave, hoping to calm himself and avoid further pain. Becky, being sensitive to abandonment, pursues him, hoping for connection and validation of her experience. The more she pursues, the deeper he can move into his cave, a dance step that leaves us both frustrated and hurting.

An easy response to such a dance step would be to back away from any topics that might evoke such pain. We've all seen the couples out to dinner with nothing to say to each other no doubt because so many topics have become "taboo," a technique that can certainly work for some, but at a cost of emotional intimacy and connection. For those of us who yearn for more, who want a deeper connection that feeds us on a more soulful level, there is a call for greater courage and determination. Why courage and determination? Because to choose vulnerability requires a decision to *risk* greater emotional pain....to trust that our partner/friend/family member will respond in a manner that is sensitive to the baring of our underbelly. How ironic that such exposure is actually the key to an emotionally *intimate* relationship.

For us, this decision to risk doesn't happen automatically when we're in the throes of great distress. We oftentimes find it difficult to focus on our own plate of feelings. It's so much easier (and safer) to metaphorically stick our fork into our partner's emotional spaghetti. No doubt our training as therapists lends itself to this habit. We've learned through experience, however, that sometimes a "time out" is necessary to give us both an opportunity to self-soothe and pause long enough to find the internal strength and courage to go deeper with our own feelings. To the reader this may all sound like hard work. It is.

But every time we are able to catch ourselves when we're headed into an emotional tidal wave, every time we can put the well-being of our relationship and each other first and "call it" before the damage occurs, and every time we can "go to the basement" with our most vulnerable feelings, we create more and more golden threads of connection. For both of us, the choice of placing our most vulnerable feelings in the hands of the other where those emotional tendrils are held with such kindness and care can generate the most healing experience of all. We believe that an intimate relationship can be an incredible spiritual journey, a call to rise each day and choose to love each other in spite of the differences that surface along the way. To be able to heal from the ruptures of our pasts while learning to love deeper and more fully in the present is the greatest opportunity of all.

Becky Jandrey, Ph.D. and Doug Bowers, Ph.D. are both licensed psychologists with private practices in Scottsdale, Arizona. In their practices they focus on different areas of interest. Becky works with adults and couples who are struggling with all life issues, including the complexities of relationships, managing stress, anxiety, depression, as well as spiritual struggles. She is EMDR trained for the management of trauma. Doug's emphasis is in Health or Health Psychology where services are coordinated with physicians from area medical institutions. His academic and clinical training include evaluation and treatment of children, adolescents and adults in multiple clinic and hospital settings.

Live brave.

RESPECT

Kim Minert

Loving for Life demands Respect...

Throughout our lives, my husband Tim and I have experienced relationships on both sides of the fence...on one side a relationship filled with conflict and contempt, and on the other... love and mutual respect.

As a 27 year old woman, I married a man for whom at the time, I had great respect. He was a college graduate with honors, had a heart for kids and worked as a teacher and coach. Over the course of 14 years, the respect I had for him diminished drastically... with his inability to maintain employment and his penchant for cancelling our family's health insurance! (And a lot more!) Grieving the loss of the marriage was over the day the divorce was final, and joy set in instantly. The heaviness of being *disrespected* by the one person who is supposed to love and respect me the most was gone.

According to a significant study at the University of Washington, the number one predictor of broken relationships is wrapped up in one word..."contempt." It is far more toxic than any other negative emotion, and reveals itself as seeing your partner "beneath you". And the opposite of contempt? Another singular word, "respect."

When I met my husband, Tim, I had been single for a year. I wanted another relationship, one in which we would enjoy deepening friendship, love and most importantly, mutual respect. He too had experienced a marriage of 14 years, in which there was contempt flowing freely! Dr. John Gottman, multi award-winning Professor of Psychology and relationship researcher at the University of Washington and his team, found this single behavior so relevant they use it to predict divorce 93% of the time! "Contempt," says Gottman, "is the kiss of death."

Gottman has written an excellent book, *The Seven Principles of Making Marriage Work*. Of the principles, I feel like there are three easy to implement strategies that can increase respect and keep contempt at bay.

Create an updated "love map" of your spouse. Fill in information such as a list of the people in his/her life, recent important events, upcoming events, and current stresses or worries. Then add your partner's hopes and aspirations.

Work to increase positive emotions about each other. The fondness and admiration aspects of couple relatedness are the antidote to contempt. It buffers the stressors by developing a fundamentally positive view of each other. List the things you appreciate about your partner.

Turn towards each other and not away. This will prevent loneliness, isolation, and apathy. It builds a path towards intimacy when you regularly practice it in the small stressors, making it easier to come together in the bigger ones.

Tim and I were married in my hometown of Billings, Montana, on June 19, 2005. My respect for him continues to grow, and it is essential that I both show *and* tell him. As a hairdresser for 38 years, I have spent countless hours talking to women, many of them older and wiser than me with years of marriage success under their belts. I have learned that a universal deep-seated need of men is to be *respected*. It is at the core of man's self-esteem that reinforces his drive to lead, protect, and provide for his family. (And of course is enjoyed by women as well.)

In 2016 I finally finished a book I had been writing for five years, to help diabetics and people at risk to create healthy lives. My research incubator was my home, and my subjects were my husband and I, both Type 1 Diabetics. The book was a labor of love, and he saw the effort that went into it. I have never felt so respected in my life, as my darling husband carries the book around, showing it off to his friends and perfectly innocent strangers who sit next to him on airplanes. He proudly announces to anyone who will pay attention, "I'm her marketing manager!"

Additionally, I am immensely proud of Tim, for his honesty and integrity as a man. He shines with work ethic, sales excellence, technology expertise, wisdom in financial planning for his clients, and in particular he shows immense care and concern for the widows he serves. He can break a horse, breed a cow, repair almost any appliance, and loves his family intensely - both his family of origin, and the family he married into. He built a room for my parents to enjoy the Arizona sunshine for months at a time. He has shown my two daughters and his son the love and support of a real dad – never ending and unwavering.

Who wouldn't respect a man like that? I'm keeping him! And to top it off, no matter the cost, he has NEVER cancelled our health insurance!

Kim Minert *is a life-long learner, never tiring of investigating what makes people tick, what defines who they are, and how they can, together, improve their lives and the lives of those they care about. She has created a vibrant career in hairdressing, working with clients for over 38 years. At the age of 44, in 2006, she was diagnosed with Type 1 (Juvenile) Diabetes. Working with her doctor who is a Type 2 Diabetic, she managed to make lifestyle changes for herself and her husband, also a Type 1 Diabetic, that eliminated confusion and stress, and created a platform for health. Today she shares those life-giving strategies with diabetics of all sizes and shapes, pre-diabetics, and those at risk. She is the author of "My New BFF, Burn Fat for Fuel, Lose Weight, Beat Diabetes" and coaches and inspires through speaking, study groups, seminars, webinars, and private coaching..*

Kim currently resides in Scottsdale, Arizona, with her husband, Tim, her two daughters Andrea and Alexa and her dog, Molly.

Live brave.

AFTERWORD

RETHINKING LOVE

Hilda

During the research and writing of *Living Brave In Love*, my thoughts took me back into my childhood and to vivid memories of my father and mother's love relationship. I never thought that I would come to realize that my father was indeed the affectionate one. My childhood perception of their relationship was generated by my father's struggle with alcohol, a dangerous medication for a Mexican Indian. Like many couples who immigrated to this country with only a few dollars in their pocket, hope in their hearts and a desire to better the lives of their children, they struggled. My father's lack of education, cultural background and social insecurities plunged him into a desperate state of anesthetizing his fears and responsibilities with alcohol. Times were tough. My perceptions were formed and I see now that I have held to a self-protection approach in my own love relationships throughout my life. Had I uncovered this observation sooner, how different my life might have evolved. Nonetheless, aside from his love of music, a sense of humor, strong work ethic as a laborer in an open-pit copper mine for over forty years, my father presented our family with a passion for rhythm and dance, a deep love and respect for the desert, affection, a heightened awareness of our environment and an array of unique family members in Mexico, including uncles, aunts, cousins and other relatives who opened our eyes to an immense feeling of gratitude that my siblings and I were born in America. I am rethinking, not what occurred in my challenging childhood, but the perception that I held on to for the rest of my life.....that falling in love would always be painful. That was simply not true.

This will be the sixth book that I have offered my readers within the past eighteen years. Although in the past I have thought that my readers would benefit from what I had researched, collected and assembled in a manuscript, I have come to the awareness that I am the one who has benefited the most. The women and men who have openly given their life stories to us to share in this book have required me to rethink my view of loving.

The first group of stories; loving, losing and loving again, softened my account of my own tale of woe and gave me a deeper sense of compassion and connection with others who have walked the journey of being devastatingly hurt. And this includes most human beings; for I can't imagine that many get away without some hurtful experiences in loving, including my own father. We are all in it together. As our research has proven scientifically, the mind is wired for love, and spiritually, for love is the essence of who we are, and we aspire to reconnect with it. We naturally experience this at different levels of discomfort, disappointments and great expectations, until we fall in love again, and then we start all over again. And there lays the greatest benefit of all, the gift of hope!

Our second group of couples has blessed me through their honesty regarding how a committed and loving relationship works and keeps on working. The diversity of their partnerships, children, religion, careers and challenges and advice for our young readers, again filled me with optimism. Yes, there will be painful times and struggles while regrouping, but the commitment to staying together and building a life-long bond is the vision that they hold for each other. One of our couple's states; "Take relationship seriously." Oh, had I been better informed, more mature, wiser, (my list of excuses could go on forever), but the truth is none of that matters any longer. I did not fully understand the seriousness of choosing a relationship that would weather the storms of life. More importantly; I did not realize the significance of my inability to commit to a relationship. I am rethinking how I loved.

For my single friends, acquaintances and clients who vow to never marry again, not to worry; our love is spreading all the way through us. As we deeply love our children, grandchildren, parents, friends, partners, our communities, country and the world (and some even love those they work with as we do in our salon) love is everywhere. And there are a million whys to offer our love. We cannot stop it. I say let it pour from us. There is plenty of love to go around and the more we love the more love is created.

And...I know this for a fact; if that certain person came along that caught your eye, warmed your heart with tender feelings of romance, and you felt completely safe...you would do it all over again. As author Eve Pell wrote in her book; Love Again, The Wisdom of Unexpected Romance, *"Do it all over again—even if for an occasional date or a cuddle."*

RETHINKING LOVE

Mary Beth

As Hilda and I sat at dinner one evening discussing the title for this particular chapter of the book, the title "Rethinking Love" seemed to be a perfect choice. We asked each other, "How did you view love through the various decades of your life? How do you now view love in your 60's?" I ask each of you to think about your view of love during each decade of YOUR life. Whether you are now 35, 55, or 75 I challenge you to take all you've experienced and learned about love up to this point, and "rethink" it. How can you love differently in the ensuing years? If in reading this book you gained insight into the challenges and rewards of relationships, take that knowledge and improve upon your current relationship or if you have been devastated by the loss of a relationship, become brave and fearless and allow yourself to fall in love again. I am challenging myself to do so.

It is Valentine's Day as I write this. I am nostalgic about the many Valentine's Day celebrations I have experienced over the years. I am happy to report that I remember all happy occasions and the occasional romantic one as well. I smile as I remember the romantic efforts put forth by men who were uneasy about preparing a special meal or not quite knowing just "how romantic" to be. I fondly remember the candy hearts we exchanged in grade school and how exciting it was to get a "love message" heart from a boy! This year I will celebrate by enjoying a delicious lobster dinner with my friends of 35 years and I can't think of a better celebration. Somehow Valentine's Day puts "rethinking love" into perspective. I want to remember romantic love as a collage of school girl crushes; two marriages that were "right" at the time and produced three fabulous children; and several post-divorce relationships that were exciting and fulfilling. In "rethinking" love I would frame it for the future as a large "safety net" of children, grandchildren, extended family, friends, and colleagues and yes, perhaps a future romantic partner. My "new" way of thinking about love and approaching love will be with more vulnerability as I believe I now better understand the choices I made in the past. "Perfect love" doesn't exist.

As I personally "rethink love" I've learned that love is not stagnant; it ebbs and flows with time based on years of experience and maturity. As is evident with the contributors to the book, they loved, they hurt, they sacrificed, they got knocked down, and they got back up----all in the name of love. Whether loving a spouse, a significant other, a child, a grandchild, a friend, or a colleague, the way in which we love can be compared to a body of water – some days it's the pounding waves of an ocean and other days it's a serene, placid lake. And yes, to carry the metaphor a bit further: it's ultimately our choice whether to sink or swim. I have chosen to swim and I so want to improve upon the way in which I love. With gratitude to the women and men who contributed to the book, I have (and hopefully you do as well) a great appreciation for the ways in which others love. I want to approach love with even more bravery than I exhibited in the past – to know when to speak with honesty and fearlessness in order to nurture a relationship or perhaps end a relationship.

So thank you to all the women and men who contributed to this book for reinforcing perhaps what we all intuitively know—to love is truly the greatest gift of all. I will leave you, our readers, with this. . . . .one of the most endearing visions of expressing love I experienced recently was when my three year old granddaughter hugged 12 of us individually (family and extended family) at the conclusion of Christmas Mass. After hugging each of us, she declared, "I have so much love"!

CONCLUSION

"Often we repeat stories, not because we are forgetful or indulgent, but because there is too much meaning to digest in one expression. So we keep sharing the story that presses on our heart until we understand it all."

Mark Nepo, The Book of Awakening

Hilda

As we complete the last words of this book, my son's birthday is just a few days away. For as long as he can remember, every year on the day of his birth, I tell him the story of the day he was born. I always begin the story the same: *'It was February 26, on a Saturday morning at five o'clock. Your father was still asleep next to me when I woke up to my water breaking.'* For over forty years, he has allowed me to repeat the story to him. Of course he pretends to want to hear every detail and listens quietly, laughing with me only at the appropriate times. He 'Oh Mom's' me when the breaking of the water is revisited and I'm sure he wishes that I will eventually omit that part. But instead, he holds that space for me to re-remember and re-feel that most treasured day of my life. Although I tell him the story of the day he was born, it is I who relishes the memory of that day. Most certainly, because I knew my life would never be the same again. I would add that kind of love into my heart that mothers feel.

Telling our stories is how we commit to memory the choices that have defined us along the way and how we've witnessed the eventual evolution of who we have become throughout the years. It's how we connect the pieces of the years that we have left behind, trailing like footsteps that will sooner or later, through the years of climate conditions wear and tear and disappear, unless we tell our stories once again. As Mark Nepo states in his quote; *"So we keep sharing the story that presses on our heart until we understand it all."*

As our years accumulate and memories capture the life that we have lived, we are able to see that our thoughts and emotions eventually materialize. We don't have to rush life as we do when we are young, nor do we have to fret as much as we do when we are older. Through our stories we can begin to understand that life takes time to reveal itself to us, and for us to expose ourselves to it. We will experience ups and downs and we will most certainly fall in love again. Our choices in the beginning of our lives will increase and then will diminish as we let others decide for us our final days. But life is unfolding all along the way. I read a revealing quote in a novel by Amor Towels, *A Gentleman in Moscow* that addressed this premise: *"Life does not proceed by leaps and bounds—it unfolds. At any given moment it is the manifestation of a thousand transitions. Our faculties wax and wane—our experiences accumulate and our opinions evolve, if not glacially, than at least gradually."*

This book has been a collection of stories of how others love...bravely. As stated in the preface, *"Your own life story of love begins the instant you are born and is still unfolding at this precise moment while reading these words."* Our stories are now a part of your story in the time you've spent with us. We trust that you have found a voice within the pages that has inspired and nurtured your soul. We wish to bring awareness that love we must, for it is a natural state of mind and a reconnection with spirit. As always, we invite you to take action in your life and fall in love again.

Yours truly,

Hilda and Mary Beth

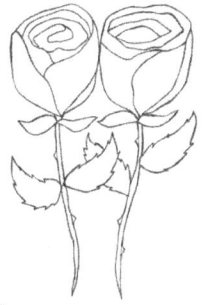

REFERENCES

Banks, Amy. *Four Ways to Click: Rewire Your Brain for Stronger, More Rewarding Relationships*. New York: Penguin Group, 2015.

Fromm, Erich. *The Art of Loving*. New York: HarperCollins, 1956.

Johnson, Sue. *Love Sense: The Revolutionary New Science of Romantic Relationships*. New York: Hachette Book Group, 2013.

Moore, Thomas. *Soul Mates: Honoring the Mysteries of Love and Relationships*. New York: HarperCollins, 1940.

Nepo, Mark. *The Book of Awakening: Having the Life You Want by Being Present to the Life You Have*. San Francisco: Conair Press, an imprint of Red Wheel/Weiser, LLC, 2011.

Ornish, Dan. *Love and Survival: 8 Pathways to Intimacy and Health*. New York: Harper Collins, 1999.

Pell, Eve. *Love, Again: The Wisdom of Unexpected Romance*. New York: Penguin Random House Company, 2015.

Villaverde, Hilda. *Blow Dry This: Stories from Behind the Chair*. Arizona: Pluma Designs Inc., 2007.